The Long Whit

"Ao Tea Roa

William Pember Reeves

Alpha Editions

This edition published in 2023

ISBN : 9789357382342

Design and Setting By
Alpha Editions
www.alphaedis.com
Email - info@alphaedis.com

Contents

Preface..- 1 -

Note of Acknowledgment ....- 3 -

Chapter I...- 5 -

   THE LONG WHITE CLOUD[1] ....- 5 -

Chapter II ....- 23 -

   THE MAORI ....- 23 -

Chapter III ....- 38 -

   THE MAORI AND THE UNSEEN ....- 38 -

Chapter IV...- 46 -

   THE NAVIGATORS...- 46 -

Chapter V ....- 56 -

   NO MAN'S LAND ....- 56 -

Chapter VI...- 65 -

   MISSION SCHOONER AND WHALE
   BOAT ....- 65 -

Chapter VII ....- 75 -

   THE MUSKETS OF HONGI...- 75 -

Chapter VIII ....- 87 -

   "A MAN OF WAR WITHOUT GUNS" ....- 87 -

Chapter IX ....- 94 -

   THE DREAMS OF GIBBON
   WAKEFIELD...- 94 -

   Chapter X...- 101 -

   IN THE CAUDINE FORKS..- 101 -

Chapter XI...- 110 -

   THROUGH WEAKNESS INTO WAR ....- 110 -

Chapter XII ....- 121 -

    GOOD GOVERNOR GREY...............................- 121 -

Chapter XIII ....- 129 -

    THE PASTORAL PROVINCES............................- 129 -

Chapter XIV ....- 139 -

    LEARNING TO WALK......................................- 139 -

Chapter XV ....- 145 -

    GOVERNOR BROWNE'S BAD
    BARGAIN ....- 145 -

Chapter XVI..- 149 -

    TUPARA[1] AGAINST ENFIELD....................- 149 -

Chapter XVII..- 159 -

    THE FIRE IN THE FERN....................................- 159 -

Chapter XVIII ....- 172 -

    GOLD-DIGGERS AND GUM-DIGGERS ....- 172 -

Chapter XIX..- 179 -

    THE PROVINCES AND THE PUBLIC
    WORKS POLICY ....- 179 -

Chapter XX ....- 185 -

    IN PARLIAMENT ....- 185 -

Chapter XXI..- 194 -

    SOME BONES OF CONTENTION ....- 194 -

Chapter XXII..- 204 -

    EIGHT YEARS OF EXPERIMENT.....................- 204 -

Chapter XXIII ....- 222 -

    THE NEW ZEALANDERS ....- 222 -

BIBLIOGRAPHY ....- 231 -

Preface

I believe that there is amongst the people of the Mother Country a minority, now ceasing to be small, which takes a quickening interest in the Colonies. It no longer consists merely of would-be investors, or emigrants who want to inquire into the resources, industries, and finances of one or other of the self-governing parts of the Empire. Many of its members never expect to see a colony. But they have come to recognise that those new-comers into the circle of civilized communities, the daughter nations of Britain, are not unworthy of English study and English pride. They have begun to suspect that the story of their struggles into existence and prosperity may be stirring, romantic, and interesting, and that some of their political institutions and experiments may be instructive, though others may seem less safe than curious. Some of those who think thus complain that it is not always easy to find an account of a colony which shall be neither an official advertisement, the sketch of a globe-trotting impressionist, nor yet an article manufactured to order by some honest but untravelled maker of books. They ask—or at least some of them, to my knowledge, ask—for a history in which the picturesque side of the story shall not be ignored, written simply and concisely by a writer who has made a special study of his subject, or who has lived and moved amongst the places, persons, and incidents he describes.

I have lived in New Zealand, have seen it and studied it from end to end, and have had to do with its affairs: it is my country. But I should not have presumed to endeavour to supply in its case the want above indicated had any short descriptive history of the colony from its discovery to the present year been available. Among the many scores of books about the Islands—some of which are good, more of which are bad—I know of none which does what is aimed at in this volume. I have, therefore, taken in hand a short sketch-history of mine, published some six months ago, have cut out some of it and have revised the rest, and blended it with the material of the following chapters, of which it forms nearly one-third. The result is something not quite so meagre in quantity or staccato in style, though even now less full than I should have liked to make it, had it been other than the work of an unknown writer telling the story of a small archipelago which is at once the most distant and well-nigh the youngest of English states. I have done my best in the later chapters to describe certain men and experiments without letting personal likes and dislikes run away with my pen; have taken pains to avoid loading my pages with the names of places and persons of no particular interest to British readers; and at the same time have tried not to forget the value of local colour and atmosphere in a book of this kind.

If *The Long White Cloud* should fail to please a discerning public, it will not prove that a good, well-written history of a colony like New Zealand is not wanted, and may not succeed, but merely that I have not done the work well enough. That may easily be, inasmuch as until this year my encounters with English prose have almost all taken the form of political articles or official correspondence. Doubtless these do not afford the best possible training. But of the quality of the material awaiting a capable writer there can be no question. There, ready to his hand, are the beauty of those islands of mid-ocean, the grandeur of their Alps and fiords, the strangeness of the volcanic districts, the lavishness, yet grace, of the forests; the mixture of quaintness, poetry, and ferocity in the Maori, and the gallant drama of their struggle against our overwhelming strength; the adventures of the gold-seekers and other pioneers; the high aims of the colony's founders, and the venturesome democratic experiments of those who have succeeded them. If in these there is not the stuff for a fine book, then I am most strangely mistaken. And if I have failed in the following pages, then let me hope that some fellow-countryman, and better craftsman, will come to the rescue, and will do with a firmer hand and a lighter touch the work attempted here.

Note of Acknowledgment

I have to thank Major-General Robley, not only for drawing the tail-piece to the second chapter, and thereby giving the book a minute but correct pattern of the Maori *moko* or face-tattooing, but for kindly lending me photographs and drawings from which several other illustrations have been taken. Two or three of the tail-pieces are after designs in Mr. Hamilton's *Maori Art*. I have also to thank Mr. A. Martin of Wanganui for his kind permission to use his fine photograph of Mount Egmont and a view on a "papa" river. Mr. W.F. Crawford was good enough to put at my disposal his photograph of the Te Reinga waterfall, a view which will be new even to most New Zealanders. The portrait of Major Kemp and that of a Muaopoko Maori standing by a carved canoe-prow were given to me by Sir Walter Buller. "A New Zealand Settler's Home" was the gift of Mr. Winckleman of Auckland, well known amongst New Zealand amateur photographers.

I have also gratefully to acknowledge the photographs which are the work of Mr. Josiah Martin of Auckland, Messrs. Beattie and Sanderson of Auckland, Mr. Iles of the Thames, and Mr. Morris of Dunedin, and to thank Messrs. Sampson, Low and Co. for the use of the blocks from which the portraits of Sir Harry Atkinson and the Hon. John McKenzie are taken.

Chapter I

THE LONG WHITE CLOUD[1]

"If to her share some female errors fall,
Look on her face—and you'll forget them all."

[Footnote 1: Ao-Tea-Roa, the Maori name of New Zealand.]

Though one of the parts of the earth best fitted for man, New Zealand was probably about the last of such lands occupied by the human race. The first European to find it was a Dutch sea-captain who was looking for something else, and who thought it a part of South America, from which it is sundered by five thousand miles of ocean. It takes its name from a province of Holland to which it does not bear the remotest likeness, and is usually regarded as the antipodes of England, but is not. Taken possession of by an English navigator, whose action, at first adopted, was afterwards reversed by his country's rulers, it was only annexed at length by the English Government which did not want it, to keep it from the French who did. The Colony's capital bears the name of a famous British commander, whose sole connection with the country was a flat refusal to aid in adding it to the Empire. Those who settled it meant it to be a theatre for the Wakefield Land System. The spirit of the land laws, however, which its settlers have gradually developed is a complete negation of Wakefield's principle. Some of the chief New Zealand settlements were founded by Church associations; but the Colony's education system has long been purely secular. From the first those who governed the Islands laboured earnestly to preserve and benefit the native race, and on the whole the treatment extended to them has been just and often generous—yet the wars with them were long, obstinate, and mischievous beyond the common. The pioneer colonists looked upon New Zealand as an agricultural country, but its main industries have turned out to be grazing and mining. From the character of its original settlers it was expected to be the most conservative of the colonies; it is just now ranked as the most democratic. Not only by its founders, but for many years afterwards, Irish were avowedly or tacitly excluded from the immigrants sent to it. Now, however, at least one person in eight in the Colony is of that race.

It would be easy to expand this list into an essay on the vanity of human wishes. It would not be hard to add thereto a formidable catalogue of serious mistakes made both in England and New Zealand by those responsible for the Colony's affairs—mistakes, some of which, at least, seem now to argue an almost inconceivable lack of knowledge and foresight. So constantly have the anticipations of its officials and settlers been reversed in the story of New Zealand that it becomes none too easy to trace any thread of guiding wisdom or consistent purpose therein. The broad result, however, has been a fine and vigorous colony. Some will see in its record of early struggles, difficulties and mistakes endured, paid for and surmounted, a signal instance of the overruling care of Providence. To the cynic the tale must be merely a minor portion of the "supreme ironic procession with laughter of gods in the background." To the writer it seems, at least, to give a very notable proof of the collective ability of a colonizing race to overcome obstacles and repair blunders. The Colony of New Zealand is not a monument of the genius of any one man or group of men. It is the outcome of the vitality and industry of a people obstinate but resourceful, selfish but honest, often ill-informed and wrong, but with the saving virtue of an ability to learn from their own mistakes.

From one standpoint the story of New Zealand ought not to take long to tell. It stretches over less time than that of almost any land with any pretensions to size, beauty, or interest. New Zealand was only discovered by Europeans in the reign of our King Charles I., and even then the Dutch explorer who sighted its lofty coasts did not set foot upon them. The first European to step on to its shores did so only when the great American colonies were beginning to fret at the ties which bound them to England. The pioneers of New Zealand colonization, the missionaries, whalers, and flax and timber traders, did not come upon the scene until the years of Napoleon's decline and fall. Queen Victoria had been on the throne for three years before the Colonial Office was reluctantly compelled to add the Islands to an Empire which the official mind regarded as already overgrown.

Yet so striking, varied, and attractive are the country's features, so full of bustle, change and experiment have its few years been, that lack of material is about the last complaint that need be made by a writer on New Zealand. The list of books on the Colony is indeed so long that its bibliography is a larger volume than this; and the chief plea to be urged for this history must be its brevity—a quality none too common in Colonial literature.

A New Zealander writing in London may be forgiven if he begins by warning English readers not to expect in the aspect of New Zealand either a replica of the British Islands or anything resembling Australia. The long, narrow, mountainous islands upon which Abel Jansen Tasman stumbled in December, 1642, are so far from being the antipodes of Britain that they lie on an average twelve degrees nearer the equator. Take Liverpool as a central city of the United Kingdom; it lies nearly on the 53rd parallel of north latitude. Wellington, the most central city of New Zealand, is not far from the 41st parallel of southern latitude. True, New Zealand has no warm Gulf Stream to wash her shores. But neither is she chilled by east winds blowing upon her from the colder half of a continent. Neither her contour nor climate is in the least Australian. It is not merely that twelve hundred miles of ocean separate the flat, rounded, massive-looking continent from the high, slender, irregular islands. The ocean is deep and stormy. Until the nineteenth century there was absolutely no going to and fro across it. Many plants are found in both countries, but they are almost all small and not in any way conspicuous. Only one bird of passage migrates across the intervening sea. The dominating trees of Australia are myrtles (called eucalypts); those of New Zealand are beeches (called birches), and various species of pines. The strange marsupials, the snakes, the great running birds, the wild dogs of Australia, have no counterpart in New Zealand. The climate of Australia, south of Capricorn, is, except on the eastern and south-eastern coast, as hot and dry as the South African. And the Australian mountains, moderate in height and flattened, as a rule, at the summit, remind one not a little of the table-topped elevations so familiar to riders on the veldt and karroo. The western coast of New Zealand is one of the rainiest parts of the Empire. Even the drier east coast only now and then suffers from drought On the west coast the thermometer seldom rises above 75° in the shade; on the other not often above 90°. New Zealand, too, is a land of cliffs, ridges, peaks, and cones. Some of the loftier volcanoes are still active, and the vapour of their craters mounts skyward above white fields of eternal snow. The whole length of the South Island is ridged by Alpine ranges, which, though not quite equal in height to the giants of Switzerland, do not lose by comparison with the finest of the Pyrenees.

No man with an eye for the beautiful or the novel would call Australia either unlovely or dull. It is not, however, a land of sharp and sudden contrasts: New Zealand is.

The Australian woods, too, are park-like: their trees, though interesting, and by no means without charm, have a strong family likeness. Their prevailing colours are yellow, brown, light green, and grey. Light and heat penetrate them everywhere.

The cool, noiseless forests of New Zealand are deep jungles, giant thickets, like those tropic labyrinths where traveller and hunter have to cut their path through tangled bushes and interlacing creepers. Their general hue is not light but dark green, relieved, it is true, by soft fern fronds, light-tinted shrubs, and crimson or snow-white flowers. Still the tone is somewhat sombre, and would be more noticeably so but for the prevalent sunshine and the great variety of species of trees and ferns growing side by side. The distinction of the forest scenery may be summed up best in the words dignity and luxuriance. The tall trees grow close together. For the most part their leaves are small, but their close neighbourhood hinders this from spoiling the effect. The eye wanders over swell after swell, and into cavern after cavern of unbroken foliage. To the botanist who enters them these silent, stately forests show such a wealth of intricate, tangled life, that the delighted examiner hardly knows which way to turn first.

A WESTERN ALPINE VALLEY
Photo by MORRIS, Dunedin.

As a rule the lower part of the trunks is branchless; stems rise up like tall pillars in long colonnades. But this does not mean that they are bare. Climbing ferns, lichens, pendant grasses, air-plants, and orchids drape the columns. Tough lianas swing in air: coiling roots overspread the ground. Bushes, shrubs, reeds and ferns of every size and height combine to make a woven thicket, filling up and even choking the spaces between trunk and trunk. Supple, snaky vines writhe amid the foliage, and bind the undergrowth together.

The forest trees are evergreens, and even in mid-winter are fresh-looking. The glowing autumnal tints of English woods are never theirs; yet they show every shade of green, from the light of the puriri to the dark of the totara, from the bronze-hued willow-like leaves of the tawa to the vivid green of the matai, or the soft golden-green of the drooping rimu. Then, though the ground-flowers cannot compare in number with those of England or Australia,[1] the Islands are the chosen land of the fern, and are fortunate in flowering creepers, shrubs, and trees. There are the koromiko bush with white and purple blossoms, and the white convolvulus which covers whole thickets with blooms, delicate as carved ivory, whiter than milk. There are the starry clematis, cream-coloured or white, and the manuka, with tiny but numberless flowers. The yellow kowhai, seen on the hillsides, shows the russet tint of autumn at the height of spring-time. Yet the king of the forest flowers is, perhaps, the crimson, feathery rata. Is it a creeper, or is it a tree? Both opinions are held; both are right. One species of the rata is an ordinary climber; another springs sometimes from the ground, sometimes from the fork of a tree into which the seed is blown or dropped. Thence it throws out long rootlets, some to earth, others which wrap round the trunk on which it is growing. Gradually this rata becomes a tree itself, kills its supporter, and growing round the dead stick, ends in almost hiding it from view.

[Footnote 1: The Alps, however, show much floral beauty, and the ground-flowers of the Auckland Islands, an outlying group of New Zealand islets, impressed the botanist Kirk as unsurpassed in the South Temperate Zone.]

In the month of February, when the rata flowers in the Alps, there are valleys which are ablaze for miles with

> "Flowers that with one scarlet gleam
> Cover a hundred leagues, and seem
> To set the hills on fire."

But the most gorgeous of all flowering trees, as distinguished from creepers, is the sea-loving pohutu kawa. When the wind is tossing its branches the contrast is startling between its blood-red flowers and the dark upper side and white, downy under side of its leaves.

Like the Australians, New Zealand Colonists call their forest "bush." What in England might be called bush or brushwood is called "scrub" in the Colonies.

The wood of many of the trees is not only useful timber, but when cut and polished is often beautiful in grain. Unhappily, their destruction goes on with rapid strides. The trees, as is usually the case with those the wood of which is hard, grow slowly. They feel exposure to wind, and seem to need the society and shelter of their fellows. It is almost impossible to restore a New Zealand forest when once destroyed. Then most of the finest trees are found on rich soil. The land is wanted for grazing and cultivation. The settler comes with axe and fire-stick, and in a few hours unsightly ashes and black funereal stumps have replaced the noble woods which Nature took centuries to grow. No attempt is made to use a great part of the timber. The process is inevitable, and in great part needful, frightfully wasteful as it seems. But the forest reserves of the Colony, large as they are, should be made even more ample. Twelve hundred thousand acres are not enough— as the New Zealanders will regretfully admit when a decade or so hence they begin to import timber instead of exporting it. As for interfering with reserves already made, any legislator who suggests it should propose his motion with a noose round his neck, after the laudable custom followed in a certain classic republic.

New Zealand is by no means a flat country, though there are in it some fair-sized plains, one of which—that of Canterbury—is about as flat a stretch of one hundred miles as is to be found in the world. On the whole, however, both North and South Islands are lands of the mountain and the flood, and not only in this, but in the contour of some of their peaks and coast-line, show more than a fanciful resemblance to the west of Scotland. But the New Zealand mountains are far loftier than anything in the British Islands. The rocky coasts as a rule rise up steeply from the ocean, standing out in many places in bold bluffs and high precipices. The seas round are not shallow, dull, or turbid, but deep, blue, wind-stirred, foam-flecked, and more often than not lit by brilliant sunshine. The climate and colouring, too, are not only essentially un-English, but differ very widely in different parts of the Islands. For New Zealand, though narrow, has length, stretching through 13 degrees of latitude, and for something like 1,100 miles from north to south. As might be looked for in a mountainous country, lying in the open ocean, the climate is windy, and except in two or three districts, moist. It is gloriously healthy and briskly cheerful. Summed up in one word, its prevailing characteristic is light!

Hot as are many summer days, they are seldom sultry enough to breed the heavy, overhanging heat-haze which shrouds the heaven nearer the tropics. Sharp as are the frosts of winter nights in the central and southern part of the South Island, the days even in mid-winter are often radiant, giving seven or eight hours of clear, pleasant sunshine. For the most part the rains are heavy but not prolonged; they come in a steady, business-like downpour, or in sharp, angry squalls; suddenly the rain ceases, the clouds break, and the sun is shining from a blue sky. Fogs and mists are not unknown, but are rare and passing visitors, do not come to stay, and are not brown and yellow in hue but more the colour of a clean fleece of wool. They do not taste of cold smoke, gas, sulphur, or mud. High lying and ocean-girt, the long, slender islands are lands of sunshine and the sea. It is not merely that their coast-line measures 4,300 miles, but that they are so shaped and so elevated that from innumerable hilltops and mountain summits distant glimpses may be caught of the blue salt water. From the peak of Aorangi, 12,350 feet in air, the Alpine climber Mannering saw not only the mantle of clouds which at that moment covered the western sea twenty miles away, but a streak of blue ocean seventy miles off near Hokitika to the north-west, and by the hills of Bank's Peninsula to the north-east, a haze which indicated the Eastern Ocean. Thus, from her highest peak, he looked right across New Zealand. The Dutch, then, its discoverers, were not so wrong in naming it Zealand or Sea-land.

Next to light, perhaps the chief characteristic of the country and its climate is variety. Thanks to its great length the north differs much from the south. Southland is as cool as northern France, with an occasional southerly wind as keen as Kingsley's wild north-easter. But in gardens to the north of Auckland I have stood under olive trees laden with berries. Hard by were orange trees, figs, and lemon trees in full bearing. Not far off a winding tidal creek was fringed with mangroves. Exotic palm trees and the cane-brake will grow there easily. All over the North Island, except at high altitudes, and in the more sheltered portions of the South Island, camellias and azaleas bloom in the open air. The grape vine bids fair to lead to wine-making in both islands—unless the total abstainers grow strong enough to put their foot on the manufacture of alcohol in any form in an already distinctly and increasingly sober Colony.

But in New Zealand not only is the north in marked contrast with the south, but the contrast between the east and west is even more sharply defined. As a rule the two coasts are divided by a broad belt of mountainous country. The words "chain" and "spine" are misnomers, at any rate in the South Island, inasmuch as they are not sufficiently expressive of breadth. The rain-bringing winds in New Zealand blow chiefly from the north-west and south-west. The moisture-laden clouds rolling up from the ocean gather and condense against the western flanks of the mountains, where an abundant rainfall has nourished through ages past an unbroken and evergreen forest. Nothing could well be more utterly different than these matted jungles of the wet west coast—with their prevailing tint of rich dark green, their narrow, rank, moist valleys and steep mountain sides—and the eastern scenery of the South Island. The sounds or fiords of the south-west are perhaps the loveliest series of gulfs in the world. Inlet succeeds inlet, deep, calm, and winding far in amongst the steep and towering mountains. The lower slopes of these are clothed with a thick tangle of forest, where foliage is kept eternally fresh and vivid by rain and mist. White torrents and waterfalls everywhere seam the verdure and break the stillness.

Cross to the east coast.

Scarcely is the watershed passed when the traveller begins to enter a new landscape and a distinct climate. The mountains, stripped of their robe of forest, seem piled in ruined, wasting heaps, or stand out bleak and bare-ribbed,

> "The skeletons of Alps whose death began
> Far in the multitudinous centuries."

Little is left them but a kind of dreary grandeur. The sunshine falls on patches of gleaming snow and trailing mist, and lights up the grey crags which start out like mushrooms on the barren slopes. On all sides streams tear down over beds of the loose shingle, of which they carry away thousands of tons winter after winter. Their brawling is perhaps the only sound you will hear through slow-footed afternoons, save, always, the whistle or sighing of the persistent wind. A stunted beech bush clothes the spurs here and there, growing short and thick as a fleece of dark wool. After a storm the snow will lie powdering the green beech trees, making the rocks gleam frostily and sharpening the savage ridges till they look like the jagged edges of stone axes. Only at nightfall in summer do the mountains take a softer aspect. Then in the evening stillness the great outlines show majesty; then in the silence after sunset rivers, winding among the ranges in many branches over broad, stony beds, fill the shadowy valleys with their hoarse murmur.

To the flock-owner, however, this severe region is what the beautiful West is not—it is useful. Sheep can find pasture there. And as the mountains decline into hills, and the hills into downs and flats, the covering of herbage becomes less and less scanty. When the colonists came to the east coast, they found plains and dales which were open, grassy, almost treeless. Easy of access, and for the most part fertile, they were an ideal country for that unaesthetic person, the practical settler. Flocks and herds might roam amongst the pale tussock grass of the slopes and bottoms without fear either of man, beast, climate, or poisonous plant.[1] A few wooden buildings and a certain extent of wire fencing represented most of the initial expenses of the pioneer. Pastoral settlement speedily overran such a land, followed more slowly and partially by agriculture. The settler came, not with axe and fire to ravage and deform, but as builder, planter and gardener. Being in nineteen cases out of twenty a Briton, or a child of one, he set to work to fill this void land with everything British which he could transport or transplant His gardens were filled with the flowers, the vegetables, the fruit trees of the old land. The oak, the elm, the willow, the poplar, the spruce, the ash grew in his plantations. His cattle were Shorthorns, Herefords, and Devons. His farm horses were of the best Clydesdale and Suffolk Punch blood. The grasses they fed upon were mixtures of cocksfoot, timothy, rye-grass, and white clover. When it was found that the red clover would not flourish for want of penetrating insects, the humble bee was imported, and with compete success, as many a field now ruddy with crimson blossom testifies. The common English bee is found wild in the forest, where it hives in hollow trees, and robs its competitors—the honey-eating native birds—of much of their food. The hedges round the fields aforesaid are also English, but with a difference. The stunted furze which beautifies English commons is at the other end of the earth a hedge plant, which makes a thick barrier from five to eight feet high, and, with its sweet-smelling blooms, has made the New Zealand fields "green pictures set in frames of gold." The very birds which rise from the clover or wheat, and nest in the trees or hedgerows of furze or quickset, are for the most part English—the skylark, the blackbird, finches, green and gold, thrushes, starlings, and that eternal impudent vagabond the house-sparrow. Heavy is the toll taken by the sparrow from the oat-crops of his new home; his thievish nature grows blacker there, though his plumage often turns partly white. He learns to hawk for moths and other flying insects. Near Christchurch rooks caw in the windy skies. Trout give excellent sport in a hundred streams, though in the lakes they grow too gross to take the fly. Many attempts have so far failed to acclimatise the salmon. The ova may be hatched out successfully, but the fish when turned out into the rivers disappears. The golden carp, however, the perch, and the rainbow trout take readily to New Zealand. The hare increases in size and weight, and has three and four leverets at a birth. The pheasant has spread from end to end of the Colony. The house-fly drives back the loathsome flesh-fly or blue-bottle, to the salvation of blankets and fresh meat. The Briton of the south has indeed taken with him all that he could of the old country.

[Footnote 1: The *tutu*, a danger to inexperienced sheep and cattle, was not eaten by horses. The berries were poisonous enough to kill an imported elephant on one occasion. Would that they had done as much for the rabbit!]

He has also brought a few things which he wishes he had left behind. The Hessian fly, the wire-worm, the flea, and grubs and scale insects thrive mischievously. The black and grey rats have driven the native rat into the recesses of the forest. A score of weeds have come, mixed with badly-screened grass-seed, or in any of a hundred other ways. The Scotch thistle seemed likely at one stage to usurp the whole grass country. Acts of Parliament failed to keep it down. Nature, more effectual, causes it to die down after running riot for a few years. The watercress, too, threatened at one time to choke half the streams. The sweetbriar, taking kindly to both soil and climate, not only grows tall enough to arch over the head of a man on horseback, but covers whole hillsides, to the ruin of pasture. Introduced, innocently enough, by the missionaries, it goes by their name in some districts. Rust, mildew, and other blights, have been imported along with plant and seed. The rabbit, multiplying in millions, became a very terror to the sheep farmers, is even yet the subject of anxious care and inspection, and only slowly yields to fencing, poison, traps, dogs, guns, stoats, weasels, ferrets, cats, and a host of instruments of destruction. In poisoning the rabbit the stock-owners have well-nigh swept the native birds from wide stretches of country. The weka, or wood-hen, with rudimentary wings like tufts of brown feathers, whose odd, inquisitive ways introduce it so constantly to the shepherd and bushman, at first preyed upon the young rabbits and throve. Now ferrets and phosphorus are exterminating it in the rabbit-infested districts. Moreover, just as Vortigern had reason to regret that he had called in the Saxon to drive out the Picts and Scots, so the New Zealanders have already found the stoat and weasel but dubious blessings. They have been a veritable Hengist and Horsa to more than one poultry farmer and owner of lambs. In addition they do their full share of the evil work of bird extermination, wherein they have active allies in the rats and wild cats. On the whole, however, though acclimatization has given the Colony one or two plagues and some minor nuisances, it would be ridiculous to pretend that these for a moment weigh in the scale against its good works. Most of the vegetable pests, though they may flourish abnormally for a few years in the virgin soil, soon become less vigorous. With the growth of population even the rabbit ceases to be a serious evil, except to a few half-empty tracts. The truth is that outside her forests and swamps New Zealand showed the most completely unoccupied soil of any fertile and temperate land on the globe. It seems possible that until about five or six hundred years ago she had no human inhabitants whatever. Her lakes and rivers had but few fish, her birds were not specially numerous, her grasses were not to be compared in their nourishing qualities with the English. Of animals there were virtually none. Even the rat before mentioned, and the now extinct dog of the Maori villages, were Maori importations from Polynesia not many centuries ago.

Not only, therefore, have English forms of life been of necessity drawn upon to fill the void spaces, but other countries have furnished their quota. The dark eucalypt of Tasmania, with its heavy-hanging, languid leaves, is the commonest of exotic trees. The artificial stiffness and regularity of the Norfolk Island pine, and the sweet-smelling golden blooms of the Australian wattle, are sights almost as familiar in New Zealand as in their native lands. The sombre pines of California and the macro carpa cypress cover thousands of acres. The merino sheep brought from Spain, _viâ_ Saxony and Australia, is the basis of the flocks. The black swan and magpie represent the birds of New Holland. The Indian minah, after becoming common, is said to be retreating before the English starling. The first red deer came from Germany. And side by side with these strangers and with the trees and plants which colonists call specifically "English"—for the word "British" is almost unknown in the Colony—the native flora is beginning to be cultivated in gardens and grounds. Neglected by the first generation, it is better appreciated by their children—themselves natives of the soil.

In the north and warmer island the traveller also meets sharp contrasts. These, however, except in the provinces of Wellington and Napier, where the Tararua-Ruahiné spine plays to some extent the part taken by the Alps in the South Island, are not so much between east and west as between the coasts and the central plateau. For the most part, all the coasts, except the south-east, are, or have been, forest-clad. Nearly everywhere they are green, hilly and abundantly watered; windy, but not plagued with extremes of cold and heat. Frost touches them but for a short time in mid-winter.

THE WHITE TERRACE, ROTOMAHANA

The extreme south and north of the North Island could hardly, by any stretch of imagination, be called rich and fertile. But the island demonstrates the "falsehood of extremes," for between them is found some of the finest and pleasantest land in the southern hemisphere. Nearly all of this, however, lies within fifty miles of one or other coast. When you have left these tracts, and have risen a thousand feet or so, you come to a volcanic plateau, clad for the most part in dark green and rusty bracken or tussocks of faded yellow. Right in the centre rise the great volcanoes,

Ruapehu, Tongariro and Tarawera, majestic in their outlines, fascinating because of the restless fires within and the outbreaks which have been and will again take place. Scattered about this plateau are lakes of every shape and size, from Taupo—called Te Moana (the sea) by the Maoris—to the tiniest lakelets and ponds. Here are found pools and springs of every degree of heat. Some are boiling cauldrons into which the unwary fall now and again to meet a death terrible, yet—if the dying words of some of them may be believed—not always agonizing, so completely does the shock of contact with the boiling water kill the nervous system. Many pools are the colour of black broth. Foul with mud and sulphur, they seethe and splutter in their dark pits, sending up clouds of steam and sulphurous fumes. Others are of the clearest green or deepest, purest blue, through which thousands of silver bubbles shoot up to the surface, flash, and vanish. But the main use of the hot springs is found in their combination of certain chemical properties,—sulphur-acid, sulphur-alkaline. Nowhere in the world, probably, are found healing waters at once so powerful and so various in their uses. Generations ago the Maori tribes knew something of their effects. Now invalids come from far and near in hundreds and thousands, and when the distractions and appliances of the sanitary stations equal those of the European spas they will come in tens of thousands, for the plateau is not only a health-resort but a wonderland. Its geysers rank with those of Iceland and the Yellowstone. Seen in the clear sunny air, these columns of water and white foam, mounting, swaying, blown by the wind into silver spray, and with attendant rainbows glittering in the light, are sights which silence even the chattering tourist for a while. Solfataras, mud volcanoes and fumaroles are counted in hundreds in the volcanic zone. If there were not such curiosities, still the beauty of the mountains, lakes, streams and patches of forest would, with the bright invigorating air, make the holiday-maker seek them in numbers. Through the middle of this curious region runs the Waikato, the longest and on the whole most tranquil and useful of that excitable race the rivers of New Zealand. Even the Waikato has its adventures. In one spot it is suddenly compressed to a sixth of its breadth, and, boiling between walls of rock, leaps in one mass of blue water and white foam into a deep, tree-fringed pool below. This is the Huka Waterfall. It is but one of the many striking falls to be met with in the Islands.

New Zealand is a land of streams of every size and kind, and almost all these streams and rivers have three qualities in common—they are cold, swift, and clear. Cold and swift they must be as they descend quickly to the sea from heights more or less great. Clear they all are, except immediately after rain, or when the larger rivers are in flood. In flood-time most of them become raging torrents. Many were the horses and riders swept away to hopeless death as they stumbled over the hidden stony beds of turbid mountain crossings in the pioneering days before bridges were. Many a foot-man—gold-seeker or labourer wandering in search of work—disappeared thus, unseen and unrecorded. Heavy were the losses in sheep and cattle, costly and infuriating the delays, caused by flooded rivers. Few are the old colonists who have not known what it is to wait through wet and weary hours, it might be days, gloomily smoking, grumbling and watching for some flood to abate and some ford to become passable. Even yet, despite millions spent on public works, such troubles are not unknown.

It is difficult, perhaps, for those living in the cool and abundantly watered British Islands to sympathise with dwellers in hotter climates, or to understand what a blessing and beauty these continual and never-failing watercourses of New Zealand seem to visitors from sultrier and drier lands. The sun is quite strong enough to make men thankful for this gift of abundant water, and to make the running ripple of some little forest rivulet, heard long before it is seen through the green thickets, as musical to the ears of the tired rider as the note of the bell-bird itself. Even pleasanter are the sound and glitter of water under the summer sunshine to the wayfarer in the open grassy plains or valleys of the east coast. As for the number of the streams—who shall count them? Between the mouths of the Mokau and Patea rivers—a distance which cannot be much more than one hundred miles of coast—no less than eighty-five streams empty themselves into the Tasman Sea, of which some sixty have their source on the slopes or in the chasms of Mount Egmont. Quite as many more flow down from Egmont on the inland side, and do not reach the sea separately, but are tributaries of two or three larger rivers.

It is true that travellers may come to the Islands and leave them with no notion of a New Zealand river, except a raging mountain torrent, hostile to man and beast. Or they may be jolted over this same torrent when, shrunk and dwindled in summer heat to a mere glittering thread, it meanders lost and bewildered about a glaring bed of hot stones. But then railways and ordinary lines of communication are chiefly along the coasts. The unadventurous or hurried traveller sticks pretty closely to these. It happens that the rivers, almost without exception, show plainer features as they near the sea.

He who wishes to see their best must go inland and find them as they are still to be found in the North Island, winding through untouched valleys, under softly-draped cliffs, or shadowed by forests not yet marred by man. Or, in the South Island, they should be watched in the Alps as, milky or green-tinted, their ice-cold currents race through the gorges.

ON A RIVER—"PAPA" COUNTRY
Photo by A. MARTIN, Wanganui.

Of forest rivers, the Wanganui is the longest and most famous, perhaps the most beautiful. Near the sea it is simply a broad river, traversed by boats and small steamers, and with grassy banks dotted with weeping willows or clothed with flax and the palm-lily. But as you ascend it the hills close in. Their sides become tall cliffs, whose feet the water washes. From the tops of these precipices the forest, growing denser and richer at every turn, rises on the flanks of the hills. In places the cliffs are so steep and impracticable that the Maoris use ladders for descending on their villages above to their canoes in the rivers below. Lovely indeed are these cliffs; first, because of the profusion of fern frond, leaf, and moss, growing from everything that can climb to, lay hold of, or root itself in crack, crevice, or ledge, and droop, glistening with spray-drops, or wave whispering in the wind; next, because of the striking form and colour of the cliffs themselves. They are formed of what is called "Papa." This is a blue, calcareous clay often found with limestone, which it somewhat resembles. The Maori word "papa" is applied to any broad, smooth, flattish surface, as a door, or to a slab of rock. The smooth, slab-like, papa cliffs are often curiously marked—tongued and grooved, as with a gouge, channelled and fluted. Sometimes horizontal lines seem to divide them into strata. Again, the lines may be winding and spiral, so that on looking at certain cliffs it might be thought possible that the Maoris had got from them some of their curious tattoo patterns. Though pale and delicate, the tints of the rock are not their least beauty. Grey, yellow, brown, fawn, terra-cotta, even pale orange are to be noted. No photograph can give the charm of the drapery that clothes these cliffs. Photographs give no light or colour, and New Zealand scenery without light and colour is Hamlet with Hamlet left out. How could a photograph even hint at the dark, glossy green of the glistening karaka leaves, the feathery, waving foliage of the lace bark, or the white and purple bloom of the koromiko? How could black-and-white suggest the play of shade and shine when, between flying clouds, the glint of sunlight falls upon the sword-bayonet blades of the flax, and the golden, tossing plumes of the toe-toe, the New Zealand cousin of the Pampas grass? Add to this, that more often than the passenger can count as he goes along the river, either some little rill comes dripping over the cliff, scattering the sparkling drops on moss and foliage, or the cliffs are cleft and, as from a rent in the earth, some tributary stream gushes out of a dark, leafy tunnel of branches. Sometimes, too, the cliffs are not cleft, but the stream rushes from their summit, a white waterfall veiling the mossy rocks. Then there are the birds. In mid-air is to be seen the little fan-tail, aptly named, zig-zagging to and fro. The dark blue tui, called parson bird, from certain throat-feathers like white bands, will sing with a note that out-rivals any blackbird. The kuku, or wild pigeon, will show his purple, copper-coloured, white and green plumage as he sails slowly by, with that easy, confiding flight that makes him the cheap victim of the tyro sportsman. The grey duck, less easy to approach, rises noisily before boat or canoe comes within gunshot. The olive and brown, hoarse-voiced ka-ka, a large, wild parrot, and green, crimson-headed parakeets, may swell the list. Such is a "papa" river! and there are many such.

Features for which the traveller in New Zealand should be prepared are the far-reaching prospects over which the eye can travel, the sight and sound of rapid water, and the glimpses of snow high overhead, or far off—glimpses to be caught in almost every landscape in the South Island and in many of the most beautiful of the North. Through the sunny, lucid atmosphere it is no uncommon thing to see mountain peaks sixty and eighty miles away diminished in size by distance, but with their outlines clearly cut. From great heights you may see much longer distances, especially on very early mornings of still midsummer days. Then, before the air is heated or troubled or tainted, but when night seems to have cooled and purged it from all impurity, far-off ridges and summits stand out clean, sharp and vivid. On such mornings, though standing low down by the sea-shore, I have seen the hills of Bank's Peninsula between sixty and seventy miles off, albeit they are not great mountains. Often did they seem to rise purple-coloured from the sea, wearing "the likeness of a clump of peaked isles," as Shelley says of the Euganean hills seen from Venice. On such a morning from a hill looking northward over league after league of rolling virgin forest I have seen the great volcano, Mount Ruapehu, rear up his 9,000 feet, seeming a solitary mass, the upper part distinctly seen, blue and snow-capped, the lower bathed and half-lost in a pearl-coloured haze. Most impressive of all is it to catch sight, through a cleft in the forest, of the peak of Mount Egmont, and of the flanks of the almost perfect cone curving upward from the sea-shore for 8,300 feet. The sentinel volcano stands alone. Sunrise is the moment to see him when his summit, sheeted with snow, is tinged with the crimson of morning and touched by clouds streaming past in the wind. Lucky is the eye that thus beholds Egmont, for he is a cloud-gatherer who does not show his face every day or to every gazer. Almost as fine a spectacle is the sight of the "Kaikouras," or "Lookers-on." When seen from the deck of a coasting steamer they seem almost to hang over the sea heaving more than 8,000 feet below their summits. Strangely beautiful are these mighty ridges when the moonlight bathes them and turns the sea beneath to silver. But more, beautiful are they still in the calm and glow of early morning, white down to the waist, brown to the feet with the sunshine full on their faces, the blue sky overhead, and the bluer sea below.

If the Southern Alps surpass the Kaikouras in beauty it is because of the contrast they show on their western flanks, between gaunt grandeur aloft, and the softest luxuriance below. The forest climbs to the snow line, while the snow line descends as if to meet it. So abrupt is the descent that the transition is like the change in a theatre-scene. Especially striking is the transformation in the passage over the fine pass which leads through the dividing range between pastoral Canterbury and Westland. At the top of Arthur's Pass you are among the high Alps. The road winds over huge boulders covered with lichen, or half hidden by koromiko, ferns, green moss, and stunted beeches, grey-bearded and wind-beaten. Here and there among the stones are spread the large, smooth, oval leaves and white gold-bearing cups of the shepherd's lily. The glaciers, snowfields, and cliffs of Mount Rolleston lie on the left. Everything drips with icy water. Suddenly the saddle is passed and the road plunges down into a deep gulf. It is the Otira Gorge. Nothing elsewhere is very like it. The coach zig-zags down at a gentle pace, like a great bird slowly wheeling downwards to settle on the earth. In a few minutes it passes from an Alpine desert to the richness of the tropics. At the bottom of the gorge is the river foaming among scarlet boulders—scarlet because of the lichen which coats them. On either side rise slopes which are sometimes almost, sometimes altogether precipices, covered, every inch of them, with thick vegetation. High above these tower the bare crags and peaks which, as the eye gazes upwards, seem to bend inwards, as though a single shock of earthquake would make them meet and entomb the gorge beneath. In autumn the steeps are gay with crimson cushion-like masses of rata flowers, or the white blooms of the ribbon-wood and koromiko. Again and again waterfalls break through their leafy coverts; one falls on the road itself and sprinkles passengers with its spray. In the throat of the gorge the coach rattles over two bridges thrown from cliff to cliff over the pale-green torrent.

In an hour comes the stage where lofty trees succeed giant mountains. As the first grow higher the second diminish. This is the land of ferns and mosses. The air feels soft, slightly damp, and smells of moist leaves. It is as different to the sharp dry air of the Canterbury ranges as velvet is to canvas; it soothes, and in hot weather relaxes. The black birch with dark trunk, spreading branches, and light leaves, is now mingled with the queenly rimu, and the stiff, small-leaved, formal white pine. Winding and hanging plants festoon everything, and everything is bearded with long streamers of moss, not grey but rich green and golden. Always some river rushes along in sight or fills the ear with its noise. Tree ferns begin to appear and grow taller and taller as the coach descends towards the sea, where in the evening the long journey ends.

On the western coast glaciers come down to within 700 feet of the sea-level. Even on the east side the snow is some 2,000 feet lower than in Switzerland. This means that the climber can easily reach the realm where life is not, where ice and snow, rock and water reign, and man feels his littleness.

Though Aorangi has been ascended to the topmost of its 12,349 feet, still in the Southern Alps the peaks are many which are yet unsealed, and the valleys many which are virtually untrodden. Exploring parties still go out and find new lakes, new passes, and new waterfalls. It is but a few years since the Sutherland Falls, 2,000 feet high, were first revealed to civilized man, nor was there ever a region better worth searching than the Southern Alps. Every freshly-found nook and corner adds beauties and interests. Falls, glaciers and lakes are on a grand scale. The Tasman glacier is eighteen miles long and more than two miles across at the widest point; the Murchison glacier is more than ten miles long; the Godley eight. The Hochstetter Fall is a curtain of broken, uneven, fantastic ice coming down 4,000 feet on to the Tasman glacier. It is a great spectacle, seen amid the stillness of the high Alps, broken only by the occasional boom and crash of a falling pinnacle of ice.

Of the many mountain lakes Te Anau is the largest, Manapouri the loveliest. Wakatipu is fifty-four miles long, and though its surface is 1,000 feet above the sea-level, its profound depth sinks below it. On the sea side of the mountains the fiords rival the lakes in depth. Milford Sound is 1,100 feet deep near its innermost end.

But enough of the scenery of the Colony. This is to be a story, not a sketch-book. Enough that the drama of New Zealand's history, now in the second act, has been placed on one of the most remarkable and favourable stages in the globe. Much—too much—of its wild and singular beauty must be ruined in the process of settlement. But very much is indestructible. The colonists are also awakening to the truth that mere Vandalism is as stupid as it is brutal. Societies are being established for the preservation of scenery. The Government has undertaken to protect the more famous spots. Within recent years three islands lying off different parts of the coast have been reserved as asylums for native birds. Two years ago, too, the wild and virgin mountains of the Urewera tribe were by Act of Parliament made inalienable, so that, so long as the tribe lasts, their ferns, their birds and their trees shall not vanish from the earth.

Chapter II

THE MAORI

"The moving finger writes; and, having writ,

Moves on. Nor all your piety or wit

Can lure it back to cancel half a line,

Nor all your tears wash out a word of it."

The first colonists of New Zealand were brown men from the South Seas. It was from Eastern Polynesia that the Maoris unquestionably came. They are of the same race as the courteous, handsome people who inhabit the South Sea Islands from Hawaii to Rarotonga, and who, in Fiji, mingle their blood with the darker and inferior Melanesians of the west. All the Polynesians speak dialects of the same musical tongue. A glance at Tregear's Comparative Maori-Polynesian Dictionary will satisfy any reader on that point. The Rarotongans call themselves "Maori," and can understand the New Zealand speech; so, as a rule, can the other South Sea tribes, even the distant Hawaiians. Language alone is proverbially misleading as a guide to identity of race. But in the case of the Polynesians we may add colour and features, customs, legends, and disposition. All are well though rather heavily built, active when they choose, and passionately fond of war and sport. The New Zealanders are good riders and capital football players. The Samoans are so fond of cricket that they will spend weeks in playing gigantic matches, fifty a side. Bold as seamen and skilful as fishermen, the Polynesians are, however, primarily cultivators of the soil. They never rose high enough in the scale to be miners or merchants. In the absence of mammals, wild and tame, in their islands, they could be neither hunters nor herdsmen. Fierce and bloodthirsty in war, and superstitious, they were good-natured and hospitable in peace and affectionate in family life.

There is no reason to think that the New Zealanders are more akin to the modern Malays than they are to the Australian blacks; nor have attempts to connect them with the red men of America or the Toltecs of Mexico succeeded. They are much more like some of the Aryans of Northern India. But the truth is, their fortunes before their race settled in Polynesia are a pure matter of guess-work. Some centuries ago, driven out by feuds or shortness of food, they left their isles of reef and palm, and found their way to Ao-tea-roa, as they called New Zealand.

On the map their new home seems at first sight so isolated and remote from the other groups of Oceania as to make it incredible that even the most daring canoe-men could have deliberately made their way thither. But this difficulty disappears upon a study of the ascertained voyages of the Polynesians. Among the bravest and most venturesome navigators of the ocean, the brown mariners studied and named the stars, winds and currents. As allies they had those friends of the sailor, the trade-winds. In cloudy weather, when the signs in the sky were hidden, the regular roll of the waves before the steady trade-wind was in itself a guide.[1] Their large double-canoes joined by platforms on which deck-houses were built were no despicable sea-boats, probably just as good as the vessels in which the Phoenicians circumnavigated Africa. Even their single canoes were sometimes between 100 and 150 feet long, and the crews of these, wielding their elastic paddles, kept time in a fashion that has won respect from the coxswain of a University eight. For their long voyages they stored water in calabashes, carried roots and dried fish, and had in the cocoa-nut both food and drink stored safely by nature in the most convenient compass. In certain seasons they could be virtually sure of replenishing their stock of water from the copious tropical or semi-tropical rains. Expert fishermen, they would miss no opportunity of catching fish by the way. They made halting-places of the tiny islets which, often uninhabited and far removed from the well-known groups, dot the immense waste of the Pacific at great intervals. The finding of their stone axes or implements in such desolate spots enables their courses to be traced. Canoe-men who could voyage to solitary little Easter Island in the wide void towards America, or to Cape York in the distant west, were not likely to find insuperable difficulties in running before the north-east winds to New Zealand from Rarotonga, Savaii or Tahiti. The discovery in the new land of the jade or greenstone— far above rubies in the eyes of men of the Stone Age—would at once give the country all the attractiveness that a gold-field has for civilized man.

[Footnote 1: S. Percy Smith on *The Geographical Knowledge of the Polynesians*.]

The Maori stories of their migration to New Zealand are a mixture of myth and legend. Among them are minute details that may be accurate, mingled with monstrous tales of the utterly impossible. For example, we are told that one chief, on his canoe first nearing the coast, saw the feathery, blood-red rata-flowers gleaming in the forest, and promptly threw overboard his Polynesian coronet of red feathers, exclaiming that he would get a new crown in the new land. Such an incident might be true, as might also the tale of another canoe which approached the shore at night. Its crew were warned of the neighbourhood of land by the barking of a dog which they had with them and which scented a whale's carcass stranded on the beach. On the other hand we are gravely told that the hero Gliding-Tide having dropped an axe overboard off the shore, muttered an incantation so powerful that the bottom of the sea rose up, the waters divided, and the axe returned to his hand. The shoal at any rate is there, and is pointed out to this day. And what are we to say to the tale of another leader, whose canoe was upset in the South Seas, and who swam all the way to New Zealand?

The traditions say that the Maori Pilgrim Fathers left the island of Hawaiki for New Zealand about the beginning of the 15th century. Hawaiki is probably one of the "shores of old romance." Other Polynesian races also claim to have come thence. Mr. Percy Smith gives good reasons for the suggestion that the ancestors of the Maoris migrated from the Society Islands and from Rarotonga, and that their principal migration took place about five hundred years ago. It seems likely enough, however, that previous immigrants had gone before them. One remnant of these, the now almost extinct Moriori, colonised the Chatham Islands, whither they were not followed by the conquering Maori until the present century. The two most famous of the great double canoes of the Maori settlers were the Arawa (shark), and the Tainui (flood-tide). On board thereof, with the men, women, and children, were brought dogs, rats, the gourd and taro root, and the invaluable kumara or sweet potato. The karaka tree, whose glossy, almost oily-looking leaves were in after days to be seen in every village, was another importation. With these tradition ranks the green parakeet and blue pukeko or swamp-hen, two birds whose rich plumage has indeed something in it of tropical gaudiness, at any rate in contrast with the sober hues of most New Zealand feathers. The Tainui canoe was said to have found its last resting-place near the mouth of the Mokau river. A stone still lies there which is treasured by the natives as the ancient anchor of their sacred craft. Some years ago, when a European carried this off, they brought an action against him and obtained an order of the Court compelling him to restore it. Not far away stands a grove of trees alleged to have sprung from the Tainui's skids. Certainly Sir James Hector, the first scientific authority in the Colony, finding that these trees grow spontaneously nowhere else in New Zealand, named them *Pomaderris Tainui*. But though, for once, at any rate, science was not indisposed to smile on tradition and Maori faith triumphed, and the unbeliever was for a while confounded, it unhappily seems now quite certain that the congener of *Pomaderris Tainui* is found only in Australia, one of the few lands nigh the Pacific which cannot have been Hawaiki.

It will be safe to say that the Maori colonists landed at different points and at widely different dates, and that later immigrants sometimes drove earlier comers inland or southward. More often, probably, each small band sought out an empty territory for itself. On this tribes and sub-tribes grew up, dwelling apart from each other. Each district became the land of a clan, to be held by tomahawk and spear. Not even temporary defeat and slavery deprived a tribe of its land: nothing did that but permanent expulsion followed by actual seizure and occupation by the conquerors. Failing this, the right of the beaten side lived on, and could be reasserted after years of exile. The land was not the property of the *arikis* or chiefs, or even of the *rangatiras* or gentry. Every free man, woman and child in each clan had a vested interest therein which was acknowledged and respected. The common folk were not supposed to have immortal souls. That was the distinction of the well born. But they had a right to their undivided share of the soil. Even when a woman married into another tribe, or—in latter days—became the wife of a white, she did not forfeit her title, though sometimes such rights would be surrendered by arrangement, to save inconvenience. Trade never entered into Maori life. Buying and selling were unknown. On and by the land the Maori lived, and he clung to it closely as any Irish peasant. "The best death a man can die is for the land," ran a proverb. "Let us die for the land!" shouted a chieftain, haranguing his fighting men before one of their first battles with the English. No appeal would be more certain to strike home.

Though the tribal estate was communal property in so far that any member could go out into the wilderness and fell trees and reclaim the waste, the fruits of such work, the timber and plantations, at once became personal property. The fields, houses, weapons, tools, clothes, and food of a family could not be meddled with by outsiders. The territory, in a word, was common, but not only products but usufructs were property attaching to individuals, who could transfer them by gift.

Though in time they forgot the way to "Hawaiki," and even at last the art of building double-canoes, yet they never wanted for pluck or seamanship in fishing and voyaging along the stormy New Zealand coasts. Their skill and coolness in paddling across flooded rivers may still sometimes be witnessed.

Always needing fish, they placed their villages near the sea beaches or the rivers and lakes. In their canoes they would paddle as far as twelve miles from land. Amongst other fish they caught sharks, killing them before they hauled them into the crank canoes; or, joining forces, they would sweep some estuary with drag nets, and, with much yelling and splashing, drive the fish into a shallow corner. There with club and spear dog-fish and smooth-hound would be done to death amid shouts and excitement. Then would come a gorge on a grand scale, followed by business—the cutting into strips and drying of the shark-meat for winter food. In the forests they found birds, and, not having the bow-and-arrow, made shift to snare and spear them ingeniously. To add to the vegetable staples which they had brought with them from their Polynesian home, they used the root of the fern or bracken, and certain wild fruits and berries—none of them specially attractive. What between fish, birds and vegetables, with occasional delicacies in the shape of dogs and rats, they were by no means badly provisioned, and they cooked their food carefully and well, chiefly by steaming in ovens lined with heated stones. Without tea, coffee, sugar, alcohol or tobacco, they had also but seldom the stimulant given by flesh meat. Their notorious cannibalism was almost confined to triumphal banquets on the bodies of enemies slain in battle. Without the aid of metals or pottery, without wool, cotton, silk or linen, without one beast of burden, almost without leather, they yet contrived to clothe, feed and house themselves, and to make some advance in the arts of building, carving, weaving and dyeing.

MAORI AND CARVED BOW OF CANOE

The labour and patience needed to maintain some degree of rude comfort and keep up any kind of organised society with the scanty means at their disposal were very great indeed. The popular notion of the lazy savage basking in the sunshine, or squatting round the fire and loafing on the labour of his women, did not fairly apply to the Maori—at any rate to the unspoiled Maori. As seen by the early navigators, his life was one of regular, though varied and not excessive toil. Every tribe, in most ways every village, was self-contained and self-supporting. What that meant to a people intelligent, but ignorant of almost every scientific appliance, and as utterly isolated as though they inhabited a planet of their own, a little reflection will suggest. The villagers had to be their own gardeners, fowlers, fishermen and carpenters. They built their own houses and canoes, and made every tool and weapon. All that they wore as well as what they used had to be made on the spot. They did not trade, though an exchange of gifts regulated by strict etiquette amounted to a rude and limited kind of barter, under which inland tribes could supply themselves with dried sea-fish and sea-birds preserved in their melted fat, or northern tribes could acquire the precious greenstone found in the west of the South Island.

Without flocks and herds or domestic fowls, theirs was the constant toil of the cultivator. Their taro and their kumara fields had to be dug, and dug thoroughly with wooden spades. Long-handled and pointed at the end, these implements resembled stilts with a cross-bar about eighteen inches from the ground on which the digger's foot rested. Two men worked them together. The women did not dig the fields, but theirs was the labour almost as severe of carrying on their backs the heavy baskets of gravel to scatter over the soil of the plantations.

Almost the only staple article of Maori vegetable food which grew wild and profusely was the fern or bracken *(pteris aquilina* var. *esculenta)*, which indeed was found on every hill and moor and in every glade, at any rate in the North Island. But the preparation of the fibrous root was tedious, calling as it did for various processes of drying and pounding.

Fishing involved not only the catching of fish, but the manufacture of seine nets, sometimes half a mile long, of eel-weirs, lines made of the fibre of the native flax, and of fish-hooks of bone or tough crooked wood barbed with human bone. The human skeleton was also laid under contribution for the material of skewers, needles and flutes.

The infinite patience and delicacy requisite in their bird-snaring and spearing are almost beyond the conception of the civilized townsmen untrained in wood-craft. To begin with, they had to make the slender bird spears, thirty feet long, out of the light wood of the *tawa* tree. A single tree could provide no more than two spears, and the making of them—with stone tools of course—took many months. Think of the dexterity, coolness and stealth required to manage such a weapon in a jungle so dense and tangled that white sportsmen often find a difficulty in handling their guns there! The silent adroitness needed to approach and spear the wild parrot or wood-pigeon without stirring the branch of a tree would alone require a long apprenticeship to wood-craft.

Maori house-building showed a knowledge of architecture decidedly above that of the builders of Kaffir kraals, to say nothing of the lairs of the Australian blacks. The poorest huts were definitely planned and securely built. The shape was oblong, the walls low, the roof high pitched and disproportionately large, though not so much so as in some of the South Sea Islands. The framework was of the durable totara-wood, the lining of reeds, the outside of dried rushes. At the end turned to the sunshine was a kind of verandah, on to which opened the solitary door and window, both low and small. The floor was usually sunk below ground, and Maori builders knew of no such thing as a chimney. Though neither cooking nor eating was done in their dwelling-houses, and offal of all kinds was carefully kept at a decent distance, the atmosphere in their dim, stifling interiors was as a rule unendurable by White noses and lungs. Even their largest tribal or meeting halls had but the one door and window; the Maori mind seemed as incapable of adding thereto, as of constructing more than one room under a single roof. On the other hand, the dyed patterns on the reed wainscoting, and the carvings on the posts, lintel and boards, showed real beauty and a true sense of line and curve.

Still less reason is there to find fault with their canoes, the larger of which were not only strangely picturesque, but, urged by as many as a hundred paddles, flew through the water at a fine speed, or under sail made long coasting voyages in seas that are pacific only in name. To the carving on these crafts the savage artists added decoration by red ochre, strips of dyed flax, gay feathers and mother-o'-pearl. Both the building of the canoes and their adornment entailed long months of labour. So did the dressing of the fibre of the flax and palm-lily, and the weaving therefrom of "mats" or mantles, and of kirtles. Yet the making of such ordinary clothing was simple indeed compared to the manufacture of a chief's full dress mat of *kiwi* feathers. The soft, hairy-looking plumage of the *kiwi* (apteryx) is so fine, each feather so minute, that one mantle would occupy a first-rate artist for two years. Many of these mantles, whether of flax, feathers or dog-skin, were quaintly beautiful as well as warm and waterproof.

Nor did Maori skill confine itself to ornamenting the clothing of man. The human skin supplied a fresh and peculiar field for durable decoration. This branch of art, that of Moko or tattooing, they carried to a grotesque perfection. Among the many legends concerning their demi-god Maui, a certain story tells how he showed them the way to tattoo by puncturing the muzzle of a dog, whence dogs went with black muzzles as men see them now. For many generations the patterns cut and pricked on the human face and body were faithful imitations of what were believed to be Maui's designs. They were composed of straight lines, angles, and cross-cuts. Later the hero Mataora taught a more graceful style which dealt in curves, spirals, volutes and scroll-work. Apart from legend it is a matter of reasonable certitude that the Maoris brought tattooing with them from Polynesia. Their marking instruments were virtually the same as those of their tropical cousins; both, for instance, before the iron age of the nineteenth century, often used the wing-bones of sea-birds to make their tiny chisels. Both observed the law of *tapu* under which the male patients, while undergoing the process of puncturing, were sacred, immensely to their own inconvenience, for they had to dwell apart, and might not even touch food with their hands. As to the source of the peculiar patterns used by the New Zealanders, they probably have some relation with the admirable wood-carving before mentioned. Either the Moko artists copied the style of the skilful carvers of panels, door-posts, clubs, and the figure-heads on the prows of canoes, or the wood-carvers borrowed and reproduced the lines and curves of the Moko. The inspiration of the patterns, whether on wood or skin, may be found in the spirals of sea-shells, the tracery on the skin of lizards and the bark of trees, and even, it may be, in the curious fluting and natural scroll-work on the tall cliffs of the calcareous clay called *papa*.

But, however the Moko artist learned his designs, he was a painstaking and conscientious craftsman in imprinting them on his subject. No black-and-white draughtsman of our time, no wood-cutter, etcher, or line-engraver, worked with slower deliberation. The outlines were first drawn with charcoal or red ochre. Thus was the accuracy of curve and scroll-work ensured. Then, inch by inch, the lines were cut or pricked out on the quivering, but unflinching, human copper-plate. The blood was wiped away and the *narahu* (blue dye) infused. In the course of weeks, months, or years, as leisure, wealth, or endurance permitted, the work was completed. In no other society did the artist have his patron so completely at his mercy. Not only was a Moko expert of true ability a rarity for whose services there was always an "effective demand," but, if not well paid for his labours, the tattooer could make his sitter suffer in more ways than one. He could adroitly increase the acute anguish which had, as a point of honour, to be endured without cry or complaint; or he could coolly bungle the execution of the design, or leave it unfinished, and betake himself to a more generous customer. A well-known tattooing chant deals with the subject entirely from the artist's standpoint, and emphasises the business principles upon which he went to work. It was this song that Alfred Domett (Robert Browning's Waring) must have had in his mind when, in his New Zealand poem, he thus described the Moko on the face of the chief Tangi-Moana:—

"And finer, closer spirals of dark blue

Were never seen than in his cheek's tattoo;

Fine as if engine turned those cheeks declared

No cost to fee the artist had been spared;

That many a basket of good maize had made

That craftsman careful how he tapped his blade,

And many a greenstone trinket had been given

To get his chisel-flint so deftly driven."

When, however, the slow and costly agony was over, the owner of an unusually well-executed face became a superior person. He united in himself the virtues and vices of a chieftain of high degree (shown by the elaborateness of his face pattern), of a tribal dandy, of a brave man able to endure pain, of the owner of a unique picture, and of an acknowledged art critic. In the rigid-looking mask, moreover, which had now taken the place of his natural face were certain lines by which any one of his fellow-tribesmen could identify him living or dead. In this way the heads of Maori chiefs have been recognised even in the glass cases of museums. On some of the earlier deeds and agreements between White and Maori, a chief would sign or make his mark by means of a rough reproduction of his special Moko.

The Maori *pas* or stockaded and intrenched villages, usually perched on cliffs and jutting points overhanging river or sea, were defended by a double palisade, the outer fence of stout stakes, the inner of high solid trunks. Between them was a shallow ditch. Platforms as much as forty feet high supplied coigns of vantage for the look-out. Thence, too, darts and stones could be hurled at the besiegers. With the help of a throwing-stick, or rather whip, wooden spears could be thrown in the sieges more than a hundred yards. Ignorant of the bow-and-arrow and the boomerang, the Maoris knew and used the sling. With it red-hot stones would be hurled over the palisades, among the rush-thatched huts of an assaulted village, a stratagem all the more difficult to cope with as Maori *pas* seldom contained wells or springs of water. The courage and cunning developed in the almost incessant tribal feuds were extraordinary. Competent observers thought the Maoris of two generations ago the most warlike and ferocious race on earth. Though not seldom guilty of wild cruelty to enemies, they did not make a business of cold-blooded torture after the devilish fashion of the North American Indians. Chivalrous on occasion, they would sometimes send warning to the foe, naming the day of an intended attack, and abide thereby. They would supply a starving garrison with provisions in order that an impending conflict might be a fair trial of strength. War was to them something more dignified than a mere lawless struggle. It was a solemn game to be played according to rules as rigidly laid down and often as honourably adhered to as in the international cricket and football matches of Englishmen and Australians.

As is so often the case with fighting races capable of cruelty, they were strictly courteous in their intercourse with strangers. Indeed, their code of manners to visitors was so exact and elaborate as to leave an impression of artificiality. No party of wayfarers would approach a *pa* without giving formal notice. When the strangers were received, they had the best of everything, and the hosts, who saw that they were abundantly supplied, had too much delicacy to watch them eat. Maori breeding went so far as to avoid in converse words or topics likely to be disagreeable to their hearers.

Their feeling for beauty was shown not merely in their art, but in selecting the sites of dwelling-places, and in a fondness for shady shrubs and trees about their huts and for the forest-flowers. The natural images and similes so common in their wild, abrupt, unrhymed chants and songs showed how closely they watched and sympathised with nature. The hoar-frost, which vanishes with the sunrise, stood with them for ephemeral fame. Rank without power was "a fountain without water." The rushing stream reminded the Maori singer, as it did the Mantuan, of the remorseless current of life and human fate.

"But who can check life's stream?

Or turn its waters back?

'Tis past,"

cried a father mourning for his dead son. In another lament a grieving mother is compared to the drooping fronds of the tree-fern. The maiden keeping tryst bids the light fleecy cloudlets, which in New Zealand so often scud across the sky before the sea-wind, to be messengers to her laggard gallant.

"The sun grows dim and hastes away

As a woman from the scene of battle,"

says the lament for a dead chief.[1] The very names given to hills, lakes, and rivers will be witnesses in future days of the poetic instinct of the Maori—perhaps the last destined to remain in his land. Such names are the expressive Wai-orongo-mai (Hear me, ye waters!); Puké-aruhé (ferny hill); Wai-rarapa (glittering water); Maunga-tapu (sacred mount); Ao-reré (flying cloud). Last, but not least, there is the lordly Ao-rangi (Cloud in the heavens), over which we have plastered the plain and practical "Mount Cook."

[Footnote 1: The Maori is deeply imbued with the poetry of the woods. His commonest phraseology shows it. 'The month when the pohutu-kawa flowers'; 'the season when the kowhai is in bloom'; so he punctuates time. And the years that are gone he softly names' dead leaves!'—HAY, *Brighter Britain*.]

Many of the Maori chiefs were, and some even now are, masterly rhetoricians. The bent of the race was always strongly to controversy and discussion. Their ignorance of any description of writing made them cultivate debate. Their complacent indifference to time made deliberative assembly a prolonged, never-wearying joy. The chiefs met in council like Homer's heroes—the commons sitting round and muttering guttural applause or dissent. The speeches abounded in short sententious utterances, in proverbs, poetic allusions and metaphors borrowed from legends. The Maori orator dealt in quotations as freely as the author of the *Anatomy of Melancholy*, and his hearers caught them with as much relish as that of a House of Commons of Georgian days enjoying an apt passage from the classics. Draped in kilt and mantle, with spear or carved staff of office in the right hand, the speakers were manly and dignified figures. The fire and force of their rhetoric were not only aided by graceful gesture but were set out in a language worthy of the eloquent. If we cannot say of the Maori tongue as Gibbon said of Greek, that it "can give a soul to the objects of sense and a body to the abstractions of philosophy," we can at any rate claim for it that it is a musical and vigorous speech. Full of vowel-sounds, entirely without sibilants, but rich in guttural and chest notes, it may be made at will to sound liquid or virile, soft or ringing.

The seamy side of Maori life, as of all savage life, was patent to the most unimaginative observer. The traveller found it not easy to dwell on the dignity, poetry and bravery of a race which contemned washing, and lived, for the most part, in noisome hovels. A chief might be an orator and skilled captain, but, squatting on the ground, smeared with oil, daubed with red ochre and grimly tattooed, he probably impressed the white visitor chiefly as an example of dirt and covetousness. The traveller might be hospitably entertained in a *pa* the gate of which was decorated with the smoke-dried heads of slain enemies by a host whose dress might include a necklace of human teeth,[1] the owner of which he had helped to eat. Though a cannibal feast was a rare orgie, putrid food was a common dainty. Without the cringing manner of the Oriental, the Maori had his full share of deceitfulness. Elaborate treachery is constantly met with in the accounts of their wars. If adultery was rare, chastity among the single women was rarer still. The affection of parents for young children was requited by no kindness on the part of youth for old age. Carving never rose higher than grotesque decoration. The attempts at portraying the human face or form resulted only in the monstrous and the obscene.

[Footnote 1: At any rate among the Ngatiporou tribe.]

A MAORI MAIDEN;
Photo by ILES, Thames

The Maori men are as a rule tall and bulky, long-bodied and short-legged, and with fairly large pyramidal skulls, showing well-developed perceptive faculties. Their colour varies from maize to dusky olive, and their features from classic to negroid; but usually the nose, though not flat, is wide, and the mouth, though not blubber-lipped, is heavy and sensual. Shorter and more coarsely built than the males, the women, even when young, are less attractive to the European eye, despite their bright glances and black, abundant hair. It might well be thought that this muscular, bulky race, with ample room to spread about a fertile and exceptionally healthy country, would have increased and multiplied till it had filled both islands. It did not, however. It is doubtful whether it ever numbered more than a hundred and fifty thousand. Except on the shores of Cook's Straits, it only planted a few scattered outposts in the South Island. Yet that is the larger island of the two. It is also the colder, and therein lies at least one secret of the check to the Maori increase. They were a tropical race transplanted into a temperate climate. They showed much the same tendency to cling to the North Island as the negroes in North America to herd in the Gulf States. Their dress, their food and their ways were those of dwellers on shores out of reach of frost and snow. Though of stout and robust figure, they are almost always weak in the chest and throat. Should the Maoris die out, the medical verdict might be summed up in the one word tuberculosis.

The first European observers noted that they suffered from "galloping" consumption. Skin disorders, rheumatism and a severe kind of influenza were other ailments.

In the absence equally of morality and medical knowledge among their unmarried women, it did not take many years after the appearance of the Whites to taint the race throughout with certain diseases. A cold-blooded passage in Crozet's journal tells of the beginning of this curse. Though not altogether unskilful surgeons, the Maoris knew virtually nothing of medicine. Nor do they show much nervous power when attacked by disease. Cheerful and sociable when in health, they droop quickly when ill, and seem sometimes to die from sheer lack of the will to live. Bright and imaginative almost as the Kelts of Europe, their spirits are easily affected by superstitious dread. Authentic cases are known of a healthy Maori giving up the ghost through believing himself to be doomed by a wizard.

There are, however, other evil influences under which this attractive and interesting people are fading away. Though no longer savages, they have never become thoroughly civilized. Partial civilization has been a blight to their national life. It has ruined the efficacy of their tribal system without replacing it with any equal moral force and industrial stimulus. It has deprived them of the main excitement of their lives—their tribal wars—and given them no spur to exertion by way of a substitute. It has fatally wounded their pride and self-respect, and has not given them objects of ambition or preserved their ancient habits of labour and self-restraint. A hundred years ago the tribes were organized and disciplined communities. No family or able-bodied unit need starve or lack shelter; the humblest could count on the most open-handed hospitality from his fellows. The tribal territory was the property of all. The tilling, the fishing, the fowling were work which could not be neglected. The chief was not a despot, but the president of a council, and in war would not be given the command unless he was the most capable captain. Every man was a soldier, and, under the perpetual stress of possible war, had to be a trained, self-denying athlete. The *pas* were, for defensive reasons, built on the highest and therefore the healthiest positions. The ditches, the palisades, the terraces of these forts were constructed with great labour as well as no small skill. The fighting was hand to hand. The wielding of their weapons—the wooden spear, the club, the quaint *mere*[1] and the stone tomahawk—required strength and endurance as well as a skill only to be obtained by hard practice. The very sports and dances of the Maori were such as only the active and vigorous could excel in. Slaves were there, but not enough to relieve the freemen from the necessity for hard work. Strange sacred customs, such as *tapu* (vulgarly Anglicized as taboo) and *muru*, laughable as they seem to us, tended to preserve public health, to ensure respect for authority, and to prevent any undue accumulation of goods and chattels in the hands of one man. Under the law of *muru* a man smitten by sudden calamity was politely plundered of all his possessions. It was the principle under which the wounded shark is torn to pieces by its fellows, and under which the merchant wrecked on the Cornish coast in bye-gone days was stripped of anything the waves had spared. Among the Maoris, however, it was at once a social duty and a personal compliment. If a man's hut caught fire his dearest friends clustered round like bees, rescued all they could from the flames, and—kept it. It is on record that a party about to pay a friendly visit to a neighbour village were upset in their canoe as they were paddling in through the surf. The canoe was at once claimed by the village chief— their host. Moreover they would have been insulted if he had not claimed it. Of course, he who lost by *muru* one week might be able to repay himself the next.

[Footnote 1: Tasman thought the meré resembled the *parang*, or heavy, broad-bladed knife, of the Malays. Others liken it to a paddle, and matter-of-fact colonists to a tennis-racket or a soda-water bottle flattened.]

Certain colonial writers have exhausted their powers ridicule—no very difficult task—upon what they inaccurately call Maori communism. But the system, in full working order, at least developed the finest race of savages the world has seen, and taught them barbaric virtues which have won from their white supplanters not only respect but liking. The average colonist regards a Mongolian with repulsion, a Negro with contempt, and looks on an Australian black as very near to a wild beast; but he likes the Maoris, and is sorry that they are dying out.

No doubt the remnants of the Maori tribal system are useless, and perhaps worse than useless. The tribes still own land in common, and much of it. They might be very wealthy landlords if they cared to lease their estates on the best terms they could bargain for. As it is, they receive yearly very large sums in rent. They could be rich farmers if they cared to master the science of farming. They have brains to learn more difficult things. They might be healthy men and women if they would accept the teachings of sanitary science as sincerely as they took in the religious teachings of the early missionaries. If they could be made to realize that foul air, insufficient dress, putrid food, alternations of feast and famine, and long bouts of sedulous idleness are destroying them as a people and need not do so, then their decay might be arrested and the fair hopes of the missionary pioneers yet be justified. So long as they soak maize in the streams until it is rotten and eat it together with dried shark—food the merest whiff of which will make a white man sick; so long as they will wear a suit of clothes one day and a tattered blanket the next, and sit smoking crowded in huts, the reek of which strikes you like a blow in the face; so long as they will cluster round dead bodies during their *tangis* or wakes; so long as they will ignore drainage—just so long will they remain a blighted and dwindling race, and observers without eyes will talk as though there was something fateful and mysterious in their decline. One ray of hope for them has quite lately been noted. They are caring more for the education of their children. Some three thousand of these now go to school, not always irregularly. Very quaint scholars are the dark-eyed, quick-glancing, brown-skinned little people sitting tied "to that dry drudgery at the desk's dull wood," which, if heredity counts for anything, must be so much harder to them than to the children of the *Pakeha*.[1] Three years ago the Government re-organized the native schools, had the children taught sanitary lessons with the help of magic lanterns, and gave power to committees of native villagers to prosecute the parents of truants. The result has been a prompt, marked and growing improvement in the attendance and the general interest. Better still, the educated Maori youths are awakening to the sad plight of their people. Pathetic as their regrets are, the healthy discontent they show may lead to better things.

[Footnote 1: Foreigner.]

Chapter III

THE MAORI AND THE UNSEEN

"Dreaming caves

Full of the groping of bewildered waves."

The Maori mind conceived of the Universe as divided into three regions—the Heavens above, the Earth beneath, and the Darkness under the Earth. To Rangi, the Heaven, the privileged souls of chiefs and priests returned after death, for from Rangi had come down their ancestors the gods, the fathers of the heroes. For the souls of the common people there was in prospect no such lofty and serene abode. They could not hope to climb after death to the tenth heaven, where dwelt Rehua, the Lord of Loving-kindness, attended by an innumerable host. Ancient of days was Rehua, with streaming hair. The lightning flashed from his arm-pits, great was his power, and to him the sick, the blind, and the sorrowful might pray.

It was not the upper world of Ao or Light, but an under world of Po or Darkness, to which the spirit of the unprivileged Maori must take its way. Nor was the descent to Te Reinga or Hades a *facilis descensus Averni*. After the death-chant had ceased, and the soul had left the body—left it lying surrounded by weeping blood-relations marshalled in due order—it started on a long journey. Among the Maoris the dead were laid with feet pointing to the north, as it was thither that the soul's road lay. At the extreme north end of New Zealand was a spot *Muri Whenua*—Land's End. Here was the Spirits' Leap. To that the soul travelled, halting once and again on the hill-tops to strip off the green leaves in which the mourners had clad it. Here and there by the wayside some lingering ghost would tie a knot in the ribbon-like leaves of the flax plant—such knots as foreigners hold to be made by the whipping of the wind. As the souls gathered at their goal, nature's sounds were hushed. The roar of the waterfall, the sea's dashing, the sigh of the wind in the trees, all were silenced. At the Spirits' Leap on the verge of a tall cliff grew a lonely tree, with brown, spreading branches, dark leaves and red flowers. The name of the tree was Spray-Sprinkled.[1] One of its roots hung down over the cliff's face to the mouth of a cavern fringed by much sea-weed, floating or dripping on the heaving sea. Pausing for a moment the reluctant shades chanted a farewell to their fellow-men and danced a last war-dance. Amid the wild yells of the invisible dancers could be heard the barking of their dogs. Then, sliding down the roots, the spirits disappeared in the cave. Within its recesses was a river flowing between sandy shores. All were impelled to cross it. The Charon of this Styx was no man, but a ferrywoman called Rohé. Any soul whom she carried over and who ate the food offered to it on the further bank was doomed to abide in Hades. Any spirit who refused returned to its body on earth and awoke. This is the meaning of what White men call a trance.

[Footnote 1: *Pohutu-kawa*.]

As there were successive planes and heights in Heaven, so there were depths below depths in the Underworld. In the lowest and darkest the soul lost consciousness, became a worm, and returning to earth, died there. Eternal life was the lot of only the select few who ascended to Rangi.

Yet once upon a time there was going and coming between earth and the place of darkness, as the legend of the origin of the later style of tattooing shows. Thus the story runs. The hero Mata-ora had to wife the beautiful Niwa Reka. One day for some slight cause he struck her, and, leaving him in anger, she fled to her father, who dwelt in the Underworld. Thither followed the repentant Mata-ora. On his way he asked the fan-tail bird whether it had seen a human being pass. Yes, a woman had gone by downcast and sobbing. Holding on his way, Mata-ora met his father-in-law, who, looking in his face, complained that he was badly tattooed. Passing his hand over Mata-ora's face he wiped out with his divine power the blue lines there, and then had him thrown down on the ground and tattooed in a novel, more artistic and exquisitely agonizing fashion. Mata-ora in his pain chanted a song calling upon his wife's name. Report of this was carried to Niwa Reka, and her heart was touched. She forgave her husband, and nursed him through the fever caused by the tattooing. Happier than Orpheus and Eurydice, the pair returned to earth and taught men to copy the patterns punctured on Mata-ora's face. But, alas! in their joy they forgot to pay to Ku Whata Whata, the mysterious janitor of Hades, Niwa Reka's cloak as fee. So a message was sent up to them that henceforth no man should be permitted to return to earth from the place of darkness. In the age of the heroes not only the realms below but the realms above could be reached by the daring. Hear the tale of Tawhaki, the Maori Endymion! When young he became famous by many feats, among others, by destroying the submarine stronghold of a race of sea-folk who had carried off his mother. Into their abode he let a flood of sunshine, and they, being children of the darkness, withered and died in the light. The fame of Tawhaki rose to the skies, and one of the daughters of heaven stole down to behold him at night, vanishing away at dawn. At last the celestial one became his wife. But he was not pleased with the daughter she bore him and, wounded by his words, she withdrew with her child to the skies. Tawhaki in his grief remembered that she had told him the road thither. He must find a certain tendril of a wild vine which, hanging down from the sky to earth, had become rooted in the ground. Therefore with his brother the hero set out on the quest, and duly found the creeper. But there were two tendrils. The brother seized the wrong one; it was loose, and he was swung away, whirled by the wind backwards and forwards from one horizon to the other. Tawhaki took the right ladder, and climbed successfully.[1] At the top he met with adventures, and had even to become a slave, and carry axes and firewood disguised as a little, ugly, old man. At last, however, he regained his wife, became a god, and still reigns above. It is he who causes lightning to flash from heaven.

[Footnote 1: Another version describes his ladder as a thread from a spider's web; a third as the string of his kite, which he flew so skilfully that it mounted to the sky; then Tawhaki, climbing up the cord, disappeared in the blue vault.]

The man in the moon becomes, in Maori legend, a woman, one Rona by name. This lady, it seems, once had occasion to go by night for water to a stream. In her hand she carried an empty calabash. Stumbling in the dark over stones and the roots of trees she hurt her shoeless feet and began to abuse the moon, then hidden behind clouds, hurling at it some such epithet as "You old tattooed face, there!" But the moon-goddess heard, and reaching down caught up the insulting Rona, calabash and all, into the sky. In vain the frightened woman clutched, as she rose, the tops of a ngaio-tree. The roots gave way, and Rona with her calabash and her tree are placed in the front of the moon for ever, an awful warning to all who are tempted to mock at divinities in their haste.

All beings, gods, heroes and men, are sprung from the ancient union of Heaven and Earth, Rangi and Papa. Rangi was the father and Earth the great mother of all. Even now, in these days, the rain, the snow, the dew and the clouds are the creative powers which come down from Rangi to mother Earth and cause the trees, the shrubs and the plants to grow in spring and flourish in summer. It is the self-same process that is pictured in the sonorous hexameters:—

"Tum pater omnipotens fecundis imbribus Aether

Coniugis in gremium laetae descendit, et omnes

Magnus alit, magno commixtus corpore, fetus."

But in the beginning Heaven lay close to the Earth and all was dim and dark. There was life but not light. So their children, tired of groping about within narrow and gloomy limits, conspired together to force them asunder and let in the day. These were Tu, the scarlet-belted god of men and war, Tané, the forest god, and their brother, the sea-god. With them joined the god of cultivated food, such as the kumara, and the god of food that grows wild—such as the fern-root. The conspirators cut great poles with which to prop up Heaven. But the father and mother were not to be easily separated. They clung to each other despite the efforts of their unnatural sons. Then Tané, the tree-god, standing on head and hands, placed his feet against Heaven and, pushing hard, forced Rangi upwards. In that attitude the trees, the children of Tané, remain to this day. Thus was the separation accomplished, and Rangi and Papa must for ever remain asunder. Yet the tears of Heaven still trickle down and fall as dew-drops upon the face of his spouse, and the mists that rise in the evening from her bosom are the sighs of regret which she sends up to her husband on high.[1]

[Footnote 1: Sir George Grey, *Polynesian Mythology*.]

Vengeance, however, fell upon the conspirators. A sixth brother had had nothing to do with their plot. This was Tawhiri-Matea, the god of winds and storms. He loyally accompanied his father to the realms above, whence he descended on his rebel brothers in furious tempests. The sea-god fled to the ocean, where he and his children dwell as fishes. The two gods of plant-food hid in the Earth, and she, forgiving mother that she was, sheltered them in her breast. Only Tu, the god of mankind, stayed erect and undaunted. So it is that the winds and storms make war to this day upon men, wrecking their canoes, tearing down their houses and fences and ruining all their handiwork. Not only does man hold out against these attacks, but, in revenge for the cowardly desertion of Tu by his weaker brethren, men, his people, prey upon the fish and upon the plants that give food whether wild or cultivated.

Space will scarcely permit even a reference to other Maori myths—to the tale, for instance, of the great flood which came in answer to the prayers of two faithful priests as punishment for the unbelief, the discords and the wickedness of mankind; then all were drowned save a little handful of men and women who floated about on a raft for eight moons and so reached Hawaiki. Of the creation of man suffice it to say that he was made by Tiki, who formed him out of red clay, or, as some say, out of clay reddened by his own blood. Woman's origin was more ethereal and poetic; her sire was a noonday sunbeam, her mother a sylvan echo. Many are the legends of the hero, Maui. He lassooed the sun with ropes and beat him till he had to go slower, and so the day grew longer. The first ropes thus used were of flax, which burned and snapped in the sun's heat. Then Maui twisted a cord of the tresses of his sister, Ina, and this stayed unconsumed. It was Maui who went to fetch for man's use the fire which streamed from the finger-nails of the fire goddess, and who fished up the North Island of New Zealand, still called by the Maoris *Te Ika a Maui*, the fish of Maui. He first taught tattooing and the art of catching fish with bait, and died in the endeavour to gain immortality for men. Death would have been done away with had

Maui successfully accomplished the feat of creeping through the body of a certain gigantic goddess. But that flippant and restless little bird, the fan-tail, was so tickled at the sight of the hero crawling down the monster's throat that it tittered and burst into laughter. So the goblin awoke, and Maui died for man in vain.

Such are some of the sacred myths of the Maori. They vary very greatly in different tribes and are loaded with masses of detail largely genealogical. The religious myths form but one portion of an immense body of traditional lore, made up of songs and chants, genealogies, tribal histories, fables, fairy-tales and romantic stories. Utterly ignorant as the Maoris were of any kind of writing or picture-drawing, the volume of their lore is amazing, and is an example of the power of the human memory when assiduously cultivated. Very great care was, of course, taken to hand it down from father to son in the priestly families. In certain places in New Zealand, notably at Wanganui, sacred colleges stood called Whare-kura (Red-house). These halls had to be built by priestly hands, stood turned to the east, and could only be approached by the purified. They were dedicated by sacrifice, sometimes of a dog, sometimes of a human being. The pupils, who were boys of high rank, went, at the time of admission, through a form of baptism. The term of instruction lasted through the autumns and winters of five years. The hours were from sunset to midnight. Only one woman, an aged priestess, was admitted into the hall, and she only to perform certain incantations. No one might eat or sleep there, and any pupil who fell asleep during instruction was at once thrust forth, was expected to go home and die, and doubtless usually did so. Infinite pains were taken to impress on the pupils' memories the exact wording of traditions. As much as a month would be devoted to constant repetitions of a single myth. They were taught the tricks of the priestly wizard's trade, and became expert physiognomists, ventriloquists, and possibly, in some cases, hypnotists. Public exhibitions afterwards tested the accuracy of their memories and their skill in witchcraft. On this their fate depended. A successful *Tohunga*, or wizard, lived on the fat of the land; a few failures, and he was treated with discredit and contempt.

Though so undoubted an authority as Mr. William Colenso sums up the old-time Maori as a secularist, it is not easy entirely to agree with him. Not only had the Maori, as already indicated, an elaborate—too elaborate— mythology, but he had a code of equally wide and minute observances which he actually did observe. Not only had he many gods both of light and evil, but the Rev. James Stack, a most experienced student, says that he conceived of his gods as something more than embodiments of power—as beings "interested in human affairs and able to see and hear from the highest of the heavens what took place on earth." Mr. Colenso himself dwells upon the Maori faith in dreams, omens, and charms, and on the universal dread felt for *kehuas* or ghosts, and *atuas* or demon spirits. Moreover, the code of observances aforesaid was no mere secular law. It was the celebrated system of *tapu* (taboo), and was not only one of the most extraordinary and vigorous sets of ordinances ever devised by barbarous man, but depended for its influence and prestige not mainly upon the secular arm or even public opinion, but upon the injunction and support of unseen and spiritual powers. If a man broke the *tapu* law, his punishment was not merely to be shunned by his fellows or—in some cases—plundered of his goods. Divine vengeance in one or other form would swiftly fall upon him—probably in the practical shape of the entry into his body of an evil spirit to gnaw him to death with cruel teeth. Men whose terror of such punishment as this, and whose vivid faith in the imminence thereof, were strong enough to kill them were much more, or less, than secularists.

The well-known principle that there is no potent, respected, and lasting institution, however strange, but has its roots in practical usefulness, is amply verified in the case of *tapu*. By it authority was ensured, dignity hedged about with respect, and property and public health protected. Any person, place or thing laid under *tapu* might not be touched, and sometimes not even approached. A betrothed maiden defended by *tapu* was as sacred as a vestal virgin of Rome; a shrine became a Holy Place; the head of a chief something which it was sacrilege to lay hands on. The back of a man of noble birth could not be degraded by bearing burdens—an awkward prohibition in moments when no slave or woman happened to be in attendance on these lordly beings. Anything cooked for a chief was forbidden food to an inferior. The author of *Old New Zealand* tells of an unlucky slave who unwittingly ate the remains of a chiefs dinner. When the knowledge of this frightful crime was flashed upon him, he was seized with internal cramps and pains and, though a strong man, died in a few hours. The weapons and personal effects of a chief were, of course, sacred even in the opinion of a thief, but *tapu* went further. Even the fire a chief had lit might not be used by commoners. As for priests, after the performance of certain ceremonies they for a time had perforce to become too sacred to feed themselves with their hands. Food would be laid down before them and kneeling, or on all-fours like dogs, they had to pick it up with their teeth. Perhaps their lot might be so far mitigated that a maiden would be permitted to convey food to their mouths on the end of a fern-stalk—a much less disagreeable process for the eater. Growing fields of the sweet potato were sacred for obvious reasons, as were those who were working therein. So were burial-places and the bones of the dead. The author above-mentioned chancing one day on a journey to pick up a human skull which had been left exposed by a land-slide, immediately became an outcast shunned by acquaintances, friends and his own household, as though he were a very leper. Before he could be officially cleansed and readmitted into decent Maori society, his clothing and furniture had to be destroyed, and his kitchen abandoned. By such means did this—to us—ridiculous superstition secure reverence for the dead and some avoidance of infection. To this end the professional grave-digger and corpse-bearer of a Maori village was *tapu*, and lived loathed and utterly apart. Sick persons were often treated in the same way, and inasmuch as the unlucky might be supposed to have offended the gods, the victims of sudden and striking misfortune were treated as law-breakers and subjected to the punishment of *Muru* described in the last chapter.

Death in Maori eyes was not the Great Leveller, as with us. Just as the destiny of the chief's soul was different from that of the commoner or slave, so was the treatment of his body.

A slave's death was proverbially that of a dog, no man regarded it. Even the ordinary free man was simply buried in the ground in a sitting posture and forgotten. But the departure of a chief of rank and fame, of great *mana* or prestige, was the signal for national mourning. With wreaths of green leaves on their heads, friends sat round the body wailing the long-drawn cry, *Aué! Aué!* or listening to some funeral chant recited in his praise. Women cut themselves with sharp sea-shells or flakes of volcanic glass till the blood ran down. The corpse sat in state adorned with flowers and red ochre and clad in the finest of mantles. Albatross feathers were in the warrior's hair, his weapons were laid beside him. The onlookers joined in the lamenting, and shed actual tears—a feat any well-bred Maori could perform at will. Probably a huge banquet took place; then it was held to be a truly great *tangi*. Often the wives of the departed killed themselves in their grief, or a slave was sacrificed in his honour. His soul was believed to mount aloft, and perhaps some star was henceforth pointed out as his eye shining down and watching over his tribe. The tattooed head of the dead man was usually reverently preserved—stored away in some secret recess and brought out by the priest to be gazed upon on high occasions. The body, placed in a canoe-shaped coffin, was left for a time to dry on a stage or moulder in a hollow tree. After an appointed period the bones were scraped clean and laid away in a cavern or cleft known only to a sacred few. They might be thrown down some dark mountain abyss or *torere*. Such inaccessible resting-places of famous chiefs—deep well-like pits or tree-fringed chasms—are still pointed out to the traveller who climbs certain New Zealand summits. But, wherever the warrior's bones were laid, they were guarded by secrecy, by the dreaded *tapu*, and by the jealous zeal of his people. Even now no Maori tribe will sell such spots, and the greedy or inquisitive *Pakeha* who profanely explores or meddles with them does so at no small risk.

Far different was the fate of those unlucky leaders who fell in battle, or were captured and slaughtered and devoured thereafter. Their heads stuck upon the posts of the victor's *pa* were targets for ribaldry, or, in later days, might be sold to the *Pakeha* and carried away to be stared at as oddities. Their bones might be used for flutes and fishing-hooks, for no fisherman was so lucky as he whose hook was thus made; their souls were doomed to successive stages of deepening darkness below, and at length, after reaching the lowest gulf, passed as earth-worms to annihilation.

Chapter IV

THE NAVIGATORS

"A ship is floating on the harbour now,

A wind is hovering o'er the mountain's brow.

There is a path on the sea's azure floor,

No keel hath ever ploughed that path before."

Nearly at the end of 1642, Tasman, a sea captain in the service of the Dutch East India Company, sighted the western ranges of the Southern Alps. He was four months out from Java, investigating the extent of New Holland, and in particular its possible continuation southward as a great Antarctic continent. He had just discovered Tasmania, and was destined, ere returning home, to light upon Fiji and the Friendly Islands. So true is it that the most striking discoveries are made by men who are searching for what they never find. In clear weather the coast of Westland is a grand spectacle, and even through the dry, matter-of-fact entries of Tasman's log we can see that it impressed him. He notes that the mountains seemed lifted aloft in the air. With his two ships, the small *Heemskirk* and tiny *Zeehan*, he began to coast cautiously northward, looking for an opening eastward, and noting the high, cloud-clapped, double range of mountains, and the emptiness of the steep desolate coast, where neither smoke nor men, ships nor boats, were to be seen. He could not guess that hidden in this wilderness was a wealth of coal and gold as valuable as the riches of Java. He seems to have regarded New Zealand simply as a lofty barrier across his path, to be passed at the first chance. Groping along, he actually turned into the wide opening which, narrowing further east into Cook's Strait, divides the North and South Islands. He anchored in Golden Bay; but luck was against him. First of all the natives of the bay paddled out to view his ships, and, falling on a boat's crew, clubbed four out of seven of the men. Tasman's account—which I take leave to doubt—makes the attack senselessly wanton and unprovoked.

He tells how a fleet of canoes, each carrying from thirteen to seventeen men, hung about his vessels, and how the strongly-built, gruff-voiced natives, with yellowish-brown skins, and with white feathers stuck in their clubbed hair, refused all offers of intercourse. Their attack on his boat as it was being pulled from the *Zeehan* to the *Heemskirk* was furious and sudden, and the crew seem to have been either unarmed or too panic-stricken to use their weapons. Both ships at once opened a hot fire on the canoes, but hit nobody. It was not until next day, when twenty-two canoes put out to attack them, that the Dutch marksmen after much more firing succeeded in hitting a native. On his fall the canoes retired. Satisfied with this Tasman took no vengeance and sailed away further into the strait. Fierce north-westerly gales checked for days his northward progress. The strait, it may be mentioned, is still playfully termed "the windpipe of the Pacific." One night Tasman held a council on board the *Heemskirk*, and suggested to the officers that the tide showed that an opening must exist to the east, for which they had better search. But he did not persevere. When next evening the north wind died away there came an easterly breeze, followed by a stiff southerly gale, which made him change his mind again. So are discoveries missed.

He ran on northward, merely catching glimpses, through scud and cloud, of the North Island. Finally, at what is now North Cape, he discerned to his joy a free passage to the east. He made one attempt to land, in search of water, on a little group of islands hard by, which, as it was Epiphany, he called Three Kings, after Caspar, Melchior, and Balthasar. But the surf was rough and a throng of natives, striding along, shaking spears and shouting with hoarse voices, terrified his boat's crew. He gave up the attempt and sailed away, glad, no doubt, to leave this vague realm of storm and savages. It says something for his judgment that amid such surroundings he saw and noted in his log-book that the country was good. He had called it Staaten Land, on the wild guess that it extended to the island of that name off the coast of Terra del Fuego. Afterwards he altered the name to New Zealand. The secretive commercial policy of the Dutch authorities made them shroud Tasman's discoveries in mystery. It is said that his discoveries were engraved on the map of the world which in 1648 was cut on the stone floor of the Amsterdam Town Hall. The full text of his log has only been quite recently published. His curt entries dealing with the appearance of the New Zealand coast and its natives seem usually truthful enough. The tribe which attacked his boat was afterwards nearly exterminated by invaders from the North Island. This would account for the almost utter absence among the Maoris of tradition concerning his visit. It is noteworthy that he describes the natives of Golden—or, as he named it, Murderers'—Bay as having double-canoes. When the country was annexed, two hundred years afterwards, the New Zealanders had forgotten how to build them.

The Dutch made no use of their Australian discoveries. They were repelled by the heat, the drought, and the barrenness of the north-western coasts of New Holland. For a century and a quarter after Tasman's flying visit, New Zealand remained virtually unknown. Then the veil was lifted once and for all. Captain James Cook, in the *Endeavour*, sighted New Zealand in 1769. He had the time to study the country, and the ability too. On his first voyage alone nearly six months were devoted to it. In five visits he surveyed the coast, described the aspect and products of the islands, and noted down a mass of invaluable details concerning the native tribes. Every one may not be able to perceive the literary charm which certain eulogists have been privileged to find in Cook's admirable record of interesting facts. But he may well seem great enough as a discoverer and observer, to be easily able to survive a worse style—say Hawkesworth's. He found New Zealand a line on the map, and left it an Archipelago, a feat which many generations of her colonists will value above the shaping of sentences. The feature of his experiences which most strikes the reader now, is the extraordinary courage and pugnacity of the natives. They took the *Endeavour* for a gigantic white-winged sea-bird, and her pinnace for a young bird. They thought the sailors gods, and the discharge of their muskets divine thunderbolts. Yet, when Cook and a boat's crew landed, a defiant war-chief at once threatened the boat, and persisted until he was shot dead. Almost all Cook's attempts to trade and converse with the Maoris ended in the same way—a scuffle and a musket-shot. Yet the savages were never cowed, and came again. They were shot for the smallest thefts. Once Cook fired on the crew of a canoe merely for refusing to stop and answer questions about their habits and customs, and killed four of them—an act of which he calmly notes that he himself could not, on reflection, approve. On the other hand he insisted on discipline, and flogged his sailors for robbing native plantations. For that age he was singularly humane, and so prudent that he did not lose a man on his first and most troubled visit to New Zealand. During this voyage he killed ten Maoris. Later intercourse was much more peaceful, though Captain Furneaux, of Cook's consort, the *Adventure*, less lucky, or less cautious, lost an entire boat's crew, killed and eaten.

Cook himself was always able to get wood and water for his ships, and to carry on his surveys with such accuracy and deliberation that they remained the standard authority on the outlines of the islands for some seventy years. He took possession of the country in the name of George the Third. Some of its coast-names still recall incidents of his patient voyaging. "Young Nick's Head" is the point which the boy Nicholas Young sighted on the 6th of October, 1769—the first bit of New Zealand seen by English eyes. At Cape Runaway the Maoris, after threatening an attack, ran away from a discharge of firearms. At Cape Kidnappers they tried to carry off Cook's Tahitian boy in one of their canoes. A volley, which killed a Maori, made them let go their captive, who dived into the sea and swam back to the *Endeavour* half crazed with excitement at his narrow escape from a New Zealand oven. The odd name of the very fertile district of Poverty Bay reminds us that Cook failed to get there the supplies he obtained at the Bay of Plenty. At Goose Cove he turned five geese ashore; at Mercury Bay he did astronomical work. On the other hand, Capes North, South, East, and West, and Capes Brett, Saunders, Stephens, and Jackson, Rock's Point, and Black Head are neither quaint nor romantic names. Cascade Point and the Bay of Islands justify themselves, and Banks' Peninsula may be accepted for Sir Joseph's sake. But it could be wished that the great sailor had spared a certain charming haven from the name of Hicks's Bay, and had not rechristened the majestic cone of Taranaki as a compliment to the Earl of Egmont.

He gave the natives seed potatoes and the seeds of cabbages and turnips. The potatoes were cultivated with care and success. One tribe had sufficient self-control not to eat any for three years; then they had abundance. Gradually the potato superseded amongst them the taro and fern-root, and even to some extent the kumara. The cabbages and turnips were allowed to run wild, and in that state were still found flourishing fifty years afterwards. The Maoris of Poverty Bay had a story that Cook gave to one of their chiefs a musket with a supply of powder and lead. The fate of the musket was that the first man to fire it was so frightened by the report and recoil that he flung it away into the sea. The powder the natives sowed in the ground believing it to be cabbage seed. Of the lead they made an axe, and when the axe bent at the first blow they put it in the fire to harden it. When it then ran about like water they tried to guide it out of the fire with sticks. But it broke in pieces, and they gave up the attempt. With better results Cook turned fowls and pigs loose to furnish the islanders with flesh-meat. To this day the wild pigs which the settlers shoot and spear in the forests and mountain valleys, are called after Captain Cook, and furnish many a solitary shepherd and farmer with a much more wholesome meal than they would get from "tame" pork. The Maoris who boarded Cook's ships thought at first that pork was whale's flesh. They said the salt meat nipped their throats, which need not surprise us when we remember what the salt junk of an eighteenth century man-of-war was like. They ate ship's biscuit greedily, though at first sight they took it for an uncanny kind of pumice-stone. But in those days they turned with loathing from wine and spirits—as least Crozet says so.

What Captain Cook thought of the Maori is a common-place of New Zealand literature. Every maker of books gives a version of his notes. What the Maori thought of Captain Cook is not so widely known. Yet it is just as interesting, and happily the picture of the great navigator as he appeared to the savages has been preserved for us. Among the tribe living at Mercury Bay when the *Endeavour* put in there was a boy—a little fellow of about eight years old, but possessing the name of Horeta Taniwha (Red-smeared Dragon)—no less. The child lived through all the changes and chances of Maori life and warfare to more than ninety years of age. In his extreme old age he would still tell of how he saw Kapene Kuku—Captain Cook. Once he told his story to Governor Wynyard, who had it promptly taken down. Another version is also printed in one of Mr. John White's volumes.[1] The two do not differ in any important particular. The amazing apparition of the huge white-winged ship with its crew of goblins, and what they said, and what they did, and how they looked, had remained clearly photographed upon the retina of Taniwha's mind's-eye for three-quarters of a century. From his youth up he had, of course, proudly repeated the story. A more delightful child's narrative it would be hard to find.

[Footnote 1: *Ancient History of the Maori*, vol. v., p. 128.]

The people at Mercury Bay knew at once, says Taniwha, that the English were goblins, because a boat's crew pulled ashore, rowing with their backs to the land. Only goblins have eyes in the backs of their heads. When these creatures stepped on to the beach all the natives retreated and the children ran into the bush. But seeing that the wondrous beings walked peaceably about picking up stones and grasses and finally eating oysters, they said to each other, "Perhaps these goblins are not like our Maori goblins," and, taking courage, offered them sweet potatoes, and even lit a fire and roasted cockles for them. When one of the strangers pointed a walking-staff he had in his hand at a cormorant sitting on a dead tree, and there was a flash of lightning and a clap of thunder, followed by the cormorant's fall there was another stampede into the bush. But the goblins laughed so good-humouredly that the children took heart to return and look at the fallen bird. Yes, it was dead; but what had killed it? and still the wonder grew!

The *Endeavour* lay in the bay for some time, and a brisk trade grew up between ship and shore. On one great, never-to-be-forgotten day little Taniwha and some of his play-fellows were taken out in a canoe and went on board the magic ship. Wrapped in their flax cloaks they sat close together on the deck, not daring to move about for fear they might be bewitched in some dark corner, and so might never be able to go away and get home again. But their sharp brown eyes noted everything. They easily made out the leader of the goblins. He was a *tino tangata* (a very man—emphatically a man). Grave and dignified, he walked about saying few words, while the other goblins chatted freely. Presently the goblin-captain came up to the boys and, after patting their heads and stroking their cloaks, produced a large nail and held it up before them temptingly. The other youngsters sat motionless, awe-struck. But the bolder Taniwha laughed cheerfully and was at once presented with the prize. The children forthwith agreed amongst themselves that Cook was not only a *tino tangata*, but a *tino rangatira*—a combination of a great chief and a perfect gentleman. How otherwise could he be so kind to them, and so fond of children, argued these youthful sages?

Then they saw the captain draw black marks on the quarter-deck and make a speech to the natives, pointing towards the coast. "The goblins want to know the shape of the country," said a quick-witted old chief, and, rising up, he drew with charcoal a map of The Fish of Maui, from the Glittering Lake at the extreme south to Land's End in the far north. Then, seeing that the goblins did not understand that the Land's End was the spot from which the spirits of the dead slid down to the shades below, the old chief laid himself down stiffly on the deck and closed his eyes. But still the goblins did not comprehend; they only looked at each other and spoke in their hard, hissing speech. After this little Taniwha went on shore, bearing with him his precious nail. He kept it for years, using it in turns as a spear-head and an auger, or carrying it slung round his neck as a sacred charm.[1] But one day, when out in a canoe, he was capsized in the breakers off a certain islet and, to use his own words, "my god was lost to me, though I dived for it."

[Footnote 1: *Heitiki*.]

Taniwha describes how a thief was shot by Lieutenant Gore for stealing a piece of calico. The thief offered to sell a dog-skin cloak, but when the calico was handed down over the bulwarks into his canoe which was alongside the *Endeavour*, he simply took it, gave nothing in return, and told his comrades to paddle to land.

> "They paddled away. The goblin went down
> into the hold of the ship, but soon came up
> with a walking-stick in his hand, and pointed it
> at the canoe. Thunder pealed and lightning
> flashed, but those in the canoe paddled on.
> Then they landed; eight rose to leave the canoe,
> but the thief sat still with his dog-skin mat and
> the goblin's garment under his feet. His
> companions called him, but he did not answer.
> One of them shook him and the thief fell back
> into the hold of the canoe, and blood was seen
> on his clothing and a hole in his back."

What followed was a capital example of the Maori doctrine of *utu*, or compensation, the cause of so many wars and vendettas. The tribe decided that as the thief had stolen the calico, his death ought not to be avenged, but that as he had paid for it with his life *he* should keep it. So it was buried with him.

The French were but a few months behind the English in the discovery of New Zealand. The ship of their captain, De Surville, just missed meeting Cook at the Bay of Islands. There the French made a fortnight's stay, and were well treated by the chief, Kinui, who acted with particular kindness to certain sick sailors put on shore to recover. Unfortunately one of De Surville's boats was stolen, and in return he not only burnt the nearest village and a number of canoes, but kidnapped the innocent Kinui, who pined away on shipboard and died off the South American coast a few days before De Surville himself was drowned in the surf in trying to land at Callao.

For this rough-handed and unjust act certain of De Surville's countrymen were destined to pay dearly. Between two and three years afterwards, two French exploring vessels under the command of Marion du Fresne entered the Bay of Islands. They were in want of masts and spars, of wood and water, and had many men down with sickness. The expedition was on the look-out for that dream of so many geographers—the great south continent. Marion was a tried seaman, a man of wealth and education, and of an adventurous spirit. It is to Crozet, one of his officers, that we owe the story of his fate. Thanks probably to the Abbé Rochon, who edited Crozet's papers, the narrative is clear, pithy, and business-like: an agreeable contrast to the Hawkesworth-Cook-Banks motley, so much more familiar to most of us.

For nearly five weeks after Marion's ships anchored in the bay all went merry as a marriage bell, though the relations of the French tars with the Maori *wahiné* were not in the strict sense matrimonial. The Maoris, at first cautious, soon became the best of friends with the sailors, conveying shooting parties about the country, supplying the ships with fish, and showing themselves expert traders, keenly appreciative of the value of the smallest scrap of iron, to say nothing of tools. Through all their friendly intercourse, however, it was ominous that they breathed no word of Cook or De Surville. Moreover, a day came on which one of them stole Marion's sword. Crozet goes out of his way to describe how the kindly captain refused to put the thief in irons, though the man's own chief asked that it should be done. But it leaks out—from the statement of another officer—that the thief was put in irons. We may believe that he was flogged also.

STERN OF CANOE

Crozet marked the physical strength of the Maori, and was particularly struck with the lightness of the complexions of some, and the European cast of their features. One young man and a young girl were as white as the French themselves. Others were nearly black, with frizzled hair, and showed, he thought, Papuan blood. To the Frenchman's eye the women seemed coarse and clumsy beside the men. He was acute enough to notice that the whole population seemed to be found by the sea-shore; though he often looked from high hill-tops he saw no villages in the interior. Children seemed few in number, the cultivations small, and the whole race plainly lived in an incessant state of war. He admired the skilful construction of the stockades, the cleanliness of the *pas*, the orderly magazines of food and fishing gear, and the armouries where the weapons of stone and wood were ranged in precise order. He praises the canoes and carving—save the hideous attempts at copying the human form. In short he gives one of the most valuable pictures of Maori life in its entirely primitive stage.

A camp on shore was established for the invalids and another for the party engaged in cutting down the tall kauri pines for masts. Crozet calls the kauri trees cedars, and is full of praises of their size and quality. He was the officer in charge of the woodcutters. On the 13th June he saw marching towards his camp a detachment from the ship fully armed and with the sun flashing on their fixed bayonets. At once it occurred to him that something must be amiss—otherwise why fixed bayonets? Going forward, Crozet bade the detachment halt, and quietly asked what was the matter. The news was indeed grave. On the day before M. Marion with a party of officers and men, seventeen strong, had gone on shore and had not been seen since. No anxiety was felt about them until morning; the French had often spent the night at one or other of the *pas*. But in the morning a terrible thing had happened. A long-boat had been sent ashore at 7 a.m. for wood and water. Two hours later a solitary sailor with two spear-wounds in his side swam back to his ship. Though badly hurt he was able to tell his story. The Maoris on the beach had welcomed the boat's crew as usual—even carrying them pick-a-back through the surf. No sooner were they ashore and separated than each was surrounded and speared or tomahawked. Eleven were thus killed and savagely hacked to pieces. The sole survivor had fought his way into the scrub and escaped unnoticed.

Crozet promptly dismantled his station, burying and burning all that could not be carried away, and marched his men to the boats. The natives met them on the way, yelling, dancing, and shouting that their chief had killed Marion. Arrived at the boats, Crozet says that he drew a line along the sand and called to a chief that any native who crossed it would be shot. The chief, he declares, quietly told the mob, who at once, to the number of a thousand, sat down on the ground and watched the French embark. No sooner had the boats pushed out than the natives in an access of fury began to hurl javelins and stones and rushed after them into the water. Pausing within easy range, the French opened fire with deadly effect and continued to kill till Crozet, wearying of the slaughter, told the oarsmen to pull on. He asks us to believe that the Maoris did not understand the effect of musketry, and yet stood obstinately to be butchered, crying out and wondering over the bodies of their fallen.

The French next set to work to bring off their sick shipmates from their camp. Strange to say they had not been attacked, though the natives had been prowling round them.

Thereafter a village on an islet close by the ship's anchorage was stormed with much slaughter of the inhabitants. Fifty were slain and the bodies buried with one hand sticking out of the ground to show that the French did not eat enemies. Next the ship's guns were tried on canoes in the bay. One was cut in two by a round shot and several of her paddle-men killed.

A day or two later the officers recovered sufficient confidence to send a party to attack the village where their captain had presumably been murdered. The Maoris fled. But Marion's boat-cloak was seen on the shoulders of their chief, and in the huts were found more clothing—blood-stained—and fragments of human flesh.

The ships were hurriedly got ready for sea. The beautiful "cedar" masts were abandoned, and jury-masts set up instead. Wood and water were taken in, and the expedition sailed for Manila, turning its back upon the quest of the great southern continent. Meanwhile the Maoris had taken refuge in the hills, whence the cries of their sentinels could be heard by day and their signal fires be descried by night.

Crozet moralizes on the malignant and unprovoked treachery of these savages. He pours out his contempt on the Parisian *philosophes* who idealized primitive man and natural virtue. For his part he would rather meet a lion or a tiger, for then he would know what to do! But there is another side to the story. The memory of the *Wi-Wi*,[1] "the bloody tribe of Marion," lingered long in the Bay of Islands. Fifty years after Captain Cruise was told by the Maoris how Marion had been killed for burning their villages. Thirty years later still, Surgeon-Major Thomson heard natives relating round a fire how the French had broken into their *tapu* sanctuaries and put their chiefs in irons. And then there were the deeds of De Surville. Apart from certain odd features in Crozet's narrative, it may be remarked that he errs in making the Maoris act quite causelessly. The Maori code was strange and fantastic, but a tribal vendetta always had a reason.

[Footnote 1: *Out-Out.*]

Thus did the Dutch, English, and French in succession discover New Zealand, and forthwith come into conflict with its dauntless and ferocious natives. The skill and moderation of Cook may be judged by comparing his success with the episodes of De Surville's roughness and the troubles which befel Tasman, Furneaux, and Marion du Fresne. Or we may please ourselves by contrasting English persistency and harsh but not unjust dealing, with Dutch over-cautiousness and French carelessness and cruelty. One after the other the Navigators revealed the islands to the world, and began at the same time that series of deeds of blood and reprisal which made the name of New Zealand notorious for generations, and only ended with the massacre of Poverty Bay a long century afterwards.

Chapter V

NO MAN'S LAND

"The wild justice of revenge."

The Maoris told Cook that, years before the *Endeavour* first entered Poverty Bay, a ship had visited the northern side of Cook's Strait and stayed there some time, and that a half-caste son of the captain was still living. In one of his later voyages, the navigator was informed that a European vessel had lately been wrecked near the same part of the country, and that the crew, who reached the shore, had all been clubbed after a desperate resistance. It is likely enough that many a roving mariner who touched at the islands never informed the world of his doings, and had, indeed, sometimes excellent reasons for secrecy. Still, for many years after the misadventure of Marion du Fresne, the more prudent Pacific skippers gave New Zealand a wide berth. When D'Entrecasteaux, the French explorer, in his voyage in search of the ill-fated *La Perouse*, lay off the coast in 1793, he would not even let a naturalist, who was on one of his frigates, land to have a glimpse of the novel flora of the wild and unknown land. Captain Vancouver, in 1791, took shelter in Dusky Bay, in the sounds of the South Island. Cook had named an unsurveyed part of that region Nobody-Knows-What. Vancouver surveyed it and gave it its present name, Somebody-Knows-What. But the chief act for which his name is noted in New Zealand history is his connection with the carrying off of two young Maoris—a chief and a priest—to teach the convicts of the Norfolk Island penal settlement how to dress flax. Vancouver had been asked by the Lieutenant-Governor of Norfolk Island to induce two Maoris to make the voyage. He therefore sent an officer in a Government storeship to New Zealand, whose notion of inducement was to seize the first Maoris he could lay hands on. The two captives, it may be mentioned, scornfully refused to admit any knowledge of the "woman's work" of flax-dressing. Soothed by Lieutenant-Governor King, they were safely restored by him to their people loaded with presents. When in Norfolk Island, one of them, at King's request, drew a map of New Zealand, which is of interest as showing how very little of his country a Maori of average intelligence then knew. Of even more interest to us is it to remember that the kindly Lieutenant-Governor's superior officer censured him for wasting time—ten whole days—in taking two savages back to their homes.

For two generations after Cook the English Government paid no attention
to the new-found land. What with losing America, and fighting the French,
it had its hands full. It colonized Australia with convicts—and found it a
costly and dubious experiment. The Government was well satisfied to
ignore New Zealand. But adventurous English spirits were not The islands
ceased to be inaccessible when Sydney became an English port, from which
ships could with a fair wind make the Bay of Islands in eight or ten days. In
the seas round New Zealand were found the whale and the fur-seal. The
Maoris might be cannibals, but they were eager to trade. In their forests
grew trees capable of supplying first-class masts and spars. Strange
weapons, ornaments, and cloaks, were offered by the savages, as well as
food and the dressed fibre of the native flax. An axe worth ten shillings
would buy three spars worth ten pounds in Sydney. A tenpenny nail would
purchase a large fish. A musket and a little powder and lead were worth a
ton of scraped flax. Baskets of potatoes would be brought down and ranged
on the sea-beach three deep. The white trader would then stretch out
enough calico to cover them. The strip was their price. The Maoris loved
the higgling of the market, and would enjoy nothing better than to spend
half a day over bartering away a single pig. Moreover, a peculiar and
profitable, if ghastly, trade sprang up in tattooed heads. A well-preserved
specimen fetched as much as twenty pounds, and a man "with a good head
on his shoulders" was consequently worth that sum to any one who could
kill him. Contracts for the sale of heads of men still living are said to have
been entered into between chiefs and traders, and the heads to have been
duly delivered "as per agreement." Hitherto hung up as trophies of victory
in the *pas*, these relics of battle were quickly turned to account, at first for
iron, then for muskets, powder, and lead. When the natural supply of heads
of slain enemies ran short, slaves, who had hitherto never been allowed the
aristocratic privilege and dignity of being tattooed, had their faces prepared
for the market. Sometimes, it is recorded, a slave, after months of painful
preparation, had the audacity to run away with his own head before the day
of sale and decapitation. Astute vendors occasionally tried the more
merciful plan of tattooing "plain" heads after death in ordinary course of
battle. But this was a species of fraud, as the lines soon became indistinct.
Such heads have often been indignantly pointed at by enthusiastic
connoisseurs. Head-sellers at times would come forward in the most
unlikely places. Commodore Wilkes, when exploring in the American
Vincennes, bought two heads from the steward of a missionary brig. It was
missionary effort, however, which at length killed the traffic, and the art of
tattooing along with it. Moved thereby, Governor Darling issued at Sydney,
in 1831, proclamations imposing a fine of forty pounds upon any one
convicted of head-trading, coupled with the exposure of the offender's
name. Moreover, he took active steps to enforce the prohibition. When

Charles Darwin visited the mission station near the Bay of Islands in 1835, the missionaries confessed to him that they had grown so accustomed to associate tattooing with rank and dignity—had so absorbed the Maori social code relating thereto—that an unmarked face seemed to them vulgar and mean. Nevertheless, their influence led the way in discountenancing the art, and it has so entirely died out that there is probably not a completely tattooed Maori head on living shoulders to-day.

Cook had found the Maoris still in the Stone Age. They were far too intelligent to stay there a day after the use of metals had been demonstrated to them. Wits much less acute than a Maori's would appreciate the difference between hacking at hardwood trees with a jade tomahawk, and cutting them down with a European axe. So New Zealand's shores became, very early in this century, the favourite haunt of whalers, sealers, and nondescript trading schooners. Deserters and ship-wrecked seamen were adopted by the tribes. An occasional runaway convict from Australia added spice to the mixture.

The lot of these unacknowledged and unofficial pioneers of our race was chequered. Some castaways were promptly knocked on the head and eaten. Some suffered in slavery. In 1815 two pale, wretched-looking men, naked, save for flax mats tied round their waists threw themselves on the protection of the captain of the *Active*, then lying in the Bay of Islands. It appeared that both had been convicts who had got away from Sydney as stowaways in a ship bound for New Zealand, the captain of which, on arrival, had handed them over to the missionaries to be returned to New South Wales. The men, however, ran away into the country, believing that the natives would reverence them as superior beings and maintain them in comfortable idleness. They were at once made slaves of. Had they been strong, handy agricultural labourers, their lot would have been easy enough. Unfortunately for them, one had been a London tailor, the other a shoemaker, and the luckless pair of feeble Cockneys could be of little use to their taskmasters. These led them such a life that they tried running away once more, and lived for a time in a cave, subsisting chiefly on fern-root. A period of this diet, joined to their ever-present fear of being found out and killed, drove them back to Maori slavery. From this they finally escaped to the *Active*—more like walking spectres than men, says an eye-witness—and resigned, if needs must, to endure once more the tender mercies of convict life in Botany Bay.

More valuable whites were admitted into the tribes, and married to one, sometimes two or three, wives. The relatives of these last occasionally resorted to an effectual method of securing their fidelity by tattooing them. One of them, John Rutherford, survived and describes the process. But as he claims to have had his face and part of his body thoroughly tattooed in four hours, his story is but one proof amongst a multitude that veracity was not a needful part of the equipment of the New Zealand adventurer of the Alsatian epoch. Once enlisted, the *Pakehas* were expected to distinguish themselves in the incessant tribal wars. Most of them took their share of fighting with gusto. As trade between whites and Maoris grew, each tribe made a point of having a white agent-general, called their *Pakeha* Maori (Foreigner Maorified), to conduct their trade and business with his fellows. He was the tribe's vassal, whom they petted and plundered as the mood led them, but whom they protected against outsiders. These gentry were for the most part admirably qualified to spread the vices of civilization and discredit its precepts. But, illiterate ruffians as most of them were, they had their uses in aiding peaceful intercourse between the races. Some, too, were not illiterate. A Shakespeare and a Lemprière were once found in the possession of a chief in the wildest part of the interior. They had belonged to his *Pakeha* long since dead. Elsewhere a tattered prayer-book was shown as the only relic of another. One of the kind, Maning by name, who lived with a tribe on the beautiful inlet of Hokianga, will always be known as *the* Pakeha Maori. He was an Irish adventurer, possessed not only of uncommon courage and acuteness, but of real literary talent and a genial and charming humour. He lived to see savagery replaced by colonization, and to become a judicial officer in the service of the Queen's Government. Some of his reminiscences, embodied in a volume entitled *Old New Zealand*, still form the best book which the Colony has been able to produce. Nowhere have the comedy and childishness of savage life been so delightfully portrayed. Nowhere else do we get such an insight into that strange medley of contradictions and caprices, the Maori's mind.

We have already seen that a lieutenant in Her Majesty's service thought it no crime in 1793 to kidnap two chiefs in order to save a little trouble. We have seen how Cook shot natives for refusing to answer questions, and how De Surville could seize and sail away with a friendly chief because some one else had stolen his boat. When in 1794 that high and distinguished body, the East India Company, sent a well-armed "snow" to the Hauraki gulf for kauri spars she did not leave until her captain had killed his quota of natives,—two men and a woman,—shot, because, forsooth, some axes had been stolen. If such were the doings of officials, it came as a matter of course that the hard-handed merchant-skippers who in brigs and schooners hung round the coasts of the Islands thought little of carrying off men or women. They would turn their victims adrift in Australia or on some South Sea islet, as their humour moved them. With even more cruel callousness, they would sometimes put Maoris carried off from one tribe on shore amongst another and maybe hostile tribe. Slavery was the best fate such unfortunates could expect. On one occasion the missionaries in the Bay of Islands rescued from bondage twelve who had in this fashion been thrown amongst their sworn enemies. Their only offence was that they had happened to be trading on board a brig in their own port when a fair wind sprang up. The rascal in command carried them off rather than waste any of the wind by sending them on shore.

An even more heartless piece of brutality was the conduct of a certain captain from Sydney, who took away with him the niece of a Bay of Islands chief, and after living with her for months abandoned her on shore in the Bay of Plenty, where she was first enslaved and finally killed and eaten by the local chief. The result was a bitter tribal war in which she was amply avenged.

Another skipper, after picking up a number of freshly-cured tattooed heads, the fruit of a recent tribal battle, put into the bay of the very tribe which had been beaten in the fighting. When a number of natives came on board to trade, he thought it a capital joke—after business was over—to roll out on the deck a sackful of the heads of their slain kinsfolk. Recognising the features, the insulted Maoris sprang overboard with tears and cries of rage.

MAORI WAHINÉ
Photo by GENERAL ROBLEY.

A third worthy, whilst trading in the Bay of Islands, missed some articles on board his schooner. He at once had the chief Koro Koro, who happened to be on board, seized and bound hand and foot in the cabin. Koro Koro, who was noted both for strength and hot temper, burst his cords, as Samson his bonds, and plunged through the cabin window into the sea. Swimming to his canoe, he gained it, and then, before taking to flight, flung his throwing-spear and transfixed a sailor on deck. The captain in return shot at the infuriated chief, but missed him, and Koro Koro paddled ashore. The wounded sailor did not die; so, on consideration, both sides decided to regard the account as settled, and the incident closed.

Such were some of the more ordinary episodes of commerce in No Man's Land. They were varied by tragedies on a larger scale. In 1809 the *Boyd*, a ship of 500 tons—John Thompson, master—had discharged a shipload of English convicts in Sydney. The captain decided to take in a cargo of timber in New Zealand, and accordingly sailed to Whangaroa, a romantic inlet to the north of the Bay of Islands. Amongst the crew were several Maoris. One of these, known as George, was a young chief, though serving before the mast. During the voyage he was twice flogged for refusing to work on the plea of illness. The captain added insult to the stripes by the words, "You are no chief!" The sting of this lay in the sacredness attached by Maori custom to a chief's person, which was *tapu*—i.e. a thing not to be touched. George—according to his own account[1]—merely replied that when they reached New Zealand the captain would see that he was a chief. But he vowed vengeance, and on reaching Whangaroa showed his stripes to his kinsfolk, as Boadicea hers to the Britons of old. The tribesmen, with the craft of which the apparently frank and cheerful Maori has so ample a share, quietly laid their plans. The captain was welcomed. To divide their foes, the Maori beguiled him and a party of sailors into the forest, where they killed them all. Then, dressing themselves in the clothes of the dead, the slayers made off to the *Boyd*. Easily coming alongside in their disguises, they leaped on the decks and massacred crew and passengers without pity. George himself clubbed half a dozen, who threw themselves at his feet begging for mercy. Yet even in his fury he spared a ship's boy who had been kind to him, and who ran to him for protection, and a woman and two girl-children. All four were afterwards rescued by Mr. Berry, of Sydney, and took refuge with a friendly neighbouring chief, Te Pehi. Meanwhile, the *Boyd* had been stripped and burned. In the orgie that followed George's father snapped a flint-lock musket over a barrel of gunpowder, and, with the followers round him, was blown to pieces. Nigh seventy lives were lost in the *Boyd* massacre. Of course the slain were eaten.

[Footnote 1: As given by him to J.L. Nicholas five years afterwards. See Nicholas' *Voyage to New Zealand*, vol. i., page 145. There are those who believe the story of the flogging to be an invention of George. Their authority is Mr. White, a Wesleyan missionary who lived at Whangaroa from 1823 to 1827, and to whom the natives are said to have admitted this. But that must have been, at least, fourteen years after the massacre, and George was by that time at odds with many of his own people. He died in 1825. His last hours were disturbed by remorse arising from an incident in the *Boyd* affair. He had not, he thought, properly avenged the death of his father—blown up by the powder-barrel. Such was the Maori conscience.]

Then ensued a tragedy of errors. The captains of certain whalers lying in the Bay of Islands, hearing that the survivors of the *Boyd* were at Te Pehi's village, concluded that that kindly chief was a partner in the massacre. Organizing a night attack, the whalers destroyed the village and its guiltless owners. The unlucky Te Pehi, fleeing wounded, fell into the hands of some of George's people, who, regarding him as a sympathiser with the whites, made an end of him. Finally, to avenge him, some of the survivors of his tribe afterwards killed and ate three seamen who had had nothing to do with any stage of the miserable drama.

Less well known than the fate of the *Boyd* is the cutting-off of the brig *Hawes* in the Bay of Plenty in 1829. It is worth relating, if only because it shows that the Maoris were not always the provoked party in these affairs, and that, moreover, vengeance, even in No Man's Land, did not always fall only on the guiltless. In exchange for fire-arms and gunpowder the captain had filled his brig with flax and pigs. He had sailed out to Whale Island in the Bay, and by a boiling spring on the islet's beach was engaged with some of his men in killing and scalding the pigs and converting them into salt pork. Suddenly the amazed trader saw the canoes of his friendly customers of the week before, headed by their chief "Lizard," sweep round and attack the *Hawes*. The seamen, still on board, ran up the rigging, where they were shot. The captain, with those on the islet, rowed away for their lives. The brig was gutted and burnt. The Maoris, perplexed by finding a number of bags of the unknown substance flour, emptied the contents into the sea, keeping the bags.[1]

[Footnote 1: Judge Wilson's *Story of Te Waharoa*.]

Certain white traders in the Bay of Islands resolved to bring "Lizard" to justice, in other words to shoot him. They commissioned a schooner, the *New Zealander*, to go down to the scene of the outrage. A friendly Bay of Islands chief offered to do the rest. He went with the schooner. On its arrival the unsuspecting "Lizard" came off to trade. At the end of a friendly visit he was stepping into his canoe when his unofficially appointed executioner stepped quietly forward, levelled his double-barrelled gun, and shot "Lizard" dead.

As a matter of course the affair did not end there: "Lizard's" tribe were bound in honour to retaliate. But upon whom? The *Pakehas* who had caused their chiefs death were far out of reach in the north. Still they were not the only *Pakehas* in the land. In quite a different direction, in the harbour which Captain Cook had dubbed Hicks's Bay, lived two inoffensive Whites who had not even heard of "Lizard's" death. What of that? They were Whites, and therefore of the same tribe as the *Pakehas* concerned! So the village in which they lived was stormed, one White killed at once, the other captured. As the latter stood awaiting execution and consumption, by an extraordinary stroke of fortune a whaling ship ran into the bay. The adroit captive offered, if his life were spared, to decoy his countrymen on shore, so that they could be massacred. The bargain was cheerfully struck; and when an armed boat's crew came rowing to land, the *Pakeha*, escorted to the seaside by a murderous and expectant throng, stood on a rock and addressed the seamen in English. What he told them to do, however, was to get ready and shoot his captors directly he dived from the rock into the water. Accordingly his plunge was followed by a volley. The survivors of the outwitted Maoris turned and fled, and the clever *Pakeha* was picked up and carried safely on board.

At that time there was living among "Lizard's" people a certain Maori from the Bay of Islands. This man, a greedy and mischievous fellow, had instigated "Lizard" to cut off the *Hawes*. This became known, and Waka Néné, a Bay of Islands chief, destined to become famous in New Zealand history, punished his rascally fellow-tribesman in a very gallant way. On a visit to the Bay of Plenty he bearded the man sitting unsuspecting among his partners in the piracy, and, after fiercely upbraiding him, shot him dead. Nor did any present venture to touch Waka Néné.

The South Island had its share of outrages. On December 12, 1817, the brig *Sophia* anchored in Otago Harbour. Kelly, her captain, was a man of strength and courage, who had gained some note by sailing round Tasmania in an open boat. He now had use for these qualities. The day after arrival he rowed with six men to a small native village outside the harbour heads, at a spot still called Murdering Beach. Landing there, he began to bargain with the Maoris for a supply of potatoes. A Lascar sailor, who was living with the savages, acted as interpreter. The natives thronged round the seamen. Suddenly there was a yell, and they rushed upon the whites, of whom two were killed at once. Kelly, cutting his way through with a bill-hook he had in his hand, reached the boat and pushed out from the beach. Looking back, he saw one of his men (his brother-in-law, Tucker) struggling with the mob. The unhappy man had but time to cry, "Captain Kelly, for God's sake don't leave me!" when he was knocked down in the surf, and hacked to death. Another seaman was reeling in the boat desperately wounded. Kelly himself was speared through one hand.

The survivors regained their ship. She was swarming with natives, who soon learned what had happened and became wildly excited. Kelly drew his men aft and formed them into a solid body. When the Maoris, headed by their chief Karaka—Kelly spells it Corockar—rushed at them, the seamen beat them off, using their large sealing-knives with such effect that they killed sixteen, and cleared the decks. The remaining natives jumped overboard. A number were swept away by the ebb-tide and drowned. Next day the crew, now only fourteen in number, repulsed an attempt made in canoes to take the vessel by boarding, and killed Karaka. Emboldened by this, they afterwards made an expedition to the shore and cut up or stove in all their enemies' canoes lying on the beach. This was on Christmas Eve. On Boxing Day they landed and burnt the principal native village, which Kelly calls the "beautiful city of Otago of about six hundred fine houses"— not the only bit of patent exaggeration in his story. Then they sailed away.[1]

[Footnote 1: *Transactions New Zealand Institute*, vol. xxviii.]

What prompted the attack at Murdering Beach is uncertain—like so much that used to happen in No Man's Land. It is said that Tucker had been to Otago some years previously and had stolen a baked head from the Maoris. It is hinted that an encounter had taken place on the coast not long before in which natives had been shot and a boat's crew cut off. As of most occurrences of the time, we can only suspect that lesser crimes which remained hidden led to the greater, which are more or less truthfully recorded.

Chapter VI

MISSION SCHOONER AND WHALE BOAT

"Behold I bring you good tidings of great joy."—Text of Samuel Marsden's first sermon at the Bay of Islands, Christmas Day, 1814.

Maoris, shipping before the mast on board whalers and traders, made some of the best seamen on the Pacific. They visited Sydney and other civilized ports, where their fine physique, bold bearing, and strangely tattooed faces, heightened the interest felt in them as specimens of their ferocious and dreaded race. Stories of the Maoris went far and wide—of their fierce fights, their cannibal orgies, their grotesque ornaments and customs, their lonely, fertile, and little-known country. Humane men conceived the wish to civilize and Christianize this people. Benjamin Franklin had planned something of the kind when the news of Cook's discovery first reached England. Thirty years later, Samuel Marsden, a New South Wales chaplain, resolved to be the Gregory or Augustine of this Britain of the South. The wish became the master-passion of his life, and he lived to fulfil it. How this resolve was carried out makes one of the pleasantest pages of New Zealand history. The first step was his rescue of Ruatara. In 1809 a roaming Maori sailor had worked his passage to London, in the hope of seeing the great city and—greatest sight of all—King George III. The sailor was Ruatara, a Bay of Islands chief. Adventurous and inquiring as he was intelligent and good-natured, Ruatara spent nearly nine years of his life away from his native land. At London his captain refused to pay him his wages or to help him to see King George, and solitary, defrauded, and disappointed, the young wanderer fell sick nigh unto death. All the captain would do for him was to transfer him to the *Ann*, a convict ship bound for Sydney. Fortunately Marsden was among her passengers. The chaplain's heart was touched at the sight of the wan, wasted Maori sitting dull-eyed, wrapped in his blanket, coughing and spitting blood. His kindness drew back Ruatara from the grave's brink and made him a grateful and attached pupil. Together they talked of the savage islands, which one longed to see and the other to regain. Nor did their friendship end with the voyage. More adventures and disappointments awaited Ruatara before he at last reached home. Once in a whale ship he actually sighted the well-beloved headlands of the Bay of Islands, and brought up all his goods and precious presents ready to go on shore. But the sulky captain broke his promise and sailed past the Bay. Why trouble to land a Maori? Ruatara had to choose between landing at Norfolk Island or another voyage to England. Cheated of his earnings and half-drowned in the surf, he struggled ashore on the convict island, whence he made his way to Sydney and to Marsden's kindly roof. The whaling captain went on towards England. But Justice caught him on the way. He and his ship were taken by an American privateer.

Ruatara gained his home at the next attempt. There he laboured to civilize his countrymen, planted and harvested wheat, and kept in touch with Marsden across the Tasman Sea. Meanwhile the latter's official superiors discountenanced his venturesome New Zealand project. It was not until 1814 that the Governor of New South Wales at last gave way to the chaplain's persistent enthusiasm, and allowed him to send the brig *Active* to the Bay of Islands with Messrs. Hall and Kendall, lay missionaries, as the advance party of an experimental mission station. Ruatara received them with open arms, and they returned to Sydney after a peaceful visit, bringing with them not only their enthusiastic host, but two other chiefs—Koro Koro and Hongi, the last-named fated to become the scourge and destroyer of his race.

At last Marsden was permitted to sail to New Zealand. With Kendall, Hall, and King, the three friendly chiefs, and some "assigned" convict servants, he reached New Zealand in December, 1814. With characteristic courage he landed at Whangaroa, among the tribe who had massacred the crew of the unhappy *Boyd*. Going on shore there, he met the notorious George, who stood to greet the strangers, surrounded by a circle of seated tribesmen, whose spears were erect in the ground. But George, despite a swaggering and offensive manner, seems to have been amicable enough. He rubbed noses with Hongi and Ruatara, and shook hands with Marsden, who passed on unharmed to the Bay of Islands. There, by Ruatara's good offices, he was enabled to preach to the assembled natives on the Sunday after arrival, being Christmas Day, from the text printed at the head of this chapter. The Maoris heard him quietly. Koro Koro walked up and down among the rows of listeners keeping order with his chief's staff. When the service ended, the congregation danced a war dance as a mark of attention to the strangers.

Marsden settled his missionaries at Rangihu, where for twelve axes he bought two hundred acres of land from a young *rangatira* named Turi. The land was conveyed to the Church Missionary Society by a deed of sale. As Turi could not write, Hongi made the ingenious suggestion that his *moko*, or face-tattoo, should be copied on the deed. This was done by a native artist. The document began as follows:

"Know all men to whom these presents shall come, That I, Ahoodee O Gunna, King of Rangee Hoo, in the Island of New Zealand, have, in consideration of twelve axes to me in hand now paid by the Rev. Samuel

Marsden, of Paramatta, in the territory of New South Wales, given, granted, bargained and sold, and by this present instrument do give, grant, bargain and sell," etc., etc.

The deed is not only the first New Zealand conveyance, but has an interest beyond that. It is evidence that, at any rate in 1815, a single Maori, a chief, but of inferior rank, could sell a piece of land without the specific concurrence of his fellow-tribesmen, or of the tribe's head chief. Five and forty years later a somewhat similar sale plunged New Zealand into long years of war.

After this Marsden returned to Sydney. The *Active* took back spars and dressed flax to the value of £450. The flax was sold at £110 a ton. Kauri timber brought half a crown a foot, and the duty charged on it at the Sydney customs house was a shilling a foot. The day of Free Trade there was not yet. One cloud was hanging over the mission when Marsden sailed. Ruatara lay dying. He had been seized with a fever, and the natives, believing him to be attacked by a devouring demon, placed him under *tapu*, and kept food, medicine, and his white friends from him. When Marsden, by threatening to bombard the village obtained access to the sick man, it was too late; he found his friend past hope. Thus was the life of this staunch ally—a life which might have been of the first value to the Maori race—thrown away. Though the missionary's friend, Ruatara died a heathen, and his head wife hung herself in customary Maori form.

Such was the setting up of the first mission station. Its founders were sterling men. Kendall had been a London schoolmaster in good circumstances. King, a master carpenter, had given up £400 a year to labour among the savages. Marsden, though he made seven more voyages to the country, the last after he had reached threescore years and ten, never settled there. Henry Williams, however, coming on the scene in 1823, became his chief lieutenant. Williams had been a naval officer, had fought at Copenhagen, and had in him the stuff of which Nelson's sailors were made. Wesleyan missionaries, following in the footsteps of Marsden's pioneers, established themselves in 1822, and chose for the place of their labours the scene of the *Boyd* disaster. Roman Catholic activity began in 1838.

It took ten years to make one convert, and up to 1830 the baptisms were very few. After that the work began to tell and the patient labourers to reap their harvest. By 1838 a fourth of the natives had been baptized. But this was far from representing the whole achievement of the missionaries. Many thousands who never formally became Christians felt their influence, marked their example, profited by their schools. They fought against war, discredited cannibalism, abolished slavery. From the first Marsden had a sound belief in the uses of trade and of teaching savages the decencies and handicrafts of civilized life. He looked upon such knowledge as the best path to religious belief. Almost alone amongst his class, he was far-sighted enough to perceive, at any rate in the latter years of his life, that the only hope of New Zealand lay in annexation, and that any dream of a Protestant Paraguay was Utopian. Quite naturally, but most unfortunately, most missionaries thought otherwise, and were at the outset of colonization placed in antagonism to the pioneers. Meanwhile they taught the elements of a rough-and-ready civilization, which the chiefs were acute enough to value. But the courage and singleness of purpose of many of them gave them a higher claim to respect. To do the Maoris justice, they recognised it, and the long journeys which the preachers of peace were able to make from tribe to tribe of cannibals and warriors say something for the generosity of the latter as well as for the devotion of the travellers. For fifty years after Marsden's landing no white missionary lost his life by Maori hands. Almost every less serious injury had to be endured. In the face of hardship, insult, and plunder, the work went on. A schooner, the *Herald*, was built in the Bay of Islands to act as messenger and carrier between the missionary stations, which—pleasant oases in the desert of barbarism—began to dot the North Island from Whangaroa as far south as Rotorua among the Hot Lakes. By 1838 there were thirteen of them. The ruins of some are still to be seen, surrounded by straggling plots run to waste, "where once a garden smiled." When Charles Darwin, during the voyage of the *Beagle*, visited the Bay of Islands, the missionary station at Waimate struck him as the one bright spot in a gloomy and ill-ordered land. Darwin, by the way, was singularly despondent in his estimate both of Australia and New Zealand. Colonial evolution was clearly not amongst his studies.

CARVED GATEWAY OF MAORI VILLAGE
From a Sketch by GENERAL ROBLEY.

Colonists as a rule shrug their shoulders when questioned as to the depth of Maori religious feeling. It is enough to point out that a Christianity which induced barbarian masters to release their slaves without payment or condition must have had a reality in it at which the kindred of Anglo-Saxon sugar-planters have no right to sneer. Odd were the absurdities of Maori lay preachers, and knavery was sometimes added to absurdity. Yet these dark-skinned teachers carried Christianity into a hundred nooks and corners. Most of them were honest enthusiasts. Two faced certain death in the endeavour to carry the Gospel to the Taupo heathen, and met their fate with cheerful courage. Comic as Maori sectarianism became, it was not more ridiculous than British. It is true that rival tribes gloried in belonging to different denominations, and in slighting converts belonging to other churches. On one occasion, a white wayfarer, when asking shelter for the night at a *pa*, was gravely asked to name his church. He recognised that his night's shelter was at stake, and had no notion what was the reigning sect of the village. Sharpened by hunger, his wit was equal to the emergency, and his answer, "the true church," gained him supper and a bed. Too much stress has been laid on the spectacle of missionaries engaging in public controversies, and of semi-savage converts wrangling over rites and ceremonies and discussing points of theology which might well puzzle a Greek metaphysician. Such incidents were but an efflorescence on the surface of what for a number of years was a true and general earnestness.

The missionaries, aided by Professor Lee, of Cambridge, gave the Maori a written language. Into this the Scriptures were translated, chiefly by William Williams, who became Bishop of Waiapu, and by Archdeacon Maunsell. Many years of toil went to the work, and it was not completed until 1853. In 1834 a printing press was set up by the Church Mission Society at the Bay of Islands, in charge of Mr. William Colenso. Neither few nor small were the difficulties which beset this missionary printer. At the outset he got his press successfully from ship to shore by lashing two canoes together and laying planks across them. Though the chiefs surveyed the type with greedy eyes and hinted that it would make good musket-balls, they did not carry it off. But on unpacking his equipment Colenso found he had not been supplied with an inking-table, composing-sticks, leads, galleys, cases, imposing-stone, or printing-paper. A clever catechist made him an imposing-stone out of two boulders of basalt found in a river-bed hard by. Leads he contrived by pasting bits of paper together, and with the help of various make-shifts, printed on February 21, 1835 the first tract published in New Zealand. It consisted of the Epistles to the Ephesians and Philippians in Maori, printed on sixteen pages of writing-paper and issued in wrappers of pink blotting-paper. Much the most capable helpers whom the lonely printer had in his first years were two one-time compositors who had turned sailors and who, tiring of foc'sle life under Yankee captains, made up their minds to resume the stick and apron in the cannibal islands. Impish Maori boys made not inappropriate "devils." With such assistants Colenso, working on, had by New Year's Day, 1838, completed the New

Testament and was distributing bound copies to the eager Maoris, who sent messengers for them from far and near. Pigs, potatoes, flax were offered for copies of the precious volume, in one case even that rarest of curiosities in No Man's Land—a golden sovereign.

Not the least debt, which any one having to do with New Zealand owes the missionaries and Professor Lee, is a scholarly method of writing Maori. In their hands the spelling of the language became simple, systematic, and pleasant to the eye. What it has done to save the names of the country's places and persons from taking fantastic and ridiculous shapes, a few examples will show. For sixty years after Cook's discovery every traveller spelt these names as seemed good to him. The books of the time offer us such things of beauty as Muckeytoo (Maketu), Kiddy-Kiddy (Keri-Keri), Wye-mattee (Waimate), Keggerigoo (Kekerangu), Boo Marray and Bowmurry (Pomaré), Shunghee and E'Ongi (Hongi), Corroradickee (Kororáreka). The haven of Hokianga figures alternately as Showkianga, Sukyanna, Jokeeangar and Chokahanga. Almost more laughable are Towackey (Tawhaki), Wycaddie (Waikare), Crackee (Karakia), Wedder-Wedder (Wera-Wera), and Rawmatty (Raumati).

These, however, are thrown into the shade by some of the courageous attempts of the two Forsters, Cook's naturalists, at the names of native birds. It must have taken some imaginative power to turn pi-waka-waka into "diggowaghwagh," and kereru into "haggarreroo," but they achieved these triumphs. Their *chef-d'oeuvre* is perhaps "pooadugghiedugghie," which is their version of putangi-tangi, the paradise-duck. After that it is not so easy to smile at the first sentences of an official statement drawn up by Governor King, of New South Wales, relative to the carrying off to Norfolk Island of the two New Zealanders before mentioned, which begins:

> "Hoodoo-Cockoty-Towamahowey is about
> twenty-four years of age, five feet eight inches
> high, of an athletic make, and very interesting.
> He is of the district of Teerawittee ... Toogee
> Teterrenue Warripedo is of the same age as
> Hoodoo, but about three inches shorter."

Poor Huru, poor Tuki

While the missionaries were slowly winning their way through respect to influence in the northern quarter of the country, and were giving the Maori a written language and the Bible, very different agents were working for civilization further south. From the last decade of the eighteenth century onwards the islands were often sought by whaling-ships. Gradually these came in greater numbers, and, until about the year 1845, were constantly to be seen in and about certain harbours—notably the Bay of Islands. But not by the utmost stretch of charity could their crews be called civilizing agencies. To another class of whalers, however, that title may not unfairly be given. These were the men who settled at various points on the coast, chiefly from Cook's Straits southward to Foveaux Straits, and engaged in what is known as shore-whaling. In schooners, or in their fast-sailing, seaworthy whale boats, they put out from land in chase of the whales which for so many years frequented the New Zealand shores in shoals. Remarkable were some of the catches they made. At Jacob's River eleven whales were once taken in seventeen days. For a generation this shore-whaling was a regular and very profitable industry. Only the senseless slaughter of the "cows" and their "calves" ruined it.

Carried on at first independently by little bands of adventurers, it in time fell into the hands of Sydney merchants, who found the capital and controlled and organized whaling-stations. At these they erected boiling-down works, shears for hoisting the huge whales' carcasses out of the water, stores, and jetties. As late as 1843 men were busy at more than thirty of these stations. More than five hundred men were employed, and the oil and whalebone they sent away in the year were worth at least £50,000. Sometimes the profits were considerable. A certain merchant, who bought the plant of a bankrupt station for £225 at a Sydney auction, took away therefrom £1,500 worth of oil in the next season. But then he was an uncommon merchant. He had been a sealer himself, and finally abandoned mercantile life in Sydney to return to his old haunts, where he managed his own establishment, joined farming to whaling, endowed a mission station,[1] and amazed the land by importing a black-coated tutor and a piano for his children. Moreover, the harpooners and oarsmen were not paid wages or paid in cash, but merely had a percentage of the value of a catch, and were given that chiefly in goods and rum. For this their employers charged them, perhaps, five times the prices current in Sydney, and Sydney prices in convict times were not low. Under this truck system the employers made profits both ways. The so-called rum was often inferior arrack—deadliest of spirits—with which the Sydney of those days poisoned the Pacific. The men usually began each season with a debauch and ended it with another. A cask's head would be knocked out on the beach, and all invited to dip a can into the liquor. They were commonly in debt and occasionally in delirium. Yet they deserved to work under a better system, for they were often fine fellows, daring, active, and skilful. Theirs was no fair-weather trade. Their working season was in the winter. Sharp winds and rough seas had to be faced, and when these were contrary it required no small strength to pull their heavy boats against them hour after hour, and mile after mile, to say nothing of the management of the cumbrous steering-oar, twenty-seven feet in length, to handle which the steersman had to stand upright in the stern sheets.

[Footnote 1: John Jones, of Waikouaiti. His first missionary found two years at a whaling-station quite enough, if we may judge from his greeting to his successor, which was "Welcome to Purgatory, Brother Creed!" Brother Creed's response is not recorded.]

The harpooning and lancing of the whale were wild work; and when bones were broken, a surgeon's aid was not always to be had. The life, however, could give change, excitement, the chance of profit, and long intervals of comparative freedom. To share these, seamen deserted their vessels, and free Australians—nicknamed currency lads—would ship at Sydney for New Zealand. Ex-convicts, of course, swelled their ranks, and were not always and altogether bad, despite the convict system. The discipline in the boats was as strict as on a man-of-war. On shore, when "trying down" the blubber, the men had to work long and hard. "Sunday don't come into this bay!" was the gruff answer once given to a traveller who asked whether the Sabbath was kept. Otherwise they might lead easy lives. Each had his hut and his Maori wife, to whom he was sometimes legally married. Many had gardens, and families of half-caste children, whose strength and beauty were noted by all who saw them. The whaler's helpmate had to keep herself and children clean, and the home tidy. Cleanliness and neatness were insisted on by her master, partly through the seaman's instinct for tidiness and partly out of a pride and desire to show a contrast to the reeking hovels of the Maori. As a rule she did her best to keep her man sober. Her cottage, thatched with reeds, was perhaps whitewashed with lime made by burning the sea-shells. With its clay floor and huge open fireplace, with its walls lined with curtained sleeping bunks, and its rafters loaded with harpoons, sharp oval-headed lances, coils of rope, flitches of bacon or bags of flour, it showed a picture of rude comfort.[1]

[Footnote 1: Wakefield, *Adventures in New Zealand*; Shortland, *Southern Districts of New Zealand*; S. Thomson, *Story of New Zealand*; Sir W.T. Power, *Sketches in New Zealand*; G.F. Angas, *Savage Scenes*.]

If the seats were the joints of a whale's backbone, there was always food in plenty, washed down with grog or tea made from manuka sprigs. Whale's heart was a delicacy set before guests, who found it rather like beef. Maoris, sharks, and clouds of sea-gulls shared much of the flesh of the captured whales' carcasses.

Maori relatives learned to envy and, to some extent, to copy what they saw. They took service as oarsmen, and even bought and equipped boats for themselves. They learned to be ashamed of some of their more odious habits, and to respect the pluck and sense of fair play shown by their whaling neighbours. As a rule, each station was held by license from the chief of the proprietary tribe. He and tenants would stand shoulder to shoulder to resist incursions by other natives. Dicky Barrett, head-man of the Taranaki whaling-station, helped the Ngatiawa to repulse a noteworthy raid by the Waikato tribe. Afterwards, when the Ngatiawa decided to abandon their much-harried land, Barrett moved with them to Cook's Straits, where, in 1839, the Wakefields found him looking jovial, round, and ruddy, dressed in a straw hat, white jacket, and blue dungaree trousers, and married to a chief's daughter—a handsome and stately woman. It was Dicky Barrett who directed Colonel Wakefield to what is now Wellington, and who, in consequence, may be recorded as the guide who pointed out to the pioneer of the New Zealand Company the future capital of the colony.

Nor was Barrett the only specimen of this rough race whom New Zealanders may remember with interest. There was Stewart, ex-Jacobite, sealer, and pilot, whose name still conceals Rakiura, and whose Highland pride made him wear the royal tartan to the last as he sat in Maori villages smoking among the blanketed savages. There was the half-caste Chaseland, whose mother was an Australian "gin," and who was acknowledged to be the most dexterous and best-tempered steersman in New Zealand—when sober. He needed his skill when he steered an open boat from the Chathams to Otago across five hundred miles of wind-vexed sea. Chaseland's mighty thews and sinews were rivalled by those of Spencer, whose claim to have fought at Waterloo was regarded as doubtful, but whose possession of two wives and of much money made by rum-selling was not doubtful. Another notable steersman was Black Murray, who once made his boatmen row across Cook's Straits at night and in a gale because they were drunk, and only by making them put out to sea could he prevent them from becoming more drunk. A congener of his, Evans—"Old Man Evans"—boasted of a boat which was as spick and span as a post-captain's gig, and of a crew who wore uniform. Nor must the best of Maori whalers be forgotten—the chief Tuhawaiki—brave in war, shrewd and businesslike in peace, who could sail a schooner as cleverly as any white skipper, and who has been most unfairly damned to everlasting fame—local fame—by his whaler's nickname of "Bloody Jack!" These, and the "hands" whom they ordered about, knocked down, caroused with, and steered, were the men who, between 1810 and 1845, taught the outside world to take its way along the hitherto dreaded shores of New Zealand as a matter of course and of business. Half heroes, half ruffians, they did their work, and unconsciously brought the islands a stage nearer civilization. Odd precursors of English law, nineteenth-century culture, and the peace of our lady the Queen, were these knights of the harpoon and companions of the rum-barrel. But the isolated coasts and savage men among whom their lot was cast did not as yet call for refinement and reflection. Such as their time wanted, such they were. They played a part and fulfilled a purpose, and then moved off the stage. It so happened that within a few years after the advent of the regular colonists whaling ceased to pay, and the rough crew who followed it, and their coarse, manly life, disappeared together.

Chapter VII

THE MUSKETS OF HONGI

"He sang of battles, and the breath

Of stormy war and violent death."

Marsden's notes help us to picture his first night in New Zealand. The son of the Yorkshire blacksmith, the voyager in convict-ships, the chaplain of New South Wales in the days of rum and chain-gangs, was not the man to be troubled by nerves. But even Marsden was wakeful on that night. Thinking of many things—thoughts not to be expressed—the missionary paced up and down on the sea beach by which a tribe was encamped. The air was pleasant, the stars shone brightly, in front of him the sea spread smoothly, peacefully folded among the wooded hills. At the head of the harbour the ripple tapped lightly upon the charred timbers of the *Boyd*. Around lay the Maori warriors sleeping, wrapped in their dyed mantles and with their spears stuck upright in the ground. It was a quiet scene. Most of the scenes of that time which have come down to us were not of quietness. Some of them have been sketched in the last two chapters, and are examples of the condition of things which the missionaries landed to confront, and amidst which they worked. More have now to be described, if only to show things as they were before annexation, and the miseries which the country, and the Maori along with it, suffered before the influences of White adventurers and their fatal gifts were tempered by a civilized government.

From 1818 to 1838 was a time of war far surpassing in bloodshed and ruin anything witnessed in the Islands before or since. For the first time the Maoris used firearms. Probably a fourth of their race perished in this ill-starred epoch. Hongi, the chief of the Ngapuhi tribe, before referred to, is usually spoken of as the first to introduce the musket into the tribal wars. This was not so. His tribe, as the owners of the Bay of Islands and other ports frequented by traders, were able to forestall their fellow-Maoris in getting firearms. A war-party of the Ngapuhi, only one hundred and forty strong, is said to have gone through the length and breadth of the North Island putting all they met to flight with the discharge of two old flint-lock guns. The cunning warriors always followed up the awe-inspiring fire with a prompt charge in which spear and tomahawk did the work for which panic had prepared the way. Another Ngapuhi chief, the leader of an attack on the men of Tauranga, managed to arm his men with thirty-five muskets, which they used with crushing effect. This was in 1818. Hongi saw the bravest warriors run before the new and terrible weapon. He never forgot the sight. To go to England and get guns became the dream of his life. A hopeful pupil of Marsden, in Sydney, he knew the ways of the white men. In 1820, he and a brother chief were taken to England by Kendall to help Professor Lee with his grammar and dictionary. The pair were lionized, and on all sides presents were made to them. They were presented to King George IV., who gave Hongi a suit of armour. On his return this grammarian's assistant heard at Sydney that his tribe was at war with the natives of the Hauraki or Thames district, and that one of his relatives had been killed. Now was his time. He at once sold all his presents, except the suit of armour, and bought three hundred muskets and a supply of powder and bullets.

The Sydney Government did not prevent him. At Marsden's table, at Parramatta, Hongi met a chief of the offending tribe. Grimly he warned his fellow-guest to take himself home, make ready for war, and prepare to be killed—and eaten. Landing in New Zealand, he determined to imitate Napoleon. Allowing for the enormous difference in his arena, he managed to be nearly as mischievous.

His luckless enemies, armed only with spears, tomahawks, stones and clubs, were shot and enslaved by thousands and eaten by hundreds. Wide districts were swept bare of people. No man cared for anything except to procure a gun and thereby have a chance to save his life. A musket was, indeed, a pearl of great price. It has been pleaded for Hongi that he protected the missionaries, and that by forcing his race to get guns at any price he unwittingly developed trade. It is indeed true that in their desperate straits the tribes sold flax, timber, potatoes, mats, tattooed heads, pigs—even their precious land—for firearms. Without them their lives were not worth a month's purchase. Men and women toiled almost frantically at growing and preparing flax or providing anything exchangeable for muskets, powder and lead. An old Brown Bess was worth three tons of scraped flax. Undoubtedly whites were welcomed, both as traders and fighters, with a readiness unknown before. In 1835, New Zealand exports to Sydney alone were valued at £113,000, her imports at £31,000. It was a poor set-off against an era of butchery.

Determined to carry out the threats he had made in Sydney, Hongi began his campaigns by sailing southward with a great fleet of war-canoes. Passing to the head of the Hauraki Gulf he sat down before the *pa* of Totara, the chief fortress of the Thames tribes—the men whom he had doomed in Sydney. The place was well garrisoned, and commanded by the head chief, Trembling-Leaf. Even the three hundred musketeers found the *pa* too strong for open assault, though those inside had but one gun and no ammunition. Hongi fell back upon fraud and offered honourable peace, if a certain sacred greenstone *mere* were handed to him as a trophy. It was solemnly handed over, and the principal invaders were feasted in the *pa*. One of them, ashamed of the intended treachery, whispered to an acquaintance in the garrison, "Beware!" In vain. That night, as Hongi's victims were sleeping securely, the Ngapuhi rushed the stockade and all within were killed or taken. The dead were variously reckoned at from two hundred to a thousand. One division of the Ngapuhi were sufficiently disgusted at Hongi's deceit to refuse to join in the surprise, and Waikato, the powerful chief who had accompanied him to England, declared he would go afield with him no more. Even his own special clan, though they had yielded to the furious exhortations of his blind wife Kiri, an Amazon who followed him in all his fights, urged him to spare some of the captives of rank. The pitiless victor spared none. Five he killed with his own spear. The death songs of two have been preserved and are quoted as choice specimens of Maori poetry.

Between 1821 and 1827 Hongi carried fire and sword into almost every corner of what is now the Province of Auckland. At first none could stand before him. He assailed in 1822 two large *pas* near where the suburbs of Auckland city now spread. In vain the terrified inmates tried to buy off the savage with presents. Nearly all were slaughtered or taken, and Hongi left naught in their villages but bones, with such flesh on them "as even his dogs had not required." He invaded the Waikato and penetrated to a famous *pa*—a triple stockade at Mataki-taki (Look-out). To get there he dragged his war-canoes overland across the Auckland isthmus, straightened winding creeks for their passage, and, when the Waikatos felled large trees across one channel, patiently spent two months in cutting through the trunks. At length the Look-out fortress was stormed with horrible slaughter. Defended on one side by a creek, on another by the Waipa river, elsewhere by deep ditches and banks that were almost cliffs, the lofty stronghold was as difficult to escape from as to enter. It was crowded with women and children: ten thousand people were in it, says one account. When the spear-men broke before the terrible musket-fire, the mass of the despairing on-lookers choked the ways of escape. In their mad panic hundreds of the flying Waikatos were forced headlong over a cliff by the rush of their fellow-fugitives. Hundreds more were smothered in one of the deep ditches of the defences, or were shot by the merciless Ngapuhi, who fired down upon the writhing mass till tired of reloading. It was the greatest of Hongi's victories, though not bloodless for the conquerors, like that of Totara, where only one Ngapuhi had been killed. Famous fighting men, the Waikato chiefs had died bravely, despite the amazement caused by the mystery of firearms. One had killed four Ngapuhi before he was shot.

Another of Hongi's triumphs was at Rotorua in the Hot Lakes district—the land of the Arawa tribe. He began by defeating them on the Bay of Plenty, and thence turning inland found the tribe gathered in strength on the green island-hill of Mokoia, encircled by the Rotorua lake. Hongi's war-canoes were twenty-five miles away on the sea-beach, and the Mokoians ridiculed him as he lay encamped by the edge of their lake, unable to get at them. Day after day they paddled to within hailing distance and insulted him with yells and gestures. But the Ngapuhi general was not to be stopped. Like Mahomet the second, he made his slaves drag their craft overland, and the astonished islanders saw his flotilla sweep across Rotorua bearing the irresistible musketeers. On their exposed strand they were easily mown down. Flying they were followed by the Ngapuhi, and few indeed were the survivors of the day. Hongi's ravages reached far to the south and east. Even the Ngatiporou, who dwelt between Cape Runaway and Poverty Bay, felt his hand. Their *pas* fell one after the other, and only those were not slaughtered who fled to the mountains.

For a while it seemed as though Hongi's dream might come true, and all New Zealand hail him as sole king. His race trembled at his name. But his cruelty deprived him of allies, and the scanty numbers of his army gave breathing time to his foes. He wisely made peace with the Waikatos, who, under Te Whero Whero, had rallied and cut off more than one Ngapuhi war-party. In the Hauraki country he could neither crush nor entrap the chief Te Waharoa, as cunning a captain and as bloodthirsty a savage as himself. His enemies, indeed, getting muskets and gaining courage, came once far north of the Auckland isthmus to meet him; and though he beat them there in a pitched battle, it cost him the life of his eldest son. He became involved in feuds with his northern neighbours, and finally marched to attack our old acquaintances the Whangaroans of *Boyd* notoriety. In a bush-fight with them he neglected to wear the suit of chain armour, the gift of George IV., which had saved his life more than once. A shot fired by one of his own men struck him in the back and passed through a lung. He did not die of the wound for fifteen months. It is said that he used to entertain select friends by letting the wind whistle through the bullet-hole in his body. Mr. Polack, who was the author of the tale, was not always implicitly believed by those who knew him; but as Surgeon-Major Thomson embodies the story in his book, perhaps a writer who is not a surgeon ought not to doubt it.

Of Hongi's antagonists none were more stubborn or successful than Te Waharoa, a fighting chief whose long life of warfare contains in it many stirring episodes of his times. Born in 1773 in a village near the upper Thames, he owed his life, when two years old, to a spasm of pity in the heart of a victorious chief from the Hot Lakes. This warrior and his tribe sacked the *pa* of Te Waharoa's father, and killed nearly all therein. The conqueror saw a pretty boy crying among the ashes of his mother's hut, and struck with the child's face, took him up and carried him on his back home to Lake Rotorua. "Oh! that I had not saved him!" groaned the old chief, when, nearly two generations later, Te Waharoa exacted ample vengeance from the Rotorua people. After twenty years of a slave's life, Te Waharoa was allowed to go back to his people. Though, in spite of the brand of slavery, his craft and courage carried him on till he became their head, he was even then but the leader of a poor three hundred fighting men.

To the north of him lay the Thames tribe, then the terror of half New Zealand; to the south, his old enemies the Arawas of the Hot Lakes. To the west the main body of the Waikatos were overwhelmingly his superiors in numbers. Eastward the Tauranga tribe—destined in aftertimes to defeat the Queen's troops at the Gate *Pa*—could in those days muster two thousand five hundred braves, and point to a thousand canoes lying on their beaches. But Te Waharoa was something more than an able guerilla chief. He was an acute diplomatist. Always keeping on good terms with the Waikatos, he made firm allies of the men of Tauranga. Protected, indeed helped, thus on both flanks, he devoted his life to harassing the dwellers by the lower Thames and the Hauraki Gulf. One great victory he won over them with the aid of his Waikato allies. Their chief *pa*, Mata-mata, he seized by a piece of callous bad faith and murder. After being admitted there by treaty to dwell as friends and fellow-citizens, his warriors rose one night and massacred their hosts without compunction. Harried from the north by Hongi, the wretched people of the Thames were between the hammer and the anvil. When at last their persecutors—the Ngapuhi and Te Waharoa—met over their bodies, Te Waharoa's astuteness and nerve were a match for the invaders from the north. In vain the Ngapuhi besiegers tried to lure him out from behind the massive palisades of Mata-mata, where, well-provisioned, he lay sheltered from their bullets. When he did make a sally it was to catch half a dozen stragglers, whom, in mortal defiance, he crucified in front of his gateway. Then he challenged the Ngapuhi captain to single combat with long-handled tomahawks. The Northerners broke up their camp, and went home; they had found a man whom even muskets could not terrify.

Te Waharoa's final lesson to the Ngapuhi was administered in 1831, and effectually stopped them from making raids on their southern neighbours. A war-party from the Bay of Islands, in which were two of Hongi's sons, ventured, though only 140 strong, to sail down the Bay of Plenty, slaying and plundering as they went. Twice they landed, and when they had slain and eaten more than their own number the more prudent would have turned back. But a blind wizard, a prophet of prodigious repute, who was with them, predicted victory and speedy reinforcement, and urged them to hold on their way. Disembarking on an islet in the bay, the inhabitants of which had fled, they encamped among the deserted gardens. Looking out next morning, they saw the sea blackened with war-canoes. Believing these to be the prophesied reinforcement, they rushed down to welcome their friends. Cruelly were they undeceived as the canoes of Te Waharoa and his Tauranga allies shot on to the beach. Short was the struggle. Only two of the Ngapuhi were spared, and as the blind soothsayer's blood was too sacred to be shed, the victors pounded him to death with their fists. Never again did the Ngapuhi come southwards. So for the remaining years of his life Waharoa was free to turn upon the Arawas, the men who had slain his father and mother. From one raid on Rotorua his men came back with the bodies of sixty enemies—cut off in an ambush. Not once did Waharoa meet defeat; and when, in 1839, he died, he was as full of fame as of years. Long afterwards his *mana* was still a halo round the head of his son Wiremu Tamihana, whom we shall meet in due time as William Thompson the king-maker, best of his race.

Hongi once dead and the Ngapuhi beaten off, the always formidable Waikato tribes began in turn to play the part of raiders. At their head was Te Whero Whero, whom in the rout at Mataki-taki a friendly hand had dragged out of the suffocating ditch of death. Without the skill of Hongi, or the craft of Te Waharoa, he was a keen and active fighter. More than once before Hongi's day he had invaded the Taranaki country, and had only been forced back by the superior generalship of the famous Rauparaha, of whom more anon. In 1831 Rauparaha could no longer protect Taranaki. He had migrated to Cook's Strait, and was warring far away in the South Island. Therefore it was without much doubt that, followed by some three thousand men, Te Whero Whero set his face towards Mount Egmont, and swept all before him. Only at a strong hill-*pa* looking down upon the Waitara river, did his enemies venture to make a stand. They easily repulsed his first assaults, but hundreds of women and children were among the refugees, and as was the wont of the Maoris, no proper stock of provisions had been laid in. On the thirteenth day, therefore, the defenders, weakened and half starved, had to make a frantic attempt to break through the Waikatos. Part managed to get away; most were either killed at once, or hunted down and taken. Many women threw themselves with their children over the cliff into the Waitara. Next day the captives were brought before Te Whero Whero. Those with the best tattooed faces were carefully beheaded that their heads might be sold unmarred to the White traders. The skulls of the less valuable were cleft with tomahawk or *mere*. Te Whero Whero himself slew many scores with a favourite greenstone weapon. A miserable train of slaves were spared to labour in the villages of the Waikato.

MOUNT EGMONT, TARANAKI
Photo by I.A. MARTIN, Wanganui

Ahead of the victorious chieftain lay yet another *pa*. It was near those quaint conical hills—the Sugar-Loaves—which, rising in and near the sea, are as striking a feature as anything can be in the landscape where Egmont's white peak dwarfs all else. Compared to the force in the Waitara *pa* the garrison of this last refuge was small—only three hundred and fifty, including women and children. But among them were eleven Whites. Some of these may have been what Mr. Rusden acidly styles them all—"dissipated Pakeha-Maoris living with Maori Delilahs." But they were Englishmen, and had four old ship's guns. They decided to make a fight of it for their women and children and their trade. They got their carronades ready, and laboured to infuse a little order and system into the excitable mob around them. So when the alarm-cry, *E! Taua! Taua!* rang out from the watchmen of the *pa*, the inmates were found resolute and even prepared. In vain the invaders tried all their wiles. Their rushes were repulsed, the firebrands they showered over the palisades were met by wet clay banking, and their treacherous offers of peace and good-will declined. Though one of the carronades burst, the others did good execution, and when shot and scrap-iron failed, the artillerymen used pebbles. Dicky Barrett, already mentioned, was the life and soul of the defence. The master of a schooner which came upon the coast in the midst of the siege tried to mediate, and stipulated for a free exit for the Whites. Te Whero Whero haughtily refused; he would spare their lives, but would certainly make slaves of them. He had better have made a bridge for their escape. The siege dragged on. The childish chivalry of the Maoris amazed the English. Waikato messengers were allowed to enter the *pa* and examine the guns and defences. On the other hand, when the besiegers resolved on a last and grand assault they sent notice thereof the day before to the garrison. Yet, after that, the latter lay down like tired animals to sleep the night through, while Barrett and his comrades watched and waited anxiously. The stormers came with the dawn, and were over the stockade before the Whites could rouse the sleepers. Then, however, after a desperate tussle—one of those sturdy hand-to-hand combats in which the Maori fighter shone—the assailants were cut down or driven headlong out. With heavy loss the astonished Waikatos recoiled in disgust, and their retreat did not cease till they reached their own country.

Even this victory could not save Taranaki. With the fear of fresh raids in their mind the survivors of its people, together with their White allies, elected to follow where so many of their tribes had already gone—to Cook's Straits, in the footsteps of Rauparaha. So they, too, chanted their farewells to their home, and turning southward, marched away. When the Waikatos had once more swept down the coast, and had finally withdrawn, it was left empty and desolate. A remnant, a little handful, built themselves a *pa* on one of the Sugar-Loaves. A few more lurked in the recesses of Mount Egmont. Otherwise the fertile land was a desert. A man might toil along the harbourless beaches for days with naught for company but the sea-gulls and the thunder of the surf; while inland,—save for a few birds,— the rush of streams and pattering of mountain-showers on the leaves were all that broke the silence of lifeless forests.

To the three warrior chiefs, whose feuds and fights have now been outlined, must be added a fourth and even more interesting figure. Rauparaha, fierce among the fierce, cunning among the cunning, was not only perhaps the most skilful captain of his time, not only a devastator second only to Hongi, but was fated to live on into another era and to come into sharp and fatal collision with the early colonists. One result among others is that we have several portraits of him with both pen and pencil. Like Waharoa and Hongi he was small, spare and sinewy; an active man even after three-score years and ten. In repose his aquiline features were placid and his manners dignified. But in excitement, his small, keen, deep-sunken eyes glared like a wild beast's, and an overhanging upper lip curled back over long teeth which suggested to colonists—his enemies—the fangs of a wolf. Born near the picturesque inlet of Kawhia, he first won fame as a youth by laying a clever ambuscade for a Waikato war-party. When later the chief of his tribe was dying and asked doubt-fully of his councillors who there was to take his place, Rauparaha calmly stepped forward and announced himself as the man for the office. His daring seemed an omen, and he was chosen. In 1819 he did a remarkable thing. He had been on a raid to Cook's Straits, and when there had been struck with the strategic value of the island of Kapiti—steep, secure from land attacks, not infertile, and handy to the shore. It was the resort, moreover, of the *Pakehas* trading-ships. Like Hongi, Rauparaha saw that the man with the most muskets must carry all before him in New Zealand. Out of the way and overshadowed by the Waikato his small tribe were badly placed at Kawhia. But if he could bring them and allies along with them to Kapiti and seize it, he could dominate central New Zealand.

He persuaded his people to migrate. Their farewell to their old dwellings is still a well-known Maori poem. Joined by a strong contingent of Waitara men under Wi Kingi—to be heard of again as late as 1860—they won their way after many fights, adventures and escapes to their goal at Kapiti. There Rauparaha obtained the coveted muskets. Not only did he trade with the visiting ships but he protected a settlement of whalers on his island who did business with him, and whose respect for the craft and subtlety of "Rowbulla" was always great. Rauparaha set out for Kapiti a year before Hongi sailed for England on his fatal quest. From his sea-fortress he kept both coasts in fear and turmoil for twenty years. More than once he was defeated, and once his much-provoked foes attacked Kapiti with a united flotilla. But though they "covered the sea with their canoes," they parleyed after landing when they should have fought. By a union of astuteness and hard fighting Rauparaha's people won, and signal was the revenge taken on his assailants. Previous to this he had almost exterminated one neighbour-tribe whose villages were built on small half-artificial islets in a forest-girt lake. In canoes and by swimming his warriors reached the islets, and not many of the lake people were left alive.

More than one story is preserved of Rauparaha's resource and ruthlessness. One night, when retreating with a weak force, he had the Waikatos at his heels. He held them back by lighting enough watchfires for a large host, and by arming and dressing his women as fighting-men. Again, when he was duck-hunting near the coast of the South Island, his enemies, led by the much-libelled "Bloody Jack," made a bold attempt to surround his party. Most of his men were cut off. Rauparaha, lowered down a sea-cliff, hid among the kelp by the rocks beneath. A canoe was found and brought, and he put to sea. It was over-loaded with fugitives, and their chief therefore ordered half to jump overboard that the rest might be saved. The lightened canoe then carried him to a place of safety. Yet, after the capture of Kaiapoi he showed generosity. Amongst the prisoners, who were lying bound hand and foot waiting for the oven, was a young brave who had killed one of Rauparaha's chiefs in a daring sortie. Him now the conqueror sought out, spared his life, cut his bonds, and took him into service and favour.

The most famous and far-reaching of Rauparaha's raids were among the Ngaitahu, whose scattered bands were masters of nearly all the wide half-empty spaces of the South Island. In one of their districts was found the famous greenstone. On no better provocation than a report which came to his ears of an insulting speech by a braggart southern chief, Rauparaha, early in 1829, manned his canoes, and sailed down the east coast to attack the boastful one's *pa*. The unsuspecting natives thronged down to the beach to meet the raiders with shouts of welcome, and on hospitable thoughts intent. Springing on to land, the invaders ran amongst the bewildered crowd, and slew or captured all they could lay hands on. Then they burned the village. Further south lay a larger *pa*, that of Kaiapoi. Here the inhabitants, warned by fugitives from the north, were on their guard. Surprise being impossible, Rauparaha tried guile, and by assurances of friendship worked upon the Kaiapois to allow his chiefs to go in and out of their *pa*, buying greenstone and exchanging hospitalities. But for once he met his match. The Kaiapois waited until they had eight of the chiefs inside their stockades, and then killed them all. Amongst the dead was Te Pehi, Rauparaha's uncle and adviser, who three years before had visited England. Powerless for the moment, Rauparaha could but go home, vow vengeance, and wait his opportunity. After two years it came.

Pre-eminent in infamy amongst the ruffianly traders of the time was a certain Stewart. At the end of 1830, he was hanging about Cook's Straits in the brig *Elizabeth*. There he agreed to become Rauparaha's instrument to carry out one of the most diabolical acts of vengeance in even Maori annals. The appearance of Stewart, ripe for any villainy, gave the Kapiti chief the chance he was waiting for. For thirty tons of flax the *Elizabeth* was hired to take Rauparaha and a war-party, not to Kaiapoi, but to Akaroa, a beautiful harbour amongst the hills of the peninsula called after Sir Joseph Banks. It lay many miles away from Kaiapoi, but was inhabited by natives of the same tribe. There, moreover, was living Tamai-hara-nui (Son-of-much-evil), best-born and most revered chief in all the South Island. Him Rauparaha determined to catch, for no one less august could be payment for Te Pehi. Arrived at Akaroa, Rauparaha and his men hid below, and waited patiently for three days until their victim came. Stewart, by swearing that he had no Maoris in the brig, but merely came to trade, tempted the chief and his friends on board. The unhappy Son-of-much-evil was invited into the cabin below. There he stepped into the presence of Rauparaha and Te Pehi's son. The three stared at each other in silence. Then Te Pehi's son with his fingers pushed open the lips of the Akaroa chief, saying, "These are the teeth which ate my father." Forthwith the common people were killed, and the chief and his wife and daughter bound. Rauparaha landed, fired the village, and killed all he could catch. Coming on board again, the victors feasted on the slain, Stewart looking on. Human flesh was cooked in the brig's coppers. The entrapped chief was put in irons—lent by Stewart. Though manacled, he signed to his wife, whose hands were free, to kill their young daughter, a girl whose ominous name was Roimata (Tear-drops). The woman did so, thus saving the child from a worse fate. Returning to Cook's Straits, Rauparaha and comrades went on shore. A Sydney merchant, Mr. Montefiore, came on board the *Elizabeth* at Kapiti and saw the chief lying in irons. As these had caused mortification to set in, Montefiore persuaded

Stewart to have them taken off, but the unhappy captive was still held as a pledge until the flax was paid over. It was paid over. Then this British sea-captain gave up his security, who with his wife was tortured and killed, enduring his torments with the stoicism of a North American Indian. The instrument of his death was a red-hot ramrod.

The *Elizabeth*, with thirty tons of flax in her hold, sailed to Sydney. But Stewart's exploit had been a little too outrageous, even for the South Pacific of those days. He was arrested and tried by order of Governor Darling, who, it is only fair to say, did his best to have him hanged. But, incredible as it seems, public sympathy was on the side of this pander to savages, this pimp to cannibals. Witnesses were spirited away, and at length the prosecution was abandoned. Soon after Stewart died at sea off Cape Horn. One authority says that he dropped dead on the deck of the *Elizabeth*, and that his carcass, reeking with rum, was pitched overboard without ceremony. Another writes that he was washed overboard by a breaking sea. Either way the Akaroa chief had not so easy a death.

Next year, Rauparaha, whose revenge was nothing if not deliberate, organized a strong attack on Kaiapoi. With complete secrecy he brought down his men from Cook's Straits, and surprised his enemies peacefully digging in the potato grounds outside their stockade. A wild rush took place. Most of the Kaiapois escaped into the *pa*, shut the gate and repulsed a hasty assault. Others fled southward, and skulking amid swamps and sand-hills got clear away, and roused their distant fellow-tribesmen. A strong relieving force was got together, and marching to the beleaguered *pa*, slipped past Rauparaha and entered it at night, bending and creeping cautiously through flax and rushes as they waved in a violent wind. But sorties were repulsed, and the garrison had to stand on the defensive. Unlike most *pas*, theirs was well supplied with food and water, and was covered on three sides by swamps and a lagoon. A gallant attempt made on a dark night to burn the besiegers' canoes on the sea-beach was foiled by heavy rain. At last Rauparaha, reaching the stockade by skilful sapping, piled up brushwood against it, albeit many of his men were shot in the process. For weeks the wind blew the wrong way for the besiegers and they could only watch their piles—could not fire them. All the while the soothsayers in the beleaguered fort perseveringly chanted incantations and prayed to the wind-god that the breeze might not change. At length one morning the north-west wind blew so furiously away from the walls that the besieged boldly set alight to the brushwood from their side. But the wilder the north-west wind of New Zealand, the more sudden and complete may be the change to the south-west. Such a shifting came about, and in a moment the flames enveloped the walls. Shouting in triumph, Rauparaha's men mustered in array and danced their frenzied war-dance, leaping high in air, and tossing and catching their muskets with fierce yells. "The earth," says an eye-witness, "shook beneath their stamping." Then they charged through the burning breach, and the defenders fell in heaps or fled before them. The lagoon was black with the heads of men swimming for life. Through the dense drifting smoke many reached the swamps and escaped. Hundreds were killed or taken, and piles of human bones were witnesses many years after to the massacre and feast which followed the fall of Kaiapoi.

Nearly seventy years have passed since these deeds were done. The name Kaiapoi belongs to a pretty little country town, noted for its woollen-mill, about the most flourishing of the colony. Kapiti, Rauparaha's stronghold, is just being reserved by the Government as an asylum for certain native birds, which stoats and weasels threaten to extirpate in the North Island. Over the English grasses which now cover the hills round Akaroa sheep and cattle roam in peace, and standing by the green bays of the harbour you will probably hear nothing louder than a cow-bell, the crack of a whip, or the creaking wheels of some passing dray. Then it is pleasant to remember that Rauparaha's son became a missionary amongst the tribes which his father had harried, and that it is now nearly a generation since Maori blood was shed in conflict on New Zealand soil.

Chapter VIII

"A MAN OF WAR WITHOUT GUNS"

"Under his office treason was no crime;

The sons of Belial had a glorious time."

Dryden.

Between 1830 and 1840, then, New Zealand had drifted into a new phase of existence. Instead of being an unknown land, peopled by ferocious cannibals, to whose shores ship-captains gave as wide a berth as possible, she was now a country with a white element and a constant trade. Missionaries were labouring, not only along the coasts, but in many districts of the interior, and, as the decade neared its end, a large minority of the natives were being brought under the influence of Christianity. The tribal wars were dying down. Partly, this was a peace of exhaustion, in some districts of solitude; partly, it was the outcome of the havoc wrought by the musket, and the growing fear thereof. Nearly all the tribes had now obtained firearms. A war had ceased to be an agreeable shooting-party for some one chief with an unfair advantage over his rivals. A balance of power, or at any rate an equality of risk, made for peace. But it would be unjust to overlook the missionaries' share in bringing about comparative tranquillity. Throughout all the wars of the musket, and the dread slaughter and confusion they brought about, most of the teachers held on. They laboured for peace, and at length those to whom they spoke began to cease to make themselves ready unto the battle. In the worst of times no missionary's life was taken. The Wesleyans at Whangaroa did indeed, in 1827, lose all but life. But the sack of their station was but an instance of the law of *Muru*. Missionaries were then regarded as Hongi's dependants. When he was wounded they were plundered, as he himself was more than once when misfortune befel him. In the wars of Te Waharoa, the mission-stations of Rotorua and Matamata were stripped, but no blood was shed. The Wesleyans set up again at Hokianga. Everywhere the teachers were allowed to preach, to intercede, to protest. At last, in 1838, the extraordinary spectacle was seen of Rauparaha's son going from Kapiti to the Bay of Islands to beg that a teacher might come to his father's tribe; and accordingly, in 1839, Octavius Hadfield, afterwards primate, took his life in his hand and his post at a spot on the mainland opposite to the elder Rauparaha's island den of rapine. By 1840 the Maoris, if they had not beaten their spears into pruning hooks, had more than one old gun-barrel hung up at the gable-end of a meeting-house to serve when beaten upon as a gong for church-goers.[1]

[Footnote 1: See Taylor's *New Zealand, Past and Present*.]

By this time there were in the islands perhaps two thousand Whites, made up of four classes—first, the missionaries; second, the *Pakeha* Maoris; third, the whalers and sealers chiefly found in the South Island; and fourth, the traders and nondescripts settled in the Bay of Islands. Of the last-named beautiful haven it was truly said that every prospect pleased, that only man was vile, and that he was very vile indeed. On one of its beaches, Kororáreka—now called Russell—formed a sort of Alsatia. As many as a thousand Whites lived there at times. On one occasion thirty-five large whaling ships were counted as they lay off its beach in the bay. The crews of these found among the rum-shops and Maori houris of Kororáreka a veritable South Sea Island paradise. The Maori chiefs of the neighbourhood shared their orgies, pandered to their vices, and grew rich thereby. An occasional murder reminded the Whites that Maori forbearance was limited.

But even Kororáreka drew the line. In 1827 a brig, the *Wellington*, arrived in the bay in the hands of a gang of convicts, who had preferred the chances of mutiny to the certainties of Norfolk Island. Forthwith Alsatia was up in arms for society and a triple alliance of missionaries, whalers, and cannibals combined to intercept the runaways. The ship's guns of the whalers drove the convicts to take refuge on shore, where the Maoris promptly secured them. The captives were duly sent to their fate in Sydney, and the services of the New Zealanders gratefully requited by a payment at the rate of a musket per convict.

Alsatia had its civil wars. In 1831 a whaling-captain deserted the daughter of a chief in the neighbourhood in order to take to himself another chief's daughter, also of a tribe by the Bay. The tribe of the deserted woman attacked that of the favoured damsel. A village was burnt, a benevolent mediator shot, and a hundred lives lost. Only the arrival on the scene of Marsden, on one of his visits to the country, restored peace. So outrageous were the scenes in the Bay that its own people had to organize some sort of government. This took the form of a vigilance committee, each member of which came to its meetings armed with musket and cutlass. Their tribunal was, of course, that of Judge Lynch. They arrested certain of the most unbearable offenders, tarred and feathered them, and drummed them out of the township. When feathers were lacking for the decoration, the white fluff of the native bullrush made a handy substitute. In the absence of a gaol, the Vigilants were known to keep a culprit in duress by shutting him up for the night in a sea-chest, ventilated by means of gimlet-holes.

They were not, however, the only representatives of law and order in New Zealand. The British authorities in New South Wales had all along, perforce, been keeping their eye on this troublesome archipelago in the south-east. In 1813 Governor Macquarie made Sydney shipmasters sailing for the country give bonds for a thousand pounds not to kidnap Maori men, take the women on board their vessels, or meddle with burying grounds. In 1814 he appointed the chiefs Hongi and Koro Koro, and the missionary Kendall, to act as magistrates in the Bay of Islands. Possibly the two first-named magistrates were thus honoured to induce them not to eat the third. No other advantage was gained by the step. A statute was passed in England in 1817 authorizing the trial and punishment of persons guilty of murder and other crimes in certain savage and disturbed countries, amongst which were specified New Zealand, Otaheite, and Honduras. Two others, in 1823 and 1828, gave the Australian courts jurisdiction over Whites in New Zealand. One White ruffian was actually arrested in New Zealand, taken back to Sydney, and executed. But this act of vigour did not come till the end of 1837. Then the crime punished was not one of the atrocities which for thirty years had made New Zealand a by-word. The criminal, Edward Doyle, paid the extreme penalty of the law for stealing in a dwelling in the Bay of Islands and "putting John Wright in bodily fear." Governor Bourke issued a special proclamation expressing hope that Doyle's punishment would be a warning to evil-doers in New Zealand. Governor Darling, as already mentioned, prohibited the inhuman traffic in preserved and tattooed heads by attaching thereto a penalty of £40, coupled with exposure of the trader's name.

In England more than one influential believer in colonies had long been watching New Zealand. As early as 1825, a company was formed to purchase land and settle colonists in the North Island. This company's agent, Captain Herd, went so far as to buy land on the Hokianga Estuary, and conduct thither a party of settlers. One of the first experiences of the new-comers was, however, the sight of a native war-dance, the terrifying effects of which, added to more practical difficulties, caused most of them to fold their tents and depart to Australia. Thus for the first time did an English company lose £20,000 in a New Zealand venture. The statesmen of the period were against any such schemes. A deputation of the Friends of Colonization waited upon the Duke of Wellington to urge that New Zealand should be acquired and settled. The Duke, under the advice of the Church Missionary Society, flatly refused to think of such a thing. It was then that he made the historically noteworthy observation that, even supposing New Zealand were as valuable as the deputation made out, Great Britain had already colonies enough. When one reflects what the British Colonial Empire was then, and what it has since become, the remark is a memorable example of the absence of the imaginative quality in statesmen.

But the Duke of Wellington was not by any means alone in a reluctance to annex New Zealand. In 1831 thirteen Maori chiefs, advised by missionaries, had petitioned for British protection, which had not been granted. The truth is, not only that the Empire seemed large enough to others besides the Duke, but that the missionaries stood in the way. As representing the most respectable and the only self-sacrificing element amongst those interested in the islands, they were listened to. It would have been strange had it been otherwise. Nevertheless, the growing trade and the increasing number of unauthorized white settlers made it necessary that something should be done. Consequently, in 1832, Lord Goderich sent to the Bay of Islands Mr. James Busby to reside there as British resident. He was paid a salary, and provided with £200 a year to distribute in presents to the native chiefs. He entered on his duties in 1833. He had no authority, and was not backed by any force. He was aptly nicknamed "a man-of-war without guns." He presented the local chiefs with a national flag. Stars and stripes appeared in the design which the chiefs selected, thanks, says tradition, to the sinister suggestion of a Yankee whaling-skipper. H.M.S. *Alligator* signalised the hoisting of the ensign with a salute of twenty-one guns. After this impressive solemnity, Mr. Busby lived at the bay for six years. His career was a prolonged burlesque—a farce without laughter, played by a dull actor in serious earnest. Personally he went through as strange an experience as has often fallen to the lot of a British official. A man of genius might possibly have managed the inhabitants of his Alsatia. But governments have no right to expect genius in unsupported officials—even when they pay them £300 a year. Mr. Busby was a well-meaning, small-minded person, anxious to justify his appointment. His Alsatians did not like him, and complained that his manners were exclusive and his wit caustic. Probably this meant nothing more than that he declined to join in their drinking-bouts. His life, however, had its own excitements. A chief whom he had offended tried to shoot him. Crouching one night in the verandah of the resident's cottage, he fired at the shadow of Mr. Busby's head as it appeared on the window-blind. As he merely hit the shadow, not the substance, the would-be assassin was not punished, but the better disposed Maoris gave a piece of land as compensation—not to the injured Busby, but to his Government.

It has been well said of Mr. Busby that "his office resembled a didactic dispatch; it sounded well, and it did nothing else." Nevertheless, New Zealand was in a state such that, from time to time, even the English Government had to do something, so urgent was the need for action. After despatching their man-of-war without guns, they next year sent a man-of-war with guns. Nor did the captain of the *Alligator* confine himself to the harmless nonsense of saluting national flags. In 1834 the brig *Harriet* was wrecked on the coast of Taranaki. Her master, Guard, an ex-convict, made his way to Sydney, asserting that the Maoris had flocked down after the wreck, and attacked and plundered the crew; had killed some, and held Guard's wife and children in captivity. As a matter of fact, it was the misconduct of his own men which had brought on the fighting, and even to his Sydney hearers it was obvious that his tale was not wholly true. But the main facts were correct. There had been a wreck and plunder; there were captives. The *Alligator* was at once sent with soldiers to the scene of the disaster to effect the rescue of the prisoners by friendly and pacific means. Arrived on the scene, the captain sent his only two interpreters on shore to negotiate. They were Guard himself and a lying billiard-marker from Kororáreka. They promised the natives ransom—a keg of gunpowder—if the captives were released; an offer which was at once accepted. They did not tell the captain of their promise, and he, most unwisely, refused to give the natives anything. All the captives were at once given up except the woman and the children, who were withheld, but kindly treated, while the natives awaited the promised payment. A chief who came down to the shore to negotiate with a boat's crew was seized, dragged on board, and so savagely mishandled that the ship's surgeon found ten wounds upon him. Yet he lived, and to get him back his tribe gave up Mrs. Guard and a child. The other child was withheld by another chief. Again a strong armed party was landed and was peacefully met by the natives, who brought the child down, but still asked, naturally, for the stipulated ransom. The sailors and soldiers settled the matter by shooting down a chief, on whose shoulders the child was sitting, and firing right and left before the officers in charge could stop them. Next day these men made a football of the chief's head. Before departing the *Alligator* bombarded *pas*, and her crew burnt villages and destroyed canoes and cultivations. If the man-of-war without guns was a figure of fun, the man-of-war with guns excited disgust by these doings even as far away as England. The whole proceeding was clumsy, cruel, and needless. A trifling ransom would have saved it all. The Maori tribal law under which wrecks were confiscated and castaways plundered was, of course, intolerable. Whites again and again suffered severely by it. But blundering and undisciplined violence and broken promises were not the arguments to employ against it. So long as England deliberately chose to leave the country in the hands of barbarians, barbaric customs had to be reckoned with.

From this discreditable business it is a relief to turn to Mr. Busby's bloodless puerilities. In 1835 he drew up a federal constitution for the Maori tribes, and induced thirty-five of the northern chiefs to accept it. This comical scheme would have provided a congress, legislation, magistrates, and other machinery of civilization for a race of savages still plunged in bloodshed and cut asunder by innumerable feuds and tribal divisions. A severe snubbing from Mr. Busby's official superiors in Australia was the only consequence of this attempt to federate man-eaters under parliamentary institutions.

The still-born constitution was Mr. Busby's proposed means of checkmating a rival. In the words of Governor Gipps, this "silly and unauthorized act was a paper pellet fired off" at the hero of an even more pretentious fiasco. An adventurer of French parentage, a certain Baron de Thierry, had proclaimed himself King of New Zealand, and through the agency of missionary Kendall bought, or imagined he bought—for thirty axes—40,000 acres of land from the natives. He landed at Hokianga with a retinue of ninety-three followers. The Maoris of the neighbourhood gravely pointed out to him a plot of three hundred acres, which was all they would acknowledge of his purchase. Unabashed, he established himself on a hill, and began the making of a carriage-road which was to cross the island. Quickly it was found that his pockets were empty. Laughed at by whites and natives alike, he at once subsided into harmless obscurity, diversified by occasional "proclamations," which a callous world allowed to drop unheeded.

Yet this little burlesque was destined to have its share in hastening the appearance of England on the scene. Thierry had tried to enlist the sympathies of the French Government. So also had another Frenchman, Langlois, the captain of a whaling ship, who professed to have bought 300,000 acres of land from the natives of Banks Peninsula in the South Island. Partly owing to his exertions, a French company called "The Nanto-Bordelaise Company" was incorporated, the object of which was to found a French colony on the shores of the charming harbour of Akaroa, on the land said to have been purchased by Langlois. In this company Louis Philippe was a shareholder. In 1837, also, the Catholic missionary Pompallier was dispatched to New Zealand to labour among the Maoris. Such were the sea-routes of that day that it took him some twelve months voyaging amid every kind of hardship and discomfort to reach his journey's end. In New Zealand the fact that he showed Thierry some consideration, and that he and his Catholic workers in the mission-field were not always on the best of terms with their Protestant competitors, aroused well-founded suspicions that the French had their eye upon New Zealand. The English missionaries were now on the horns of a dilemma. They did not want a colony, but if there was to be annexation, the English flag would, of course, be far preferable.

Moreover, a fresh influence had caused the plot to thicken, and was also making for annexation. This was the appearance on the scene of the "land-sharks"—shrewd adventurers, from Sydney and elsewhere, who had come to the conclusion that the colonization of New Zealand was near at hand, and were buying up preposterously large tracts of land on all sides. Most of the purchases were either altogether fictitious, or else were imperfect and made for absurdly low prices. Many of the deeds of sale may be dismissed with the brief note, "no consideration specified"! A hundred acres were bought for a farthing. Boundaries were inserted after signature. Some land was bought several times over. No less than eight purchasers claimed the whole or part of Kapiti Island. The whole South Island was the subject of one professed sale by half a dozen natives in Sydney. Certain purchased blocks were airily defined by latitude and longitude. On the other hand, the Maoris often played the game in quite the same spirit, selling land which they did not own, or had no power to dispose of, again and again. In some cases diamond cut diamond. In others both sides were playing a part, and neither cared for the land to pass. The land-shark wanted a claim with which to harass others; the Maori signed a worthless document on receipt of a few goods. By 1840 it was estimated that, outside the sweeping claim on the South Island, 26,000,000 acres, or more than a third of the area of New Zealand, was supposed to have been gobbled up piecemeal by the land-sharks. The claims arising out of these transactions were certain at the best to cause confusion, ill-feeling, and trouble, and indeed did so. Some legally-constituted authority was clearly wanted to deal with them. Otherwise armed strife between the warlike Maoris and adventurers claiming their lands was inevitable. Before Marsden's death in 1838 both he and his ablest lieutenant, Henry Williams, had come to see that the only hope for the country and the natives lay in annexation and the strong hand of England.

Chapter IX

THE DREAMS OF GIBBON WAKEFIELD

Twin are the gates of sleep: through that of Horn,

Swift shadows winged, the shapes of truth are borne.

Fair wrought the Ivory gate gleams white anigh,

But false the dreams dark gods despatch thereby.

The founder of the Colony now comes on the scene. It was time he came. The Islands were neither to fall into the hands of the French nor remain the happy hunting-ground of promiscuous adventurers. But the fate which ordained that Edward Gibbon Wakefield should save them from these alternatives interposed in the way of the great colonizer a series of difficulties from which any mind less untiring and resourceful than his must have recoiled. The hour had come and the man. Yet few bystanders could have thought either the hour propitious or the man promising. The word colony was not in favour when William the Fourth came to the throne. It was associated with memories of defeat and humiliation in America, and with discontent and mutterings of rebellion in Canada. Australia was scarcely more than an expensive convict station. Against the West Indian planters the crusade of Wilberforce was in full progress, and the very name of "plantation" had an evil savour. South Africa promised little but the plentiful race troubles, which indeed came. The timid apathy of the Colonial Office was no more than the reflex of the dead indifference of the nation. None but a man of genius could have breathed life into it. Fortunately the genius appeared.

Though the name of Gibbon Wakefield will probably be remembered as long as the history of Australia and New Zealand is read, the man himself was, during most of his active career, under a cloud. The abduction of an heiress—a mad freak for which he paid by imprisonment and disgrace—deprived him of the hope of ordinary public distinction. For many years he had to work masked—had to pour forth his views in anonymous tracts and letters, had to make pawns of dull men with respectable names. This and more he learned to do. He found information and ideas for personages who had neither, and became an adept at pulling strings and manipulating mediocrities. All things to all men, plausible to the old, magnetic to the young, persuasive among the intellectual, impressive to the weak-minded, Gibbon Wakefield was always more than the mere clever, selfish schemer which many thought him. Just as his fresh face and bluff British manner concealed the subtle mind ever spinning webs and weaving plans, so, behind and above all his plots and dodging, was the high dream and ideal to which he was faithful, and which redeemed his life. He saw, and made the commonplace people about him see, that colonization was a national work worthy of system, attention, and the best energies of England. The empty territories of the Empire were no longer to be treated only as gaols for convicts, fields for negro slavery, or even as asylums for the persecuted or refuges for the bankrupt and the social failures of the Mother Country. To Wakefield the word "colony" conveyed something more than a back yard into which slovenly Britain could throw human rubbish, careless of its fate so long as it might be out of sight.

His advocacy revived "Ships, Colonies, Commerce!" as England's motto. But for colonies to be worthy, they must be, not fortuitous congregations of outcasts, but orderly bands of representative British citizens, going forth into the wilderness with some consciousness of a high mission. From the outset his colonies were to be civilized communities where men of culture and intellect need not find themselves companionless exiles. Capital and labour, education and religion, were all to work together as in the Mother Country, but amid easier, happier surroundings. For Wakefield conceived of his settlements not as soulless commercial outposts, but as free, self-governing communities.

How was all this to be brought about? Whence was the money to come? Whence the organizing power? At that point came in Wakefield's conception of the sale of waste lands at a "sufficient price." He saw the immense latent value of the fertile deserts of the Empire. He grasped the full meaning of the truth that the arrival of a population with money and industry instantly gives good land a value. His discernment showed him the absurdity of giving colonial lands away in indefinite areas to the first chance grabbers, and the mistake of supposing that wage labour would not be required in young countries. His theory, therefore, was that colonizing associations should be formed in England—not primarily to make money; that these bodies should hold tracts of land in the colonies as capital; that the sale of these lands at a "sufficient price" to intending colonists, selected for character and fitness, should provide the funds for transporting the colony across the earth, for establishing it in working order on its land, and for recruiting it with free labour.

The numerous *ex post facto* assailants of Wakefield's theory usually assume that he wished to keep labour divorced from the soil and in a state of permanent political and industrial inferiority. That is sheer nonsense. There are few more odd examples of the irony of fate in colonial history than that the man who warred against the convict system, fought the battle of colonial self-government, was ever the enemy of the land-shark and monopolist, who denounced low wages, and whose dream it was that the thrifty, well-paid colonial labourer could and should develop into the prospering farmer, should be railed at in the Colonies as the enemy of the labourer. The faults of Wakefield's "sufficient price" theory were indeed grave enough. But compare them with the lasting mischief wrought in New Zealand by Grey's unguarded scheme of cheap land for everybody, and they weigh light in the balance. Later on I shall return to Wakefield's system and its defects. Here I have but to say that, as a temporary expedient for overcoming at that time the initial difficulties of a colony, it ought not to be hastily condemned. It has long ago been abandoned after working both good and evil, and in the same way the schemes of Church Settlement Wakefield made use of are now but interesting chapters of colonial history. But we must not forget that these things were but some of the dreams of Gibbon Wakefield. At the most he regarded them as means to an end. His great dream of lifting colonization out of disrepute, and of founding colonies which should be daughter-states worthy of their great mother, has been no false or fleeting vision. That dream, at any rate, came to him through the Gate of Horn and not through the Ivory Gate.

By Wakefield it was that the Colonial Office was forced to annex New Zealand. In the face of the causes making for annexation sketched in the last chapter, the officials hung back to the last. In 1837 a body of persons appeared on the scene, and opened siege before Downing Street, whom even permanent officials could not ignore. They were composed of men of good standing, in some cases of rank and even personal distinction. They were not traders, but colonizers, and as such could not be ignored, for their objects were legitimate and their hands as clean as those of the missionaries. They first formed, in 1837, a body called "The New Zealand Association." At their head was Mr. Francis Baring. Their more prominent members included John Lambton Earl of Durham, Lord Petre, Mr. Charles Enderby, Mr. William Hutt, Mr. Campbell of Islay, Mr. Ferguson of Raith, Sir George Sinclair, and Sir William Molesworth. The Earl of Durham was an aristocratic Radical of irregular temper, who played a great part in another colonial theatre—Canada. Sir William Molesworth did much to aid the agitation which put an end to the transportation of convicts to Australia. For the rest, the Association thought the thoughts, spoke the words, and made the moves of Gibbon Wakefield. Yet though he pervaded it sleeplessly, its life was but an episode in his career. He fought against the convict system with Molesworth and Rentoul of the *Spectator*. He went to Canada as Lord Durham's secretary and adviser. He was actively concerned in the foundation of South Australia, where his system of high prices for land helped to bring about one of the maddest little land "booms" in colonial history. And as these things were not enough to occupy that daring, original, and indefatigable spirit, he threw himself into the colonization of New Zealand. He and his brother, Colonel Wakefield, became the brain and hand of the New Zealand colonizers.

For years they battled against their persistent opponents the Church Missionary Society and the officials of the Colonial Office. The former, who hit very hard at them in controversy, managed Lord Glenelg, then Colonial Secretary; the latter turned Minister after Minister from friends of the colonizers into enemies. Thus Lord Melbourne and Lord Howick had to change face in a fashion well-nigh ludicrous. The Government offered the Association a charter provided it would become a joint-stock company. Baring and his friends refused this on the ground that they did not want any money-making element to come into their body. Moreover, in those days joint-stock companies were concerns with unlimited liability. The Association tried to get a bill of constitution through Parliament and failed. Mr. Gladstone spoke against it, and expressed the gloomiest apprehensions of the fate which the Maoris must expect if their country were settled. New Zealand, be it observed, was already a well-known name in Parliament. The age of committees of inquiry into its affairs began in 1836. Very interesting to us to-day is the evidence of the witnesses before the committee of that year; nor are the proceedings of those of 1838, 1840, and 1844, less interesting. In the third of the four Gibbon Wakefield, under examination, tells the story of the New Zealand Association. In 1839 it became the New Zealand Land Company. Baffled in Parliament, as already described, the colonizers changed their ground, decided to propitiate the powers, and become a joint-stock company. Having done so, and subscribed a capital of £100,000, they tried to enlist the sympathies of Lord Normanby, who had just succeeded Lord Glenelg at the Colonial Office. They found the new-made Secretary of State very affable indeed, and departed rejoicing. But, like many new-made ministers, Lord Normanby had spoken without reckoning with his permanent officials. A freezing official letter, following swiftly on the pleasant interview, dashed the hopes of the Company. They were getting desperate. Lord Palmerston had, in November, 1838, promised them to send a consul to New Zealand to supersede poor Mr. Busby, but the permanent officials thwarted him, and nothing was done for eight months. At last, in May, 1839, Gibbon Wakefield crossed the Rubicon. As the Government persisted in treating New Zealand as a foreign country, let the Company do the same, and establish settlements there as in a foreign land! Since repeated efforts to obtain the help and sanction of the English Government had failed, let them go on unauthorized. Secretly, therefore, the ship *Tory*, bearing Colonel Wakefield, as Agent for the Company, was despatched in May to Cook's Straits to buy tracts of land for the Company. He was given a free hand as to locality, though Port Nicholson was hinted at as the likeliest port. With him went Gibbon Wakefield's son, Jerningham

Wakefield, whose book, *Adventures in New Zealand*, is the best account we New Zealanders have of the every-day incidents of the founding of our colony.

Arriving in August among the whalers then settled in Queen Charlotte's Sound, Colonel Wakefield enlisted Dicky Barrett's services, and, passing on to Port Nicholson, entered into a series of negotiations with the Maori chiefs, which led to extensive land purchases. Ultimately Colonel Wakefield claimed that he had bought twenty millions of acres—nearly the whole of what are now the provincial districts of Wellington and Taranaki, and a large slice of Nelson. It is quite probable that he believed he had. It is certain that the Maoris, for their part, never had the least notion of selling the greater portion of this immense area. It is equally probable that such chiefs as Rauparaha and Rangihaeata, who were parties to the bargain, knew that Wakefield thought he was buying the country. Fifty-eight chiefs in all signed the deeds of sale. Even if they understood what they were doing, they had no right, under the Maori law and custom, thus to alienate the heritage of their tribes. Had Colonel Wakefield's alleged purchases been upheld the Company would have acquired nine-tenths of the lands of no less than ten well-known tribes. The price paid for this was goods valued at something less than £9,000. The list of articles handed over at the Wakefield purchases is remarkable enough to be worth quoting:—

300 red blankets.
200 muskets.
16 single-barrelled guns.
8 double-barrelled guns.
2 tierces tobacco.
15 cwt. tobacco.
148 iron pots.
6 cases soap.
15 fowling pieces.
81 kegs gunpowder.
2 casks ball cartridges.
4 kegs lead slates.
200 cartouche boxes.
60 tomahawks.
2 cases pipes.
10 gross pipes.
72 spades.
100 steel axes.
20 axes.
46 adzes.
3,200 fish-hooks.

24 bullet moulds.
1,500 flints.
276 shirts.
92 jackets.
92 trousers.
60 red nightcaps.
300 yards cotton duck.
200 yards calico.
300 yards check.
200 yards print.
480 pocket-handkerchiefs.
72 writing slates.
600 pencils.
204 looking glasses.
276 pocket knives.
204 pairs scissors.
12 pairs shoes.
12 hats.
6 lbs. beads.
12 hair umbrellas.
100 yards ribbons.
144 Jews' harps.
36 razors.
180 dressing combs.
72 hoes.
2 suits superfine clothes.
36 shaving boxes.
12 shaving brushes.
12 sticks sealing wax.
11 quires cartridge paper.
12 flushing coats.
24 combs.

The purchasing took three months. While it was going on Henry Williams and other missionaries urged the chiefs not to sell. But with the goods spread out before them—especially the muskets—the chiefs were not to be stopped. The Wakefields justified the transactions on the ground that population would rapidly make the ten per cent. of the country reserved for the natives more valuable than the whole. Gibbon Wakefield talked airily to the parliamentary committee next year of a value of 30s. an acre, which, on a reserve of two million acres, would mean three million sterling for the Maoris! Nothing can justify the magnitude of Colonel Wakefield's claims, or the payment of fire-arms for the land. But at the bottom of the mischief was the attempt of the missionaries and officials at home to act as though a handful of savages—not then more, I believe, than 65,000 in all, and rapidly dwindling in numbers—could be allowed to keep a fertile and healthy Archipelago larger than Great Britain. The haste, the secrecy, the sharp practice, of the New Zealand Company were forced on the Wakefields by the mulish obstinacy of careless or irrational people. Their land-purchasing might have taken place legally, leisurely, and under proper Government supervision, had missionaries been business-like, had Downing-Street officials known what colonizing meant, and had Lord Glenelg been fitted to be anything much more important than an irreproachable churchwarden.

Meanwhile the Company had been advertising, writing, canvassing, and button-holing in England, had kept a newspaper on foot, and was able to point to powerful friends in Parliament and in London mercantile circles. By giving scrip supposed to represent plots and farms in its New Zealand territory, it secured numbers of settlers, many of whom were men of worth, education, and ability. The character of the settlers which it then and afterwards gave New Zealand may well be held to cover a multitude of the Company's sins. Towards the end of 1839 its preparations were complete, and, without even waiting to hear how Colonel Wakefield had fared, the first batch of its settlers were shipped to Port Nicholson. They landed there on January 22nd, 1840, and that is the date of the true foundation of the colony. But for some weeks after that New Zealand remained a foreign country. Not for longer, however. In June, 1839, the Colonial Office had at length given way. What between the active horde of land-sharks in New Zealand itself—what between the menace of French interference, and the pressure at home of the New Zealand Company, the official mind could hold out no longer. Captain Hobson, of the Royal Navy, was directed to go to the Bay of Islands, and was armed with a dormant commission authorizing him, after annexing all or part of New Zealand, to govern it in the name of Her Majesty. In Sydney a royal proclamation was issued under which New Zealand was included within the political boundary of the colony of New South Wales. Captain Hobson was to act as Lieutenant-Governor, with the Governor of New South Wales as his superior officer. On January 29th, 1840, therefore, he stepped on shore at Kororáreka, and was loyally received by the Alsatians. The history of New Zealand as a portion of the British Empire now begins.

Chapter X

IN THE CAUDINE FORKS

I would rather be governed by Nero on the spot than by a Board of Angels in London.—*John Robert Godley.*

Though Governor Hobson landed in January, the formal annexation of the Colony did not take place until May. He had first to take possession; and this could only be effectually done with the consent of the native tribes. The northern chiefs were therefore summoned, and came to meet the Queen's representative at Waitangi (Water of Weeping). Tents and a platform were erected, and the question of annexation argued at length. The French Bishop Pompallier appeared in full canonicals, and it was found that chiefs under his influence had been well coached to oppose the new departure. Behind the scenes, too, that worst of beachcombers, Jacky Marmon, secretly made all the mischief he could. On the other hand, Henry Williams, representing the Protestant missionaries, threw his weight into the scale on the Governor's side and acted as translator. While many of the chiefs were still doubtful, if not hostile, Waka Nene, the most influential of the Ngapuhi tribe, spoke strongly and eloquently for annexation. His speech gained the day, and a treaty was drawn up and signed. By the preamble, Queen Victoria invited the confederated and independent Chiefs of New Zealand to concur in Articles to the following effect:—

(1) The Chiefs of New Zealand ceded to Her Majesty, absolutely and without reservation, all their rights and powers of Sovereignty.

(2) Her Majesty guaranteed to the Chiefs and Tribes of New Zealand, full, exclusive, and undisturbed possession of their Lands and Estates, Forests, Fisheries and other properties; but the Chiefs yielded to Her Majesty the exclusive right of Pre-emption over such lands as the proprietors thereof might be disposed to alienate, at such prices as might be agreed upon.

(3) Her Majesty gave to the natives of New Zealand all the Rights and Privileges of British Subjects.

Nearly fifty chiefs signed the treaty there and then, and within six months— so energetically did the missionaries and Government agents carry it throughout the tribes—it had been signed by five hundred and twelve. Only about one chief of first-class rank and importance refused to sign it. This was that fine barbarian, Te Heu Heu, whose home lay at the foot of the great volcanoes by Lake Taupo on the plateau in the centre of the North Island. Te Heu Heu was the last of the old heathen warriors. Singularly fair-skinned, and standing fully six feet high, he looked what he was, a patriarch and leader of his people. Scoffing at the White men and their religion, he defied Governor and missionaries alike until his dramatic end, which came in 1846, when he and his village were swallowed up in a huge landslide. At present, as he could neither be coerced nor persuaded, he was let alone. For the rest, it may fairly be claimed that the Maori race accepted the Treaty of Waitangi.

They had very good reason to do so. To this day they regard it as the Magna Charta of their liberties. They were fully aware that under it the supreme authority passed to the Queen; but they were quite able to understand that their tribal lands were guaranteed to them. In other words, they were recognised as the owners in fee simple of the whole of New Zealand. As one of them afterwards expressed it, "The shadow passes to the Queen, the substance stays with us."

At the same time Governor Hobson had announced to the white settlers by proclamation that the Government would not recognise the validity of any of their land titles not given under the Queen's authority. It is not easy to see how else he could have dealt with the land-sharks, of whom there had been an ugly rush from Sydney on the news of the coming annexation, and most of whom as promptly retreated on finding the proclamation to be a reality. But at the same time his treaty and his proclamation were bound to paralyse settlement, to exasperate the entire white population, and to plunge the infant colony into a sea of troubles. Outside the missionaries and the officials every one was uneasy and alarmed. All the settlers were either landowners, land claimants, or would-be land purchasers. Yet they found themselves at one and the same time left without titles to all that they thought they possessed, and debarred from the right of buying anything more except from the Crown. And as the Governor was without funds, and the Crown, therefore, could not buy from the natives, there was a deadlock. Space will not admit here of a full discussion of the vexed question of the land clause in the Treaty of Waitangi. As a rule civilized nations do not recognise the right of scattered handfuls of barbarians to the ownership of immense tracts of soil, only a fraction of which they cultivate or use. However, from the noblest and most philanthropic motives an exception to this rule was made in the case of New Zealand, and by treaty some sixty to seventy thousand Maoris were given a title guaranteed by England—the best title in the world—to some sixty-six million acres of valuable land. Putting aside the question of equity, it may be observed that, had not this been done, the Maoris, advised by the missionaries, would certainly have refused their assent to the Treaty. The millions sterling which have had to be spent in New Zealand, directly and indirectly, in acquiring Maori land for settlement, supply of course no argument whatever against the equity of the Treaty. When honour is in the scale, it outweighs money. Yet had Captain Hobson been able to conceive what was entailed in the piecemeal purchase of a country held under tribal ownership, it is difficult to think that he would have signed the Treaty without hesitation. He could not, of course, imagine that he was giving legal force to a system under which the buying of a block of land would involve years of bargaining even when a majority of its owners wished to sell; that the ascertainment of a title would mean tedious and costly examination by courts of experts of a labyrinth of strange and conflicting barbaric customs; that land might be paid for again and again, and yet be declared unsold; that an almost empty wilderness might be bought first from its handful of occupants, then from the conquerors who had laid it waste, and yet after all be reclaimed by returned slaves or fugitives who had quitted it years before, and who had been paid for the land on which they had been living during their absence. Governor Hobson could not foresee that cases would occur in which the whole purchase money of broad lands would be swallowed up in the costs of sale, or that a greedy tribe of expert middlemen would in days to come bleed Maori and settler alike. Yet it would have been but reasonable for the Colonial Office to exert itself to palliate the effects of the staggering blows it thus dealt the pioneer colonists of New Zealand. They were not all land-sharks; most of them were nothing of the sort. It was but natural that they felt with extreme bitterness that the Queen's Government only appeared on the scene as the friend and protector of the aborigines. For the Whites the Government had for years little but suspicion and restraint.

It would have been only just and statesmanlike if the recognition of Maori ownership had been accompanied by a vigorous policy of native land purchase by the authorities. But it was not. Captain Hobson was only scantily supplied with money—he had £60,000 sent him in three years—and did not himself appear to recognise the paramount need for endowing the Colony with waste land for settlement. He is said to have held that there need be no hurry in the matter inasmuch as the steady decrease of the Maoris would of itself solve the problem. Nearly sixty years have passed since then, and the Maori race is by no means extinct. But Captain Hobson, though a conscientious and gallant man, was no more imbued with the colonizing spirit than might be expected of any honest English naval officer. Of such money as he had he wasted £15,000 at the outset in buying a site for a town in the Bay of Islands on a spot which he quickly had to abandon. Moreover, he was just what a man in his irksome and difficult position should not have been—an invalid. Within a few weeks after the signing of the Treaty of Waitangi he was stricken with paralysis. Instead of being relieved he was left to be worried slowly to death at his post. To have met the really great difficulties and the combination of petty annoyances which beset him, the new governor should have had the best of health and spirits. The complications around him grew daily more entangled. In the North the excellent settlers, who with their children were to make the province of Auckland what it is, were scarcely even beginning to arrive. The Whites of his day there were what tradesmen call a job lot. There were the old Alsatian; the new speculator; genuine colonists, *rari nantes*; a coterie of officials; and the missionaries, regarding all with distrust. The whole barely numbered two thousand. Confronting the Whites were the native tribes, who, if united and irritated, could have swept all before them. Hobson, a man accustomed to command rather than to manage, was instructed to control the Maoris by moral suasion. He was to respect their institutions and customs when these were consistent with humanity and decency, otherwise not. How in the last resort he was to stamp out inhuman and indecent customs was left unexplained, though he asked for an explanation. Certainly not by force; for it would have been flattery to apply such a term to the tiny handful of armed men at his back. Troops were not sent until the war of 1844. During the five years after that the defence of New Zealand probably cost the Imperial Government a round million, the result of the starving policy of the first five years.

VIEW OF NELSON
Photo by HENRY WRIGHT

Moreover, for the reasons already sketched, the English in New Zealand formed a house divided against itself. The differences in the north between Maoris' officials, Alsatians of the old school, and settlers of the new, were sufficient to supply the Governor with a daily dish of annoyance. But the main colony of New Zealand was not in the north round Governor Hobson, but in Cook's Straits. There was to be found the large and daily increasing antagonistic element being brought in by the New Zealand Company. With an energy quite unchecked by any knowledge of the real condition of New Zealand, the directors of the Company in London kept on sending out ship-load after ship-load of emigrants to the districts around Cook's Straits. The centre of their operations was Port Nicholson, but bodies of their settlers were planted at Wanganui, at the mouth of the fine river described in the first chapter; at New Plymouth, hard by the Sugar-Loaves, in devastated almost empty Taranaki; and at pleasant but circumscribed Nelson in the South Island. Soon these numbered five times as many Whites as could be mustered in the north. Upon them at the very outset came the thunderbolt of Governor Hobson's proclamation refusing recognition to their land purchases. Of this and of the land clause in the Treaty of Waitangi the natives were made fully aware by the missionaries. Rauparaha, before told of and still the most influential chief near Cook's Straits, was exactly the man to take advantage of the situation. He had taken the muskets and gunpowder of the Company, and was now only too pleased to refuse them the price they thought to receive. It was, as already said, impossible to justify all, or nearly all, of Colonel Wakefield's gigantic purchase. But it was certainly incumbent on the Government to find a *modus vivendi* with the least possible delay. On the one hand they had thousands of decent, intelligent English colonists newly landed in a savage country, and not in any way responsible for the Company's haste and ignorance. The settlers at any rate had paid ample value for their land. They had given £1 for each acre of it. Angry as the English Government had been with the New Zealand Company for the defiant dispatch of its settlers, Lord John Russell had instructed Hobson's superior, Sir George Gibbs, that the emigrants should be regarded with kindness and consideration. On the other side were the native tribes, who, as the price of land went in those days, had certainly received the equivalent for a considerable territory. There was room for an equitable arrangement just as there was most pressing need for promptitude. Speed was the first thing needful, also the second, and the third. Instead of speed the settlers got a Royal Commission. A Commissioner was appointed, who did not arrive until two years after the Governor, and whose final award was not given for many months more. When he did give it, he cut down the Company's purchase of twenty million acres to two hundred and eighty-three thousand. As for land-claims of private persons, many of them became the subjects of litigation and petition, and some were not settled for twenty years. Why three or four Commissioners were not sent instead of one, and sent sooner, the official mind alone knows. Meantime, the weary months dragged on, and the unfortunate settlers of the Company were either not put in possession of their land at all, or had as little security for their farms as for their lives. They were not allowed to form volunteer corps, though living in face of ferocious and well-armed savages. Yet the Governor who forbade them to take means to defend themselves had not the troops with which to defend them. To show the state of the country it may be noted that the two tribes from whom Colonel Wakefield bought the land round Port Nicholson quarrelled amongst themselves over the sale. The Ngatiraukawa treacherously attacked the Ngatiawa, were soundly beaten, and lost seventy men. At first, it is true, settlers and natives got on excellently well together. The new-comers had money, and were good customers. But as time went on, and the settlers exhausted their funds and hopes, they ceased to be able to buy freely. And when they found the Maoris refusing to admit them to the farms for which they had paid £1 an acre in London, feeling grew more and more acute. The Company's settlement at Port Nicholson was perversely planted just on that place in the inner harbour which is exposed to the force of the ocean. It had to be shifted to a more sheltered spot, and this the natives denied they ever sold. That was but one of a series of disputes which led to murder and petty warfare, and were hardly at an end seven years later. The settlers, though shut out of the back country, did, however, hold the townland on which they had squatted, and which is now the site of Wellington, the capital of New Zealand.

Cooped up in their narrow plots by the sea, Colonel Wakefield and his settlers established a provisional Government. Captain Hobson, hearing probably some very exaggerated account of this, sent down his Lieutenant, Mr. Willoughby Shortland, in a Government vessel, with sailors and marines, to put down this act of insubordination. Mr. Shortland, who suffered from the not uncommon failing of a desire to magnify his office made the process as ridiculous as possible. He began by stealthily sending a scout on shore at daybreak to haul down the Company's flag in Wellington and hoist the Union Jack instead. Then he landed amongst the settlers, who had gathered to welcome him, in the fashion of a royal commander sent to suppress a rebellion. The settlers consoled themselves by laughing at him. Apart from one circular visit occupying two months, Captain Hobson himself kept sedulously away from the southern settlements, and stayed in the north, then a longer journey away from Wellington than Australia is now. Under the rather high-sounding title of Chief Protector of the Aborigines, Mr. Clarke, a missionary, was appointed to be the Governor's adviser on native matters; yet Mr. Clarke, the settlers complained, was a larger land claimant than any of themselves. It is not to be wondered at if a feeling grew up among the New Zealand settlers directed against both officials and missionaries, which at times intensified to great bitterness, and which took many years to die down. Even now its faint relics may be observed in a vague feeling of dislike and contempt for the Colonial Office.

The New Zealand Company, however, cannot be acquitted of blame in more respects than one. The foundation of the Wakefield theory rested on a secure supply of useful land. This not available, the bottom dropped out of the whole scheme. When in New Zealand the Company's estate was put into chancery, the Wakefield system could not, of course, work. Not only were the Company's purchases such as could not be sustained, not only did the directors hurry out thousands of settlers without proper knowledge or consideration, but they also committed a capital error in their choice of localities for settlements. Wellington, with its central position and magnificent harbour, is undeniably the key of New Zealand. It was in after years very properly made the seat of government, and is always likely to remain so. But it was an almost criminal error on the part of the Company to plump down its settlers in districts that were occupied and certain to be stubbornly held by warlike natives. Nearly the whole of the South Island had no human occupants. Shut off by the Kaikoura mountains from the more dangerous tribes, the east and south-east of that island lay open to the first comer. Moreover, the country there was not only fertile, but in large part treeless, and therefore singularly suited for rapid and profitable settlement. It is quite easy to see now that had the New Zealand Company begun its first operations there, a host of failures and troubles would have been avoided. The settlement of the North Island should not have been begun until after an understanding had been come to with the Imperial authorities and missionaries, and on a proper and legal system of land purchase. This and other things the Company might have found out if it had taken early steps to do so. The truth is that the first occupation of New Zealand was rushed, and, like everything else that is done in a hurry, it was in part done very badly.

So little was known or thought of the South Island that sovereignty was not proclaimed over it until four months after the Governor's arrival in the north, and even then the royal flag was not hoisted there. The consequence was a narrow escape from an attempt by the French to plant a colony at Akaroa in Banks Peninsula. The French frigate *L'Aube* put in at the Bay of Islands in July, 1840, bound for the south. Her captain, hospitably entertained by Hobson, let fall some incautious words about the object of his voyage. Hobson took the alarm, and promptly dispatched the *Britomart* to hoist the English flag at Akaroa. Thanks to bad weather, the *Britomart* only reached the threatened port a few days before the Frenchmen. Then it was found that an emigrant ship, with a number of French settlers, was coming with all the constituent parts of a small colony. The captain of *L'Aube*, finding himself forestalled, good-humouredly made the best of it. A number of the immigrants did indeed land. Some of them were afterwards taken away to the Marquesas Islands in the South Seas: others remained permanently settled at Akaroa. There around a bay, still called French Bay, they planted vineyards and built cottages in a fashion having some pathetic reminiscences of rural France. There they used to be visited from time to time by French men-of-war; but they gave no trouble to any one, and their children, by removal or intermarriage, became blended with the English population which in later days surrounded them.

Captain Hobson had to choose a capital. After throwing away much good money at Russell in the Bay of Islands, he saw that he must come further south. A broader-minded man might have gone at once to Wellington, and planted himself boldly amongst the English settlers. But the prejudice of the officials and the advice of the missionaries combined with Hobson's own peculiar views of the Cook's Straits colonists, to keep him in the north. From his despatches it is clear that he regarded the immigrants in the south—one of the finest bodies of settlers that ever left England—as dangerous malcontents of anarchical tendencies. As he would not go to Wellington and take his natural position at the head of the main English colony and at the centre of New Zealand, he did the next best thing in going to Auckland. In pitching upon the Waitemata isthmus he made so good a choice that his name is likely to be remembered therefore as long as New Zealand lasts. By founding the city of Auckland he not only took up a strategic position which cut the Maori tribes almost in half, but selected a very fine natural trading centre. The narrow neck of land on which Auckland stands between the winding Waitemata on the east and the broader Manu-kau Harbour on the west, will, before many years, be overspread from side to side by a great mercantile city. The unerring eye of Captain Cook had, seventy years before, noted the Hauraki Gulf as an admirable position. Hobson's advisers, in choosing it as his seat of Government, are said to have been the missionary, Henry Williams, and Captain Symonds, a surveyor. As the capital of New Zealand it was the wrong place from the first. From every other standpoint the selection was a master-stroke. Twenty-four years later Auckland ceased to be the capital of the Colony; but though in this she had to yield to the superior claims of Wellington, she could afford to lose the privilege. First in size and beauty, she is to-day second to no other New Zealand city in prosperity and progress.

In 1841, however, by way of making as bad a start as possible, little Auckland began with a land boom. Forty-four acres were sold at auction by the Government for £24,275. Small suburban lots a few months later fetched £45 an acre, and cultivation lots £8 an acre. For one or two picked city frontages as much as £7 10s. a foot was paid. The hanging up of the northern land claims, and the inability of the Government to buy native land while it refused to let private persons do so, joined, with a trade collapse in Australia, to make the condition of the Auckland settlers soon almost as unenviable as that of their fellow-colonists in the Company's settlements.

Governor Hobson died at Auckland after ruling New Zealand for a little less than three years. His best monument is the city which he founded, and the most memorable verdict on his life is written in a letter addressed by a Maori chief to the Queen. "Let not," said this petition, "the new Governor be a boy or one puffed up. Let not a troubler come amongst us. Let him be a good man like this Governor who has just died." When these words were written, the judgment of the English in New Zealand would have been very different. But time has vindicated Hobson's honesty and courage, and in some important respects even his discernment. He anticipated the French, baffled the land-sharks, kept the peace, was generous to the Maori, and founded Auckland. No bad record this for the harassed, dying sailor, sent to stand between his own countrymen and savages at the very end of the earth, and left almost without men or money! If under him the colonists found their lot almost unbearable, the fault was chiefly that of his masters. Most of his impolicy came from Downing Street; most of his good deeds were his own. It must be remembered that he was sent to New Zealand, not to push on settlement, but to protect the natives and assert the Queen's authority. These duties he never forgot.

Chapter XI

THROUGH WEAKNESS INTO WAR

"Awhile he makes some false way, undebarred

By thwarting signs, and braves

The freshening wind and blackening waves,

And then the tempest strikes him; and between

The lightning-bursts is seen

Only a driving wreck,
And the pale master on his spar-strewn deck."

In 1842 it took eight months before an official, when writing from New Zealand to England, could hope to get an answer. The time was far distant when the results of a cricket match in the southern hemisphere could be proclaimed in the streets of London before noon on the day of play. It was not therefore surprising that Hobson's successor did not reach the Colony for more than a year after his death. Meantime the Government was carried on by Mr. Secretary Shortland, not the ablest of his officials. He soon very nearly blundered into war with the Maoris, some of whom had been killing and eating certain of another tribe—the last recorded instance of cannibalism in the country. The Acting-Governor was, however, held back by Bishop Selwyn, Chief Justice Martin, and Swainson the Attorney-General, a trio of whom more will be said hereafter. The two former walked on foot through the disturbed district, in peril but unharmed, to proffer their good advice. The Attorney-General advised that what the Acting-Governor contemplated was *ultra vires*, an opinion so palpably and daringly wrong that some have thought it a desperate device to save the country. He contended that as the culprits in the case were not among the chiefs who had signed the Treaty of Waitangi, they were not subject to the law or sovereignty of England. Though it is said that Dr. Phillimore held the same opinion, the Colonial Office put its foot upon it heavily and at once. Her Majesty's rule, said Lord Stanley, having once been proclaimed over all New Zealand, it did not lie with one of her officers to impugn the validity of her government.

Mr. Shortland's day was a time of trial for the land claimants. After nearly two years' delay Mr. Spain, the Commissioner for the trial of the New Zealand Company's claims, had landed in Wellington in December, 1841, and had got to work in the following year. As the southern purchases alone gave him work enough for three men, Messrs. Richmond and Godfrey were appointed to hear the Auckland cases. By the middle of 1843 they had disposed of more than half of 1,037 claims. Very remorselessly did they cut them down. A well-known missionary who had taken over a block of 50,000 acres to prevent two tribes going to war about it, was allowed to keep 3,000 acres only. At Hokianga a purchaser who claimed to have bought 1,500 acres for £24 was awarded 96 acres. When we remember that among the demands of the greater land-sharks of the Colony had been three for more than a million acres each, three for more than half a million each, and three for more than a quarter of a million each, we can appreciate what the early Governors and their Commissioners had to face. The Old Land Claims, now and afterwards looked into, covered some eleven million acres. Of these a little less than one twenty-second part was held to have passed from the natives, and was divided between the Crown and the claimants. A number of the Church of England missionaries had to go through the ordeal with the rest. Some twenty-four of these, together with members of their families, had, between 1830 and 1843, bought about 216,000 acres of land from the natives. The Commissioners cut down this purchase to about 66,000 acres. Even then there was some litigation and much bitterness. Some of the very missionaries who had been most prominent in thwarting and denouncing the land purchases of the New Zealand Company were themselves purchasers of land. As may be imagined, the criticisms directed at them were savage, noisy, and often unjust and exaggerated. Years afterwards Governor Grey became involved in this miserable controversy, which only slowly died away when he passed ordinances that did much to settle doubtful and disputed claims.

Not all the missionaries laid themselves open to these attacks. Neither Hadfield, Maunsell, nor the printer Colenso were amongst the land-buyers, and the same honourable self-denial was shown by all the Catholic missionaries, and by all the Wesleyans but two. Nor were the lay land-claimants always ravenous. Maning, the Pakeha Maori, had paid £222 for his 200 acres at Hokianga. At Tauranga £50 had been given for a building site fifty feet square, in a *pa*. At Rotorua the price given for half an acre had been £12 10s. Many of the most monstrous claims, it may be noted, were never brought into court.

In the Cook's Straits settlements Mr. Spain strove to do equity. The very sensible plan was adopted of allowing the Company to make some of their incomplete purchases good by additional payments. But this, which might have brought about a tolerable adjustment in 1840, led to little but delays and recriminations in 1843. After three years of stagnation the Company was as exasperated and impecunious as the settlers. The positions of

Colonel Wakefield in Wellington, and his brother and fellow-agent, Arthur Wakefield, in Nelson, were almost unbearable. It is hardly to be wondered at that the latter, in June, 1843, committed the very great mistake which led to the one misfortune from which the unhappy Colony had so far escaped—war.

In the north-east corner of the South Island lies the grassy valley of the Wairau. Rich in alluvial soil, open and attractive to the eye, and near the sea, it wanted only greater extent to be one of the finest districts in the Islands. The Company claimed to have bought it from Rauparaha and Rangihaeata, whose ownership—for they did not live in it—was based on recent conquest, and on occupation by some members of their tribe. The chiefs denied the sale, and, when the Company's surveyors came into the valley, warned them off, and burned down the huts they had put up. Commissioner Spain was coming almost at once to try the dispute as to the title. But the delays and vexations of the previous years had infuriated Captain Wakefield. He looked upon the chiefs as a pair of "travelling bullies" who wanted but firmness to cow them. With hasty hardihood he obtained a warrant for the arrest of Rauparaha on a charge of arson, and set out to arrest him, accompanied by the Nelson police magistrate, at the head of a *posse* of some fifty Nelson settlers very badly equipped. Rauparaha, surrounded by his armed followers, was found in a small clearing backed by a patch of bush, his front covered by a narrow but deep creek. The leaders of the arresting party crossed this, and called on the chief to give himself up. Of course he defied them. After an argument the police magistrate, an excitable man, made as though to arrest him. There was a scuffle; a gun went off, and in the conflict which followed the undisciplined settlers, fired upon by hidden natives, and divided by the stream, became panic-stricken, and retreated in confusion, despite Wakefield's appeals and entreaties to them to stand. As he could do nothing with them, Wakefield held up a white handkerchief, and with four gentlemen and four labourers gave himself up to Rauparaha. But Rangihaeata had a blood-feud with the English. A woman-servant of his—not his wife—had been accidentally shot in the fray. Moreover, some time before, another woman, a relative of his, had been murdered by a white, who, when tried in the Supreme Court, had been acquitted. Now was the hour for vengeance. Coming up wild with rage, Rangihaeata fell upon the unresisting prisoners and tomahawked them all. Captain Wakefield, thus untimely slain, was not only an able pioneer leader, but a brave man of high worth, of singularly fine and winning character, and one of whom those who knew him spoke with a kind of enthusiasm. Twenty-two settlers in all were killed that day and five wounded. The natives, superior in numbers, arms, and position, had lost only four killed and eight wounded. So easily was the first tussle between Maori and settler won by the natives. In the opinion of some the worst feature of the whole unhappy affair was that something very like cowardice had been shown on the losing side. Naturally the Wairau Massacre, as it was called, gave a shock to the young Colony. The Maoris triumphantly declared that the *mana* (prestige) of the English was gone.

A Wesleyan missionary and a party of whalers buried the dead. No attempt was ever made to revenge them. Commissioner Spain visited Rauparaha, at the request of the leading settlers of Wellington, to assure him that the matter should be left to the arbitrament of the Crown. The Crown, as represented by Mr. Shortland, was, perhaps, at the moment more concerned at the defenceless position of Auckland, in the event of a general rising, than at anything else. Moreover, the philo-Maori officials held that Rauparaha and Rangihaeata were aggrieved persons. A company of fifty-three Grenadiers was sent to Wellington and a man-of-war to Nelson. Strict orders were given to the disgusted settlers not to meet and drill. On the whole, in the helpless state of the Colony, inaction was wisest. At any rate Mr. Shortland's successor was on his way out, and there was reason in waiting for him. Now had come the result of Hobson's error in fixing the seat of government in Auckland, and in keeping the leading officials there. Had Wellington been the seat of government in 1843, the Wairau incident could hardly have occurred.

Not the least of poor Mr. Shortland's troubles were financial. He inherited debts from his predecessor. Indeed, the New Zealand Treasury may be said to have been cradled in deficits. In 1841 Hobson's expenditure had been £81,000 against a revenue of £37,000, most of which was the product of land sales. In 1842 the revenue was £50,000, of which only £11,000 came from land sales; and in 1843 this source of income fell to £1,600. The southern settlers complained, truly enough, that whilst they found much of the money, nearly all of it was spent in Auckland. In 1844—if I may anticipate—Mr. Shortland's successor had the melancholy duty of warning the Colonial Office that to meet an inevitable outlay of £35,000 he could at the best hope for a revenue of £20,000. Mr. Shortland himself, in 1843, tried to replenish the treasury chest by borrowing £15,000 in Sydney. But New Zealand, which has lately borrowed many times that sum at about three per cent. interest, could not then raise the money at fifteen per cent. Mr. Shortland next drew bills on the English treasury, which were dishonoured, though the mother country afterwards relented so far as to lend the sum, adding it to the public debt of the Colony. Finally, the Governor, who on arrival superseded Mr. Shortland, made a beginning by publicly insulting that gentleman. With proper spirit the Secretary at once resigned, and was sent by Downing Street to govern a small island in the West Indies.

If neither Captain Hobson nor Mr. Shortland found official life in New Zealand otherwise than thorny, their career was smooth and prosperous compared to that of the Governor who now appears on the scene. Admiral—then Captain—Robert Fitzroy will have a kind of immortality as the commander of the *Beagle*—Darwin's *Beagle*. His scientific work as a hydrographer at the Admiralty is still spoken of in high terms. He was unquestionably a well-meaning sailor. But his short career in New Zealand is an awful example of the evils which the Colonial Office can inflict on a distant part of the Empire by a bad appointment. It is true that, like his predecessors, Fitzroy was not fairly supported by the authorities at Home. They supplied him with neither men nor money, and on them therefore the chief responsibility of the Colony's troubles rest. But a study of his two years of rule fails to reveal any pitfall in his pathway into which he did not straightway stumble.

Captain Fitzroy was one of those fretful and excitable beings whose manner sets plain men against them, and who, when they are not in error, seem so. Often wrong, occasionally right, he possessed in perfection the unhappy art of doing the right thing in the wrong way. Restless and irascible, passing from self-confidence to gloom, he would find relief for nerve tension in a peevishness which was the last quality one in his difficult position should have shown. An autocratic official amid little rough, dissatisfied communities of hard-headed pioneers was a king with no divinity to hedge him round. Without pomp, almost without privacy, everything he said or did became the property of local gossips. A ruler so placed must have natural dignity, and requires self-command above all things. That was just the quality Captain Fitzroy had not. It was said that the blood of a Stuart king ran in his veins; and, indeed, there seemed to be about the tall, thin, melancholy man something of the bad luck, as well as the hopeless wrong-headedness, of that unteachable House.

For he landed at Auckland in November, 1843, to find an ample legacy of trouble awaiting him. The loyal and patriotic address with which the Aucklanders welcomed him was such as few viceroys have been condemned to receive at the outset of their term of office. It did not mince matters. It described the community as bankrupt, and ascribed its fate to the mistakes and errors of the Government. At New Plymouth a similar address declared that the settlers were menaced with irretrievable ruin. Kororáreka echoed the wail. Nor was the welcome of Wellington one whit more cheerful—a past of bungling, a present of stagnation, a future of danger: such was the picture it drew. It was not much exaggerated. On the coasts of New Zealand some twelve thousand colonists were divided into eight settlements, varying in population from 4,000 at Wellington to 200 at Akaroa. Not one of them was defensible in military eyes. There were no troops, no militia, no money. Neither at Wellington nor Nelson had more than one thousand acres of land been cleared and cultivated. Labourers were riotously clamouring for work or rations. Within fifty miles of Wellington was Rauparaha, who, had he appealed to his race, could probably have mustered a force strong enough to loot and burn the town. Some wondered why he did not; perhaps Hadfield's influence amongst his tribe supplied the answer.

Governor Fitzroy began at his first *levee* at Wellington by scolding the settlers, inveighing against the local newspaper, and grossly insulting Gibbon Wakefield's son when he was presented to him. At Nelson he rated the magistrates after such a fashion that they threw up their commissions. He then went to Rauparaha's *pa* at Waikanae near Kapiti. A dozen whites were with the Governor; five hundred Maoris surrounded the chief. After lecturing the latter for the slaughter of the captives at Wairau, Fitzroy informed him that, as the slain men had been the aggressors, he was to be freely forgiven. Only one utterly ignorant of the Maori character could have fancied that this exaggerated clemency would be put down to anything but weakness. Even some missionaries thought that compensation should have been demanded for the death of the prisoners. As for the settlers, their disgust was deep. Putting together the haste, violence, and want of dignity of his proceedings, they declared the new Governor could not be master of his own actions. That Gibbon Wakefield's brother should have been savagely butchered and not avenged was bad enough; that his fellow-settlers should be rated for their share in the disaster seemed a thing not to be endured. The Maoris grew insolent, the settlers sullen, and for years afterward a kind of petty warfare lingered on in the Wellington district.

Governor Fitzroy was no more successful in Taranaki. There the Company, after claiming the entire territory, had had their claim cut down by the Commissioners' award to 60,000 acres. But even this was now disputed, on the ground that it had been bought from a tribe—the Waikato—who had indeed conquered it, and carried away its owners as slaves, but had never taken possession of the soil by occupation. When Colonel Wakefield bought it, the land was virtually empty, and the few score of natives living at the Sugar-Loaves sold their interest to him readily enough. But when the enslaved Ngatiawa and Taranaki tribesmen were soon afterwards released through the influence of Christianity, they returned to the desolated land, and disputed the claim of the Company. Moreover, there were the Ngatiawas, who, led by Wiremu Kingi, had migrated to Cook's Straits in the days of devastation. They claimed not only their new possessions—much of which they sold to the Company—but their old tribal lands at Waitara, from which they had fled, but to which some of them now straggled back. On this nice point Captain Fitzroy had to adjudicate. He decided that the returned slaves and Ngatiawa fugitives were the true owners of the land. Instead of paying them fairly for the 60,000 acres—which they did not require—he handed the bulk of it back to them, penning the unhappy white settlers up in a miserable strip of 3,200 acres. The result was the temporary ruin of the Taranaki settlement, and the sowing of the seeds of an intense feeling of resentment and injustice which bore evil fruit in later days.

Nor did Captain Fitzroy do any better with finance than in his land transactions. His very insufficient revenue was largely derived from Customs duties. Trade at the Bay of Islands had, by this time, greatly fallen away. Whalers and timber vessels no longer resorted there as in the good old Alsatian days. Both natives and settlers grumbled at the change, which they chose to attribute to the Government Customs duties. To conciliate them, the Governor abolished Customs duties at Kororáreka. Naturally a cry at once went up from other parts of the Colony for a similar concession. The unhappy Governor, endeavouring to please them all, like the donkey-owner in Æsop's Fables, abolished Customs duties everywhere. To replace them he devised an astounding combination of an income-tax and property-tax. Under this, not only would the rich plainly pay less in proportion than the poor, but a Government official drawing £600 a year, but owning no land, would pay just half the sum exacted from a settler who, having invested £1,000 in a farm, was struggling to make £200 a year thereby. The mere prospect of this crudity caused such a feeling in the Colony that he was obliged to levy the Customs duties once more. His next error was the abandonment of the Government monopoly of land purchase from the Maoris. As might be expected, the pressure upon all rulers in New Zealand to do this, and to allow private bargaining with the natives for land, has always been very strong, especially in the Auckland district. Repeated experience has, however, shown that the results are baneful to all concerned—demoralizing to the natives, and by no means always profitable to the white negotiators. When Fitzroy proclaimed that settlers might purchase land from the natives, he imposed a duty of ten shillings an acre upon each sale. Then, when this was bitterly complained of, he reduced the fee to one penny. Finally, he fell back on the desperate expedient of issuing paper money, a thing which he had no right to do. All these mistakes and others he managed to commit within two short years. Fortunately for the Colony, he, in some of them, flatly disregarded his instructions. The issue of paper money was one of the few blunders the full force of which Downing Street could apprehend. Hence his providential recall.

Before this reached him he had drifted into the last and worst of his misfortunes, an unsuccessful war, the direct result of the defeat at the Wairau and the weakness shown thereafter. It was not that he and his missionary advisers did not try hard enough to avert any conflict with the

Maoris. If conciliation pushed to the verge of submission could have kept the peace, it would have been kept. But conciliation, without firmness, will not impress barbarians. The Maoris were far too acute to be impressed by the well-meaning, vacillating Governor. They set to work, instead, to impress him. They invited him to a huge banquet near Auckland, and danced a war-dance before their guest with the deliberate intention of overawing him. Indeed, the spectacle of fifteen hundred warriors, stripped, smeared with red ochre, stamping, swaying, leaping, uttering deep guttural shouts, and brandishing their muskets, while their wild rhythmic songs rose up in perfect time, and their tattooed features worked convulsively, was calculated to affect even stronger nerves than the Governor's.

It was among the discontented tribes in the Bay of Islands, where Alsatia was now deserted by its roaring crews of whalers and cheated of its hoped-for capital, that the outbreak came.

In the winter of 1844, Honé Heké, son-in-law of the great Hongi, presuming on the weakness of the Government, swaggered into Kororáreka, plundered some of the houses, and cut down a flagstaff on the hill over the town on which the English flag was flying. Some White of the beach-comber species is said to have suggested the act to him by assuring him that the flag-staff represented the Queen's sovereignty—the evil influence which had drawn trade and money away to Auckland. Heké had no grievance whatever against the Government or colonists, but he and the younger braves of the Northern tribes had been heard to ask whether Rangihaeata was to do all the *Pakeha*-killing? At the moment Fitzroy had not two hundred soldiers in the country. He hurried up to the scene of disturbance. Luckily Heké's tribe—the Ngapuhi—were divided. Part, under Waka Nené, held with the English. Accepting Nené's advice Fitzroy allowed Heké to pay ten muskets in compensation for the flagstaff, and then foolishly gave back the fine as a present and departed. Nené and the friendly chiefs undertook to keep peace—but failed, for Heké again cut down the flagstaff. This, of course, brought war definitely on. The famous flagstaff was re-erected, guarded by a block-house, and a party of soldiers and sailors were sent to garrison Kororáreka. As H.M.S. *Hazard* lay off the beach in the Bay and guns were mounted in three block-houses, the place was expected to hold out. Heké, however, notified that he would take it— and did so. He marched against it with eight hundred men. One party attacked the flagstaff, another the town. The twenty defenders of the flag-staff were divided by a stratagem by which part were lured out to repel a feigned attack. In their absence the stockade was rushed, and, for the third time, the flagstaff hewn down. During the attack the defenders of the town, however, under Captain Robertson of the *Hazard*, stood their ground and repulsed a first attack. Even when Robertson fell, his thigh-bone shattered by a bullet, Lieutenant Philpotts, taking command, had the women and children sent safely on board the ships, and all was going well when the outnumbered garrison were paralysed by the blowing up of their powder magazine. The townsmen began to escape, and a council of war decided to abandon the place. This was done. Lovell, a gunner, would not leave his piece until he had spiked it, and was killed, but not before doing so. Bishop Selwyn, landing from his mission ship in the Bay, had been doing the work of ten in carrying off women and children and succouring the wounded, aided therein by Henry Williams. To Selwyn, as he toiled begrimed with smoke and sweat, came running a boy, young Nelson Hector, whose father, a lawyer, was in charge of a gun in position on one of the hillsides outside the town. The boy had stolen away unnoticed, and crept through the Maoris to find out for his father how things stood. The bishop offered to take him on board with the women, but the youngster scouted the notion of leaving his father. "God bless you, my boy!" said the big-hearted Selwyn; "I have nothing to say against it"; and the lad, running off, got back safely. Out in the Bay the American corvette *St. Louis* lay at anchor. Her men were keen to be allowed to "bear a hand" in the defence. Though this could not be, her captain sent boats through the fire while it was still hot to bring off the women and children, and gave them shelter on board. Anglo-Saxon brotherhood counted for something even in 1845. The scene became extraordinary. The victorious Maoris, streaming gleefully into the town, began to plunder in the best of good tempers. Some of the townspeople went about saving such of their goods as they could without molestation, indeed, with occasional help from the Maoris, who considered there was enough for all. Presently a house caught fire, the flames spread, and the glowing blaze, the volumes of smoke, and the roar of the burning under the red-lit sky, gave a touch of dignity to the end of wicked old Kororáreka.

Loaded with booty, Heké's men went off inland in high spirits. Three vessels crowded with the ruined Alsatians sailed to Auckland, where for a while the astonished people expected nightly to be roused from their beds by the yells of Ngapuhi warriors. Our loss had been thirty-one killed and wounded, and it was small consolation to know that, thanks to the ship's guns, the Maoris' had been three times as great. The disaster was a greater blow to the English *Mana* than even the Wairau Massacre. But the settlements showed spirit everywhere, and under the stress of the time the Governor forgot some of his prejudices. Even those much-suspected people, the Wellington settlers, were allowed to form themselves into a militia at last.

Thanks to the divisions among the Ngapuhi, Heké did not follow up his victory. Troops were procured from Sydney, but they had no artillery. The natives relied on their *pas* or stockades. These, skilfully constructed by means of double or triple rows of heavy palisades, masked by flax and divided by shallow ditches which did duty for rifle-pits, could not be carried without being breached by cannon. A fruitless attack upon one of them soon demonstrated this. The *pa*, called Okaihau, though strong in front, was weak in the rear. Four hundred soldiers, supported by as many Ngapuhi friendlies under Waka Nené, marched against it. Fruitlessly Nené advised the English Colonel to assail the place from behind. The Colonel, who had seen Nené yelling in a war-dance, and looked upon him as a degraded savage, approached the front, where Okaihau was really strong. As he had no guns he tried the effect of rockets, but though terrified by the strange fire, the defenders gained heart when they found that the rockets hit nothing. They even charged the English in the open with long-handled tomahawks, and only fell back before a bayonet charge in regular form. After skirmishing all day and losing fifty-four in killed and wounded with but negative results, the English retreated to Auckland to request artillery. Waka Nené carried on the fighting on his own account, and in a skirmish with him Heké was badly wounded. Guns were fetched from Australia, and Heké's men were brought to bay at their principal *pa*, Ohaeawai. Colonel Despard commanded the besiegers, who outnumbered the defenders by more than three to one. After bombarding the palisades for some days, the colonel, in defiance of the advice of his artillery officer—who declared there was no practicable breach—ordered an assault. Two hundred soldiers and sailors were told off for the duty, and at four o'clock on a pleasant, sunny afternoon they charged up a gentle, open slope to the simple-looking stockade. Only two or three got inside. In a quarter of an hour half the force were shot down, and the survivors only saved by the bugle-call which Despard ordered to be sounded. Forty, including a captain and two lieutenants, were killed on the spot or died of their wounds. Sixty-two others were wounded. Gallant Lieutenant Philpotts, the first through the stockade, lay dead, sword in hand, inside the *pa*. At the outset of the war he had been captured by the natives whilst scouting, and let go unharmed with advice to take more care in future. Through no fault of his own he had lost Kororáreka. Stung by this, or, as some say, by a taunt of Despard's, he led the way at Ohaeawai with utterly reckless courage, and, to the regret of the brave brown men his enemies, was shot at close quarters by a mere boy. The wounded could not be removed for two days. During the night the triumphant Maoris shouted and danced their war-dance. They tortured—with burning kauri gum—an unfortunate soldier whom they had captured alive, and whose screams could be plainly heard in the English camp. Despard, whose artillery ammunition had run short, remained watching the *pa* for several days. But when he was in a position to renew his bombardment, the natives quietly abandoned the place by night, without loss. According to their notions of warfare, such a withdrawal was not a defeat.

Such are the facts of one of the worst repulses sustained by our arms in New Zealand. It will scarcely be believed that after this humiliation Captain Fitzroy, on missionary advice, endeavoured to make peace—of course, without avail. Heké became a hero in the eyes of his race. The news of Ohaeawai reached England, and the Duke of Wellington's language about Colonel Despard is said to have been pointed. But already the Colonial Office had made up its mind for a change in New Zealand. Fitzroy was recalled, and Captain Grey, the Governor of South Australia, whose sense and determination had lifted that Colony out of the mire, was wisely selected to replace him.

Chapter XII

GOOD GOVERNOR GREY

"No hasty fool of stubborn will,
But prudent, wary, pliant still,
Who, since his work was good,
Would do it as he could."

Captain Grey came in the nick of time. That he managed because he wasted no time about coming. The despatch, removing him from South Australia to New Zealand, reached Adelaide on the 15th of October, 1845, and by the 14th of November he was in Auckland.

He arrived to find Kororáreka in ashes, Auckland anxious, the Company's settlers in the south harassed by the Maoris and embittered against the Government, the missionaries objects of tormenting suspicions, and the natives unbeaten and exultant. The Colonists had no money and no hope. Four hundred Crown grants were lying unissued in the Auckland Land Office because land-buyers could not pay the fee of £1 apiece due on them.

But the Colonial Office, now that it at last gave unfortunate New Zealand a capable head, did not do things by halves. It supplied him with sufficient troops and a certain amount of money. The strong hand at the helm at once made itself felt. Within a month the circulating debentures were withdrawn, the pre-emptive right of the Crown over native lands resumed, the sale of fire-arms to natives prohibited, and negotiations with Heké and his fellow insurgent chief, Kawiti, sternly broken off.

The Governor set to work to end the war. High in air, on the side of a thickly-timbered hill, lay Kawiti's new and strongest *pa*, Rua-peka-peka (the Bat's Nest). Curtained by a double palisade of beams eighteen feet high by two feet thick, strengthened by flanking redoubts, ditches, and traverses, honeycombed with rifle-pits and bomb-proof chambers below ground, "large enough to hold a whist-party," it was a model Maori fortification of the later style.

SIR GEORGE GREY
Photo by RUSSELL, Baker St., W.

Against it the Governor and Despard moved with 1,200 soldiers and sailors, a strong native contingent, and what for those days and that corner of the earth was a strong park of artillery. The first round shot fired carried away the *pa's* flagstaff; but though palisades were splintered and sorties were repulsed, the stubborn garrison showed no sign of yielding, and the Bat's Nest, for all our strength, fell but by an accident. Our artillery fire, continued for several days, was—rather to the surprise of our Maori allies—not stopped on Sunday. The defenders, Christians also, wishing to hold divine service, withdrew to an outwork behind their main fort to be out of reach of the cannon balls. A few soldiers and friendly natives, headed by Waka Nené's brother, struck by the deserted aspect of the place, crept up and got inside before they were discovered. The insurgents, after a plucky effort to retake their own fortress, fled with loss. Our casualties were but forty-three. The blow thus given ended the war. Heké, weakened by his wound, sued for peace. Even tough little Kawiti wrote to the Governor that he was "full." Grey showed a wise leniency. Waka Nené was given a pension of £100 a year, and ostentatiously honoured and consulted. As time went on the Ngapuhi themselves re-erected the historic flagstaff in token of reconciliation. From that day to this there has been no rebellion amongst the tribes north of Auckland. Heké's relation and name-sake, Honé Heké, M.H.R., is now a member of the New Zealand House of Representatives, which he addresses in excellent English, and only in May of this year the good offices' of Mr. Honé Heké were foremost in quelling what threatened to be a troublesome riot among the Ngapuhi on the Hokianga.

The petty warfare against Rangihaeata in the Cook's Straits district took longer to end. It was a series of isolated murders, trifling skirmishes, night surprises, marchings and counter-marchings. Their dreary insignificance was redeemed by the good-tempered pertinacity shown by our troops in enduring month after month of hardship and exposure in the rain-soaked bush and the deep mud of the sloughs, miscalled tracks, along which they had to crawl through the gloomy valleys. And there was one story of heroism. An out-post of the fifty-eighth regiment had been surprised at dawn. The bugler, a lad named Allen, was raising his bugle to sound the alarm, when a blow from a tomahawk half severed his arm. Snatching the bugle with the other hand, he managed to blow a warning note before a second tomahawk stroke stretched him dead. Grey adopted the Fabian plan of driving the insurgents back into the mountain forests and slowly starving them out there. In New Zealand, thanks to the scarcity of wild food plants and animals, even Maoris suffer cruel hardships if cut off long from their plantations.

Rauparaha, now a very old man, was nominally not concerned in these troubles. He lived quietly in a sea-coast village by the Straits, enjoying the reputation earned by nearly fifty years of fighting, massacring and plotting. The Governor, however, satisfied himself that the old chief was secretly instigating the insurgents. By a cleverly managed surprise he captured Rauparaha in his village, whence he was carried kicking and biting on board a man-of-war. The move proved successful. The *mana* of the Maori Ulysses was fatally injured in the eyes of his race by the humiliation. The chief, who had killed Arthur Wakefield and laughed under Fitzroy's nose, had met at length a craftier than himself. Detained at Auckland, or carried about in Grey's train, he was treated with a studied politeness which prevented him from being honoured as a martyr. His influence was at an end.

Peace quickly came. It is true that at the end of the year 1846 there came a small outbreak which caused a tiny hamlet, now the town of Wanganui, to be attacked and plundered. But the natives, who retired into the bush, were quietly brought to submission by having their trade stopped, and in particular their supply of tobacco cut off. Fourteen years of quiet now followed the two years of disturbance. During the fighting from the Wairau conflict onwards, our loss had been one hundred and seven Whites killed and one hundred and seventy-two wounded. To this must be added several "murders" of settlers and the losses of our native allies. Small as the total was, it was larger than the casualties of the insurgents.

For his success Governor Grey was made Sir George, and greatly pleased the natives by choosing Waka Nené and Te Whero Whero, our old Waikato acquaintance, to act as esquires at his investiture. But it was in the use he made of the restored tranquillity that he showed his true capacity. He employed the natives as labourers in making roads, useful both for war and peace. They found wages better than warfare. As navvies, they were paid half a crown a day, and were reported to do more work as spade-men than an equal number of soldiers would. At no time did the Maoris seem to make such material progress as during the twelve peaceful years beginning with 1848.

With his brown subjects, Grey, after once beating them, trod the paths of pleasantness and peace. The chiefs recognised his imperturbable courage and self-control, and were charmed by his unfailing courtesy and winning manners. He found time to learn their language. The study of their character, their myths, customs, and art was not only to him a labour of love, but bore practical fruit in the knowledge it gave him of the race. So good were the volumes in which he put together and published the fruits of his Maori studies, that for nearly half a century students of Maori literature have been glad to follow in the way pointed out by this busy administrator. Few men have ever understood the Natives better. He could humour their childishness and respect their intelligence. When a powerful chief refused to allow one of the Governor's roads to be pushed through his tribe's land, Grey said nothing, but sent the chief's sister a present of a wheeled carriage. Before long the road was permitted. But on the all-important question of the validity of the land clause in the treaty of Waitangi, the Governor always gave the Maoris the fullest assurance. Striving always to keep liquor and fire-arms from them, he encouraged them to farm, helped to found schools for them, and interested himself in the all-important question of their physical health, on which he consulted and corresponded with Florence Nightingale.

After a good deal of tedious litigation Grey was able to settle nearly all the outstanding land claims. By a misuse of one of Fitzroy's freakish ordinances land-grabbers had got hold of much of the land near Auckland. Grey was able to make many of them disgorge. His influence with the Maoris enabled him to buy considerable tracts of land. By him the Colonial Office was persuaded to have a reasonable force retained for the protection of the Colony. He put an end to the office of "Protector of the Aborigines," the source of much well-meant but unpractical advice. When Earl Grey sent out in 1846 a constitution prematurely conferring upon the Colonists the right of governing themselves—and also of governing the Maoris—Sir

George had the moral courage and good sense to stand in the way of its adoption. For this, and for refusing to allow private purchase of native land, he was bitterly attacked; but he stood his ground, to the advantage of both races. Especially in the settlements of the New Zealand Company was the agitation for free institutions carried on with vigour and ability.

It is scarcely needful now to scan in detail the various compromises and expedients by which Grey vainly endeavoured to satisfy the Colonists, first with nominated councils, then with local self-governing powers; or how, finally, he completely changed front, went further than Lord Grey, and drafted and sent home a constitution which, for that day, seemed the quintessence of Radicalism.

Meanwhile he remained an autocrat. Even an autocrat has his advisers, and in some of them he was fortunate. Mr. William Swainson, his Attorney-General, was an English lawyer of striking abilities of more than one kind. Fortunately one of these lay in drafting statutes. On him devolved the drawing-up of the laws of the infant Colony. In doing so he ventured to be much simpler in language and much less of a slave to technical subtleties than was usual in his day. By an ordinance dealing with conveyancing he swept away a host of cumbrous English precedents relating to that great branch of law. Other excellent enactments dealt with legal procedure and marriage. Mr. Swainson's ordinances were not only good in themselves, but set an example in New Zealand which later law reformers were only too glad to follow and improve upon. Another official of ability and high character was Sir William Martin, Chief Justice, long known, not only as a refined gentleman and upright judge, but as an enthusiastic and unswerving champion of what he believed to be the rights of the Maori race. But a more commanding figure than either Martin or Swainson was George Augustus Selwyn, the first Bishop of the Colony. No better selection could have been made than that by which England sent this muscular Christian to organize and administer a Church of mingled savages and pioneers. Bishop Selwyn was both physically and mentally a ruler of men. When young, his tall, lithe frame, and long, clean-cut aquiline features were those of the finest type of English gentleman. When old, the lines on his face marked honourably the unresting toil of the intellectual athlete. Hard sometimes to others, he was always hardest to himself. When in the wilderness, he could outride or outwalk his guides, and could press on when hunger made his companions flag wearily. He would stride through rivers in his Bishop's dress, and laugh at such trifles as wet clothes, and would trudge through the bush with his blankets rolled up on his back like any swag-man. When at sea in his missionary schooner, he could haul on the ropes or take the helm—and did so.[1] If his demeanour and actions savoured at times somewhat of the dramatic, and if he had more of iron than honey in his manner, it must be remembered that his duty lay in wild places and amongst rough men, where strength of will and force of character were more needed than gentler virtues. For more than a generation he laboured strenuously amongst Maoris and Europeans, loved by many and respected by all. He organized the Episcopal Church in New Zealand upon a basis which showed a rare insight into the democratic character of the community with which he had to deal. The basis of his system is found in the representative synods of clergy and laity which assemble annually in each New Zealand diocese. The first draft of this Church constitution came indeed from the brain and hand of Sir George Grey, but for the rest the credit of it belongs to Selwyn.

[Footnote 1: The lines with which Mr. Punch in December, 1867, saluted "Selwyn the pious and plucky," then just translated to Lichfield, had truth in them as well as fun:—

> "Where lawn sleeves and silk apron had turned
> with a shiver,
>   From the current that roared 'twixt his
> business and him,
> If no boat could be come at he breasted the
> river,
>   And woe to his chaplain who craned at a
> swim!
>
> "What to him were short commons, wet jacket,
> hard-lying
>   The savage's blood-feud, the elements' strife,
> Whose guard was the Cross, at his peak
> proudly flying,
>   Whose fare was the bread and the water of
> life?"]

Among the many interesting figures on the stage of the New Zealand of the first generation three seem to me to rise head and shoulders above the crowd—Gibbon Wakefield, Grey, and Selwyn, the founder, the ruler, the pastor. Nor must it be supposed, because these towered above their fellow-actors, that the latter were puny men. Plenty of ability found its way to the Colony, and under the stress of its early troubles wits were sharpened and faculties brightened. There is nothing like the colonial grindstone for putting an edge on good steel. Grey, Selwyn, and Wakefield, as unlike morally as they were in manner, had this in common, that they were leaders of men, and that they had men to lead. That for thirty years the representatives of the English Government, from Busby to Browne, were, with the exception of Grey, commonplace persons or worse, must not blind us to the interest of the drama or to the capacity of many of the men whom these commonplace persons were sent to guide.

Of the trio referred to, Grey is the greatest figure, and most attractive and complex study. Of such a man destiny might have made a great visionary, a capable general, an eloquent tribune, or a graceful writer. He had in him the stuff for any of these. But the south wing of the British Empire had to be built, and the gods made Grey a social architect in the guise of a pro-consul. Among the colonies of the southern hemisphere he is already a figure of history, and amongst them no man has played so many parts in so many theatres with so much success. Not merely was he the saviour and organizer of New Zealand, South Australia, and South Africa; not merely was he an explorer of the deserts of New Holland, and a successful campaigner in New Zealand bush-warfare, but he found time, by way of recreation, to be an ethnologist, a literary pioneer, and an ardent book-collector who twice was generous enough to found libraries with the books which had been the solace and happiness of his working life. A mere episode of this life was the fanning of the spark of Imperialism into flame in England thirty years ago. There are those who will think the eloquence with which he led the New Zealand democracy, the results he indirectly obtained for it, and the stand which at the extreme end of his career he made with success for a popular basis for the inevitable Australian Federation, among the least of his feats. To the writer they do not seem so. Before a life so strenuous, so dramatic, and so fruitful, criticism—at least colonial criticism—is inclined respectfully to lay down its pen. But when we come to the man himself, to the mistakes he made, and the misunderstandings he caused, and to the endeavour to give some sort of sketch of what he *was*, the task is neither easy nor always pleasant. I have known those who thought Grey a nobler Gracchus and a more practical Gordon; and I have known those who thought him a mean copy of Dryden's Achitophel. His island-retreat, where Froude described him as a kind of evangelical Cincinnatus, seemed to others merely the convenient lurking-place of a political rogue-elephant. The viceroy whose hated household the Adelaide tradesmen would not deal with in 1844, and the statesman whose visit to Adelaide in 1891 was a triumphal progress, the public servant whom the Duke of Buckingham insulted in 1868, and the empire-builder whom the Queen delighted to honour in 1894, were one and the same man. So were the Governor against whom New Zealanders inveighed as an arch-despot in 1848, and the popular leader denounced as arch-demagogue by some of the same New Zealanders thirty years afterwards. In a long life of bustle and change his strong but mixed character changed and moulded circumstances, and circumstances also changed and moulded him. The ignorant injustice of some of his Downing Street masters might well have warped his disposition even more than it did. The many honest and acute men who did not keep step with Grey, who were disappointed in him, or repelled by and embittered against him, were not always wrong. Some of his eulogists have been silly. But the student of his peculiar nature must be an odd analyst who does not in the end conclude that Grey was on the whole more akin to the Christian hero painted by Froude and Olive Schreiner than to the malevolent political chess-player of innumerable colonial leader-writers.

Grey had the knightly virtues—courage, courtesy, and self-command. His early possession of official power in remote, difficult, thinly-peopled outposts gave him self-reliance as well as dignity. Naturally fond of devious ways and unexpected moves, he learned to keep his own counsel and to mask his intentions; he never even seemed frank. Though wilful and quarrelsome, he kept guard over his tongue, but, pen in hand, became an evasive, obstinate controversialist with a coldly-used power of exasperation. He learned to work apart, and practised it so long that he became unable to co-operate, on equal terms, with any fellow-labourer. He would lead, or would go alone. Moreover, so far as persons went, his antipathies were stronger than his affections, and led him to play with principles and allies. Those who considered themselves his natural friends were never astonished to find him operating against their flank to the delight of the common enemy. Fastidiously indifferent to money, he was greedy of credit; could be generous to inferiors, but not to rivals; could be grateful to God, but hardly to man.

When he landed in New Zealand, he was a pleasant-looking, blue-eyed, energetic young officer, with a square jaw, a firm but mobile mouth, and a queer trick of half closing one eye when he looked at you. For all his activity he suffered from a spear-wound received from an Australian blackfellow. He was married to a young and handsome wife; and, though this was not his first Governorship, was but thirty-three. The colonists around him were quite shrewd enough to see that this was no ordinary official, and that beneath the silken surcoat of courtesy and the plate-armour of self-confidence lay concealed a curious and interesting man. The less narrow of them detected that something more was here than a strong administrator, and that they had among them an original man of action, with something of the aloofness and mystery that belong to

"a mind for ever
Voyaging through strange seas of thought alone."

None imagined that his connection with the Islands would not terminate for half a century, and that the good and evil of his work therein would be such as must be directly felt—to use his own pet phrase—by unborn millions in distant days.

Chapter XIII

THE PASTORAL PROVINCES

"Whose even thread the Fates spin round and full
Out of their choicest and their whitest wool."

The Company's settlements were no longer confined to the shores of
Cook's Straits. In 1846, Earl Grey, formerly Lord Howick, came to the
Colonial Office, and set himself to compensate the Company for former
official hostility. He secured for it a loan of £250,000, and handed over to it
large blocks of land in the South Island, which—less certain reserves—was
in process of complete purchase from its handful of Maori owners. The
Company, gaining thus a new lease of life, went to work. In 1848 and 1850
that was done which ought to have been done a decade sooner, and the
void spaces of Otago and Canterbury were made the sites of settlements of
a quasi-religious kind. The Otago settlement was the outcome of the
Scottish Disruption; its pioneers landed in March, 1848. They were a band
of Free Kirk Presbyterians, appropriately headed by a Captain Cargill, a
Peninsular veteran and a descendant of Donald Cargill, and by the Rev.
Thomas Burns, a minister of sterling worth, who was a nephew of the poet.
Otago has this year celebrated her jubilee, and the mayor of her chief city,
Captain Cargill's son, is the first citizen of a town of nearly 50,000
inhabitants which in energy and beauty is worthy of its name—Dunedin.
For years, however, the progress of the young settlement was slow.
Purchasers of its land at the "sufficient price"—£2 an acre—were
provokingly few, so few indeed that the regulation price had to be reduced.
It had no Maori troubles worth speaking of, but the hills that beset its site,
rugged and bush-covered, were troublesome to clear and settle, the winter
climate is bleaker than that of northern or central New Zealand, and a good
deal of Scottish endurance and toughness was needed before the colonists
won their way through to the more fertile and open territory which lay
waiting for them, both on their right hand and on their left, in the broad
province of Otago. Like General Grant in his last campaign, they had to
keep on "pegging away," and they did. They stood stoutly by their kirk, and
gave it a valuable endowment of land. Their leaders felt keenly the difficulty
of getting good school teaching for the children, a defect so well repaired
later on that the primary schools of Otago are now, perhaps, the best in
New Zealand, while Dunedin was the seat of the Colony's first university
college. They had a gaol, the prisoners of which in early days were
sometimes let out for a half-holiday, with the warning from the gaoler,

Johnnie Barr, that if they did not come back by eight o'clock they would be locked out for the night.[1] The usual dress of the settlers was a blue shirt, moleskin or corduroy trousers, and a slouch hat. Their leader, Captain Cargill, wore always a blue "bonnet" with a crimson knob thereon. They named their harbour Port Chalmers, and a stream, hard by their city, the Water of Leith. The plodding, brave, clannish, and cantankerous little community soon ceased to be altogether Scotch. Indeed, the pioneers, called the Old Identities, seemed almost swamped by the flood of gold-seekers which poured in in the years after 1861. Nevertheless, Otago is still the headquarters of that large and very active element in the population of the Colony which makes the features and accent of North Britain more familiar to New Zealanders than to most Englishmen.

[Footnote 1: An amusing article might be written on the more primitive gaols of the early settlements. At Wanganui there were no means of confining certain drunken bush-sawyers whose vagaries were a nuisance; so they were fined in timber—so many feet for each orgie—and building material for a prison thus obtained. When it was put up, however, the sawyers had departed, and the empty house of detention became of use as a storehouse for the gaoler's potatoes.

In a violent gale in the Southern Alps one of these wooden "lock-ups" was lifted in air, carried bodily away and deposited in a neighbouring thicket. Its solitary prisoner disappeared in the whirlwind. Believers in his innocence imagined for him a celestial ascent somewhat like that of Elijah. What is certain is that he was never seen again in that locality.

A more comfortable gaol was that made for himself by a high and very ingenious provincial official. Arrested for debt, he proclaimed his own house a district prison, and as visiting Justice committed himself to be detained therein.]

The next little colony founded in New Zealand dates its birth from 1850. Though it was to be Otago's next-door neighbour, it was neither Presbyterian nor Scottish, but English and Episcopalian. This was the Canterbury settlement. It owed its existence to an association in which the late Lord Lyttelton was prominent. As in the case of Otago, this association worked in conjunction with the New Zealand Company, and proposed to administer its lands on the Wakefield system. Gibbon Wakefield himself (his brother, the Colonel, had died in 1847) laboured untiringly at its foundation, amid troubles which were all the more annoying in that the association was in financial difficulties from its birth.[1] Three pounds an acre was to be the price of land in the Canterbury Block, of which one pound was to go to the church and education, two pounds to be spent on the work of development. The settlers landed in December, 1850, from four vessels, the immigrants in which have ever since had in their new home the exclusive right to the name of Pilgrims. The dream of the founders of Canterbury was to transport to the Antipodes a complete section of English society, or, more exactly, of the English Church. It was to be a slice of England from top to bottom. At the top were to be an Earl and a Bishop; at the bottom the English labourer, better clothed, better fed, and contented. Their square, flat city they called Christchurch, and its rectangular streets by the names of the Anglican Bishoprics. One schismatic of a street called High was alone allowed to cut diagonally across the lines of its clerical neighbours. But the clear stream of the place, which then ran past flax, koromiko, and glittering toé-toé, and now winds under weeping-willows, the founders spared from any sacerdotal name; it is called Avon. When wooden cottages and "shedifices" began to dot the bare urban sections far apart, the Pilgrims called their town the City of Magnificent Distances, and cheerfully told you how new-comers from London rode through and out of Christchurch and thereafter innocently inquired whether the town still lay much ahead. The Canterbury dream seems a little pathetic as well as amusing now, but those who dreamed it were very much in earnest in 1850, and they laid the foundation stones of a fine settlement, though not precisely of the kind they contemplated. Their affairs for some years were managed by John Robert Godley, a name still well remembered at the War Office, where he afterwards became Under-Secretary. He had been the life and soul of the Canterbury Association, and as its agent went out to New Zealand, partly in search of health and partly with the honourable ambition to found a colony worthy of England. He made a strong administrator. Their Earl and their Bishop soon fled from the hard facts of pioneer life, but the Pilgrims as a rule were made of sterner stuff, and sticking to their task, they soon spread over the yellow, sunny plains, high-terraced mountain valleys, and wind-swept hillsides of their province. Their territory was better suited than Otago for the first stages of settlement, and for thirty years its progress was remarkable.

[Footnote 1: It was when he was at this work that Dr. Garnett pictures him so vividly—"the sanguine, enthusiastic projector, fertile, inventive creator, his head an arsenal of expedients and every failure pregnant with a remedy, imperious or suasive as suits his turn; terrible in wrath or exuberant in affection; commanding, exhorting, entreating, as like an eminent personage of old he

"With head, hands, wings or feet pursues his way,

And swims, or wades, or sinks, or creeps, or
flies."]

On the surface there were certain differences between the Canterbury
colonists and those of Otago, which local feeling intensified in a manner
always paltry, though sometimes amusing. When the stiff-backed Free-
Churchmen who were to colonize Otago gathered on board the emigrant
ship which was to take them across the seas, they opened their psalm-
books. Their minister, like Burns' cottar, "waled a portion wi' judicious
care," and the Puritans, slowly chanting on, rolled out the appeal to the
God of Bethel:—

"God of our fathers, be the God
of their succeeding race!"

Such men and women might not be amusing fellow-passengers on a four
months' sea-voyage,—and, indeed, there is reason to believe that they were
not,—but settlers made of such stuff were not likely to fail in the hard fight
with Nature at the far end of the earth; and they did not fail. The
Canterbury Pilgrims, on the other hand, bade farewell to old England by
dancing at a ball. In their new home they did not renounce their love of
dancing, though their ladies had sometimes to be driven in a bullock-dray to
the door of the ballroom, and stories are told of young gentlemen,
enthusiastic waltzers, riding on horseback to the happy scene clad in
evening dress and with coat-tails carefully pinned up. But the Canterbury
folk did not, on the whole, make worse settlers for not taking themselves
quite so seriously as some of their neighbours. The English gentleman has a
fund of cheery adaptiveness which often carries him through Colonial life
abreast of graver competitors. So the settler who built a loaf of station-
bread into the earthen wall of his house, alleging that it was the hardest and
most durable material he could procure, did not, we may believe, find a
sense of humour encumber him in the troubles of a settler's life. For there
were troubles. The pastoral provinces were no Dresden-china Arcadia.
Nature is very stubborn in the wilderness, even in the happier climes, where
she offers, for the most part, merely a passive resistance. An occasional
storm or flood was about her only outburst of active opposition in South-
eastern New Zealand. Nevertheless, an educated European who finds
himself standing in an interminable plain or on a windy hillside where
nothing has been done, where he is about to begin that work of reclaiming
the desert which has been going on in Europe for thousands of years, and
of which the average civilized man is the calm, self-satisfied, unconscious
inheritor, finds that he must shift his point of view! The nineteenth-century
Briton face to face with the conditions of primitive man is a spectacle fine
in the general, but often ludicrous or piteous in the particular. The

loneliness, the coarseness, the everlasting insistence of the pettiest and most troublesome wants and difficulties, harden and brace many minds, but narrow most and torment some. Wild game, song-birds, fish, forest trees, were but some of the things of which there were few or none round nearly all the young pastoral settlements. Everything was to make. The climate might be healthy and the mountain outlines noble. But nothing but work, and successful work, could reconcile an educated and imaginative man to the monotony of a daily outlook over league after league of stony soil, thinly clothed by pallid, wiry tussocks bending under an eternal, uncompromising wind; where the only living creatures in sight might often be small lizards or a twittering grey bird miscalled a lark; or where the only sound, save the wind aforesaid, might be the ring of his horse's shoe against a stone, or the bleat of a dull-coated merino, scarcely distinguishable from the dull plain round it. To cure an unfit new-comer, dangerously enamoured of the romance of colonization, few experiences could surpass a week of sheep-driving, where life became a prolonged crawl at the heels of a slow, dusty, greasy-smelling "mob" straggling along at a maximum pace of two miles an hour. If patience and a good collie helped the tyro through that ordeal, such allies were quite too feeble to be of service in the supreme trial of bullock-driving, where a long whip and a vocabulary copious beyond the dreams of Englishmen were the only effective helpers known to man in the management of the clumsy dray and the eight heavy-yoked, lumbering beasts dragging it. Wonderful tales are told of cultivated men in the wilderness, Oxonians disguised as station-cooks, who quoted Virgil over their dish-washing or asked your opinion on a tough passage of Thucydides whilst baking a batch of bread. Most working settlers, as a matter of fact, did well enough if they kept up a running acquaintance with English literature; and station-cooks, as a race, were ever greater at grog than at Greek.

Prior to about 1857 there was little or no intercourse between the various settlements. Steamers and telegraphs had not yet appeared. The answer to a letter sent from Cook's Straits to Auckland might come in seven weeks or might not. It would come in seventy hours now. Despatches were sometimes sent from Wellington to Auckland *viâ* Sydney, to save time. In 1850 Sir William Fox and Mr. Justice Chapman took six days to sail across Cook's Straits from Nelson to Wellington, a voyage which now occupies eight hours. They were passengers in the Government brig, a by-word for unseaworthiness and discomfort. In this vessel the South Island members of the first New Zealand parliament spent nearly nine weeks in beating up the coast to the scene of their labours in Auckland. But the delight with which the coming of steamships in the fifties was hailed was not so much a rejoicing over more regular coastal communication, as joy because the English Mail would come sooner and oftener. How they did wait and watch for the letters and newspapers from Home, those exiles of the early days! Lucky did they count themselves if they had news ten times a year, and not more than four months old. One of the best of their stories is of a certain lover whose gallant grace was not unworthy a courtier of Queen Elizabeth. One evening this swain, after securing at the post-office his treasured mail budget, was escorting his lady-love home through the muddy, ill-lighted streets of little Christchurch. A light of some sort was needed at an especially miry crossing. The devoted squire did not spread out his cloak, as did Sir Walter Raleigh. He had no cloak to spread. But he deftly made a torch of his unread English letters, and, bending down, lighted the way across the mud. His sacrifice, it is believed, did not go wholly unrewarded.

THE CURVING COAST
Photo by HENRY WRIGHT

One first-rate boon New Zealand colonists had—good health. Out of four thousand people in Canterbury in 1854 but twenty-one were returned as sick or infirm. It almost seemed that but for drink and drowning there need be no deaths. In Taranaki, in the North Island, among three thousand people in 1858-59 there was not a funeral for sixteen months. Crime, too, was pleasantly rare in the settlements. When Governor Grey, in 1850, appointed Mr. Justice Stephen to administer law in Otago, that zealous judge had nothing to do for eighteen months, except to fine defaulting jurors who had been summoned to try cases which did not exist and who neglected to attend to try them. Naturally the settlers complained that he did not earn his £800 a year of salary. His office was abolished, and for seven years the southern colonists did very well without a judge. Great was the shock to the public mind when in March, 1855, a certain Mackenzie, a riever by inheritance doubtless, "lifted" a thousand sheep in a night from the run of a Mr. Rhodes near Timaru, in South Canterbury, and disappeared with them among the Southern Alps. When he was followed and captured, it was found that he had taken refuge in a bleak but useful upland plain, a discovery of his which bears his name to this day. He was set on horseback, with his hands tied, and driven to Christchurch, 150 miles, by captors armed with loaded pistols. That he was a fellow who needed such precautions was shown by three bold dashes for freedom, which he afterwards made when serving a five years' sentence. At the third of these attempts he was shot at and badly wounded. Ultimately, he was allowed to leave the country.

A sheep-stealer might easily have fallen into temptation in Canterbury at that time. In three years the settlers owned 100,000 sheep; in four more half a million. Somewhat slower, the Otago progress was to 223,000 in ten years.

Neither in Canterbury nor Otago were the plough and the spade found to be the instruments of speediest advance. They were soon eclipsed by the stockwhip, the shears, the sheep-dog, and the wire-fence. Long before the foundation of New Zealand, Macarthur had taught the Australians to acclimatize the merino sheep. Squatters and shepherds from New South Wales and Tasmania were quick to discover that the South Island of New Zealand was a well-nigh ideal land for pastoral enterprise, with a climate where the fleece of a well-bred merino sheep would yield 4 lbs. of wool as against 21/2 lbs. in New South Wales. Coming to Canterbury, Otago, and Nelson, they taught the new settlers to look to wool and meat, rather than to oats and wheat, for profit and progress. The Australian *coo-ee*, the Australian buck-jumping horse, the Australian stockwhip and wide-awake hat came into New Zealand pastoral life, together with much cunning in dodging land-laws, and a sovereign contempt for small areas. In a few years the whole of the east and centre of the island, except a few insignificant cultivated patches, was leased in great "runs" of from 10,000 to 100,000 acres to grazing tenants. The Australian term "squatter" was applied to and accepted good-humouredly by these. Socially and politically, however, they were the magnates of the colony; sometimes financially also, but not always. For the price of sheep and wool could go down by leaps and bounds, as well as up; the progeny of the ewes bought for 30s. each in 1862 might have to go at 5s. each in 1868, and greasy wool might fluctuate in value as much as 6d. a lb. Two or three bad years would deliver over the poor squatter as bond-slave to some bank, mortgage company or merchant, to whom he had been paying at least 10 per cent. interest, *plus* 21/2 per cent. commission exacted twice a year, on advances. In the end, maybe, his mortgagee stepped in; he and his children saw their homestead, with its garden and clumps of planted eucalypts, willows, and poplars—an oasis in the grassy wilderness—no more. Sometimes a new squatter reigned in his stead, sometimes for years the mortgagee left the place in charge of a shepherd—a new and dreary form of absentee ownership. Meanwhile, in the earlier years the squatters were merry monarchs, reigning as supreme in the Provincial Councils as in the jockey clubs. They made very wise and excessively severe laws to safeguard their stock from infection, and other laws, by no means so wise, to safeguard their runs from selection, laws which undoubtedly hampered agricultural progress. The peasant cultivator, or "cockatoo" (another Australian word), followed slowly in the sheep farmer's wake. As late as 1857 there were not fifty thousand acres of land under tillage in the South Island. Even wheat at 10s. a bushel did not tempt much capital into agriculture, though such were the prices of cereals that in 1855 growers talked dismally of the low price of oats—4s. 6d. a bushel. Labour, too, preferred in many cases, and not unnaturally, to earn from 15s. to £1 a day at shearing or harvest-time to entering on the early struggles of the cockatoo. Nevertheless, many workers did save their money and go on the land, and many more would have done so but for that curse of the pioneer working-man—drink.

The Colony's chief export now came to be wool. The wool-growers looked upon their industry as the backbone of the country. So, at any rate, for many years it was. But then the system of huge pastoral leases meant the exclusion of population from the soil. A dozen shepherds and labourers were enough for the largest run during most of the year. Only when the sheep had to be mustered and dipped or shorn were a band of wandering workmen called in. The work done, they tramped off to undertake the next station, or to drink their wages at the nearest public-house.

The endowed churches, the great pastoral leases, high-priced land (in Canterbury), and the absence of Maori troubles, were the peculiar features of the southern settlements of New Zealand. These new communities, while adding greatly to the strength and value of the Colony as a whole, brought their own special difficulties to its rulers. With rare exceptions the settlers came from England and Scotland, not from Australia, and were therefore quite unused to despotic government. Having no Maori tribes in overwhelming force at their doors, they saw no reason why they should not at once be trusted with self-government. They therefore threw themselves heartily into the agitation for a free constitution, which by this time was in full swing in Wellington amongst the old settlers of the New Zealand Company. Moreover, in this, for the first time in the history of the Colony, the settlers were in accord with the Colonial Office. As early as 1846, Earl Grey had sent out the draft of a constitution the details of which need not detain us, inasmuch as it never came to the birth. Sir George Grey refused to proclaim it, and succeeded in postponing the coming-in of free institutions for six years For many reasons he was probably right, if only because the Maoris still much outnumbered the Whites; yet under Earl Grey's proposed constitution they would have been entirely governed by the white minority. Warlike and intelligent, and with a full share of self-esteem, they were not a race likely to put up with such an indignity. But Governor Grey's action, though justifiable, brought him into collision with the southern settlers. Godley, with questionable discretion, flung himself into the constitutional controversy.

Grey was successful in inducing the Maoris to sell a fair amount of their surplus land. During the last years of his rule and the four or five years after he went, some millions of acres were bought in the North Island. This, following on the purchase of the whole of the South Island, had opened the way for real progress. The huge estate thus gained by the Crown brought to the front new phases of the eternal land problem. The question had to be faced as to what were to be the terms under which this land was to be sold and leased to the settlers. Up to 1852 the settlers everywhere, except in Auckland, had to deal, not with the Crown, but with the New Zealand Company. But in 1852 the Company was wound up, and its species of overlordship finally extinguished. By an English Act of Parliament its debt to the Imperial Government was forgiven. The Colony was ordered to pay it £263,000 in satisfaction of its land lien. This was commuted in the end for £200,000 cash, very grudgingly paid out of the first loan raised by a New Zealand parliament. Thereafter, the Company, with its high aims, its blunders, its grievances, and its achievements, vanishes from the story of New Zealand.

In the Church settlements of the South the Wakefield system came into full operation under favourable conditions. Three pounds an acre were at the outset charged for land. One pound went to the churches and their schools. This system of endowment Grey set himself to stop, when the Company's fall gave him the opportunity, and he did so at the cost of embittering his relations with the Southerners, which already were none too pleasant. For the rest, Canterbury continued within its original special area to sell land at £2 an acre. When Canterbury was made a province this area was enlarged by the inclusion of a tract in which land had been sold cheaply, and in which certain large estates had consequently been formed. Otherwise land has never been cheap in Canterbury. The Wakefield system has been adhered to there, has been tried under favourable conditions, and on the whole, at any rate up to the year 1871, could not be called a failure. As long as the value of land to speculators was little or nothing above the "sufficient price," things did not go so badly. The process of free selection at a uniform price of £2 an acre had amongst other merits the great advantage of entire simplicity. A great deal of good settlement went on under it, and ample funds were provided for the construction of roads, bridges, and other public works.

Meantime, Grey was called upon to devise some general system of land laws for the rest of the Colony. The result was the famous land regulations of 1853, a code destined to have lasting and mischievous effects upon the future of the country. Its main feature was the reduction of the price of land to ten shillings an acre. Had this been accompanied by stringent limitations as to the amount to be purchased by any one man, the result might have been good enough. But it was not; nor did those who ruled after Grey think fit to impose any such check until immense areas of the country had been bought by pastoral tenants and thus permanently locked up against close settlement. Grey's friends vehemently maintain that it was not he, but those who afterwards administered his regulations, who were responsible for this evil. They point out that it was not until after his departure that the great purchases began. Possibly enough Sir George never dreamt that his regulations would bring about the bad results they did. More than that one can hardly say. In drawing them up his strong antipathy to the New Zealand Company and its system of a high price for land doubtless obscured his judgment. His own defence on the point, as printed in his life by Rees, is virtually no defence at all. It is likely enough that had he retained the control of affairs after 1853 he would have imposed safeguards. He is not the only statesman whose laws have effects not calculated by their maker.

Chapter XIV

LEARNING TO WALK

"Some therefore cried one thing and some
another; for the Assembly was confused; and
the more part knew not wherefore they were
come together."

The Constitution under which the colonists were granted the management of their own affairs was partly based on Grey's suggestions, though it was drafted in England by Mr. Adderley under Gibbon Wakefield's supervision. Its quality may be judged from its duration. It worked almost without alteration for twenty-two years, and in the main well. Thereafter it was much cut about and altered. Briefly described, it provided the Colony with a dual system of self-government under a Viceroy appointed by the Colonial Office, who was to be Commander-in-Chief of the Queen's forces in the Colony, and might reserve Bills for the consideration of Her Majesty—in effect for that of the Home Government. Under this proviso laws restricting immigration from other parts of the Empire or affecting mercantile marine have, it may be mentioned, been sometimes reserved and vetoed. Foreign affairs and currency were virtually excluded from the scope of the Colonial Government. The Viceroy might use his judgment in granting or withholding dissolutions of Parliament. Side by side with the central Parliament were to exist a number of provincial assemblies. The central Parliament was to have two Chambers, the Provincial Councils one. Over the Parliament was to be the Viceroy ruling through Ministers; over each Provincial Council, a superintendent elected, like the Councils, by the people of his province. Each superintendent was to have a small executive of officials, who were themselves to be councillors—a sort of small Cabinet. The central Parliament, called the General Assembly, was to have an Upper House called the Legislative Council, whose members were, Grey suggested, to be elected by the Provincial Councils. But in England, Sir John Pakington demurred to this, and decided that they should be nominated for life by the Crown. Their number was not fixed by law. Had Grey's proposal been carried out, New Zealand would have had a powerful Senate eclipsing altogether the Lower Chamber. The thirty-seven members of the Lower House were, of course, to be elected—on a franchise liberal though not universal. To be eligible, a member must be qualified to have his name on an electoral roll, and not have been convicted of any infamous offence, and would lose his seat by bankruptcy. Until 1880 the ordinary duration of Parliament was five years. The Provinces numbered six: Auckland, Taranaki, Nelson, Wellington, Canterbury, and Otago. Maoris had no special representation. They might register as landowners, and vote with the white electors, but as a matter of fact not many did so, and after a foolish and unfair delay of fifteen years they were given four members solely chosen by Maoris, and who must themselves be Maoris or half-castes. Two of their chiefs were at the same time called to the Legislative Council.

In 1853, the year of the land regulations, the Governor was entrusted with the task of proclaiming the constitution. He took the rather curious course of bringing the Provincial Councils into existence, and leaving the summoning of the central Parliament to his successor. He left the Colony in December of the same year, praised and regretted by the Maoris, regarded by the settlers with mixed feelings. Nevertheless, it would not be easy now to find any one who would refuse a very high meed of praise to Governor Grey's first administration. It was not merely that he found the Colony on the brink of ruin, and left it in a state of prosperity and progress. Able subalterns, a rise in prices, the development of some new industry, might have brought about the improvement. Such causes have often made reputation for colonial rulers and statesmen. But in Grey's case no impartial student can fail to see that to a considerable extent the change for the better was due to him. Moreover, he not only grappled with the difficulties of his time, but with both foresight and power of imagination built for the future, and—with one marked exception—laid foundations deep and well.

If the Colonial Office did not see its way to retain Grey in the Colony until his constitution had been put into full working order, it should, at least, have seen that he was replaced by a capable official. This was not done. His successor did not arrive for two years, and meanwhile the Vice-regal office devolved upon Colonel Wynyard, a good-natured soldier, unfitted for the position. The first Parliament of New Zealand was summoned, and met at Auckland on the Queen's birthday in 1854. Many, perhaps most, of its members were well-educated men of character and capacity. The presence of Gibbon Wakefield, now himself become a colonist, added to the interest of the scene. At last, those who had been agitating so long for self-government had the boon apparently within their grasp. In their eyes it was a great occasion—the true commencement of national life in the Colony. The irony of fate, or the perversity of man, turned it into a curious anticlimax. The Parliament, indeed, duly assembled. But it dispersed after weeks of ineffectual wrangling and intrigue, amid scenes which were discreditable and are still ridiculous. Those who had drawn up the constitution had forgotten that Government, through responsible Ministers forming a Cabinet and possessing the confidence of the elective Chamber, must be a necessary part of their system. Not only was no provision made for it in the written constitution, but the Colonial Office had sent the Governor no instructions on the subject. The Viceroy was surrounded by Patent Officers, some of whom had been administering since the first days of the Colony. No place of refuge had been prepared for them, and, naturally, they were not going to surrender their posts without a struggle. Colonel Wynyard was wax in the hands of the cleverest of these—Mr. Attorney-General Swainson. When the Parliament met, he asked three members to join with his old advisers in forming a Cabinet. They agreed to do so, and one of them, Mr. James Edward Fitzgerald, a Canterbury settler of brilliant abilities, figured as the Colony's first Premier. An Irish gentleman, an orator and a wit, he was about as fitted to cope with the peculiar and delicate imbroglio before him as Murat would have been to conceive and direct one of Napoleon's campaigns. In a few weeks he and his Parliamentary colleagues came to loggerheads with the old officials in the Cabinet, and threw up the game. Then came prorogation for a fortnight and another hybrid ministry, known to New Zealand history as the "Clean-Shirt Ministry," because its leader ingenuously informed Parliament that when asked by the Governor to form an administration, he had gone upstairs to put on a clean shirt before presenting himself at Government House. The Clean-Shirt Ministry lived for just two days. It was born and died amid open recrimination and secret wire-pulling, throughout which Mr. Attorney Swainson, who had got himself made Speaker of the Upper House while retaining his post as the Governor's legal adviser, and Mr. Gibbon Wakefield, who was ostensibly nothing but a private member of the Lower House, pulled the strings behind the scenes. Wakefield began by putting himself at the head of the agitation for responsible Ministers. When later, after negotiating with the Governor's *entourage*, he tried compromise, the majority of the House turned angrily upon him. At last a compromise was arrived at. Colonel Wynyard was to go on with his Patent Officers until a Bill could be passed and assented to in England establishing responsible government; then the old officials were to be pensioned off and shelved. At one stage in this singular session, the Governor sent a message to the House written on sheets of paper, one of the leaves of which the clerk found to be missing. Gibbon Wakefield thereupon coolly pulled the missing portion out of his pocket and proposed to hand it in—a piece of effrontery which the House could not stomach. On another occasion the door of the House had to be locked to prevent the minority running away to force on a count-out, and one honourable member assaulted another with his fists. Australia laughed at the scene, which, it may here be said, has never been repeated in the New Zealand Legislature. The greatest man in the Parliament was the greatest failure of the session. Gibbon Wakefield left Auckland unpopular and distrusted. Soon afterwards his health broke down, and the rest of his life was passed in strict retirement in the Colony which he had founded and in which he died.

The Colonial Office snubbed Colonel Wynyard and Mr. Swainson, and informed them that responsible government could be initiated without an Act of Parliament. A year, however, passed before the General Assembly was summoned together, and then it merely did formal work, as the Acting-Governor had taken upon himself to ordain that there should be a dissolution previous to the establishment of responsible Ministers. This put everything off till the middle of 1856, by which time Colonel Wynyard had left the Colony. To his credit be it noted that he had kept out of native wars. Moreover, in his time, thanks to the brisk trade caused by the gold discoveries in Australia and the progress of sheep-farming in the South Island, the Colony was waxing prosperous.

The second Parliament met in 1856, and still for a time there was confusion. First, Mr. Sewell formed a ministry which lived for thirteen days; then Sir William Fox another which existed for thirteen days more. After that, Sir Edward Stafford took the helm and made headway. A loan of £600,000 was the fair wind which filled his sails. Judgment in choosing colleagues and officials, very fair administrative abilities, attention to business, and an indisposition to push things to extremes in the House were some of the qualities which enabled him to retain office for four years, and to regain it more than once afterwards. Until 1873 he and his rival, Mr. Fox, were considered inevitable members of almost any combination. Native affairs were in the forefront during that period. Mr. Fox, the most impulsive, pugnacious, and controversial of politicians, usually headed the peace party; Sir Edward Stafford, much more easy going in ordinary politics, was usually identified with those who held that peace could only be secured by successful war.

The other principal moving cause in public affairs between 1856 and 1876 was the Provincial system. That had had much to do with the confusion of the sessions of 1854 and 1856. Then and afterwards members were not so much New Zealanders, or Liberals, or Conservatives, as they were Aucklanders, or men of Otago, or some other Province. The hot vigorous local life which Provincial institutions intensified was in itself an admirable thing. But it engendered a mild edition of the feelings which set Greek States and Italian cities at each others' throats. From the first many colonists were convinced that Provincialism was unnatural and must go. But for twenty years the friends of the Provinces were usually ready to forego quarrelling with each other when the Centralists in Parliament threatened the Councils. There were able men in the Colony who devoted their energies by preference to Provincial politics. Such was Dr. Featherston, who was for eighteen years the trusted superintendent of

Wellington, and who, paternally despotic there, watched and influenced Parliament, and was ever vigilant on the Provinces' behalf.

In truth the Provinces had been charged with important functions. The management and sale of Crown lands, education, police, immigration, laws relating to live-stock and timber, harbours, the making of roads and bridges—almost the entire work of colonization—came within their scope. By a "compact" arrived at in the session of 1856 each Province was in effect given the entire control of its public lands—an immense advantage to those of the South Island, where these were neither forest-covered nor in Maori hands. On the other hand, it would have been grossly unfair to confiscate them for general purposes. The Wakefield system in Canterbury would have been unbearable had the £2 paid by the settlers for each acre been sent away to be spent elsewhere. The Wakefield price was a local tax, charged and submitted to to get a revenue to develop the lands for which it was paid. As it was, half a crown an acre was handed over by each Province to the Central Treasury as a contribution for national purposes. Loans were also raised by Parliament to buy native land for the North Island Provinces.

On the other hand, the Provinces enjoyed their land revenue—when there was any—their pastoral rents, a dog tax, and such fag-ends of customs revenue as the central Government could spare them. Their condition was quite unequal. Canterbury, with plenty of high-priced land, could more than dispense with aid from the centre. Other Provinces, with little or no land revenue, were mortified by having to appear at Wellington as suppliants for special grants. When the Provinces borrowed money for the work of development, they had to pay higher rates of interest than the Colony would have had. Finally, the colonial treasurer had not only to finance for one large Colony, but for half a dozen smaller governments, and ultimately to guarantee their debts. No wonder that one of her premiers has said that New Zealand was a severe school of statesmanship.

Yet for many years the ordinary dissensions of Liberal and Tory, of classes and the parties of change and conservatism, were hardly seen in the Parliament which sat at Auckland until 1864 and thereafter at Wellington. Throughout the settlements labour as a rule was in demand, often able to dictate its own terms, nomadic, and careless of politics. The land question was relegated to the Provincial councils, where round it contending classes and rival theories were grouped. It was in some of the councils, notably that of Otago, that the mutterings of Radicalism began first to be heard. The rapid change which bred a parliamentary Radical party after the fall of the Provinces in 1876 was the inevitable consequence of the transfer of the land problem to the central legislature and the destruction of those local safety-valves—the councils. Meanwhile, the ordinary lines of division were not found in the central legislature. According as this or that question came into the foreground, parties and groups in the House of Representatives shifted and changed like the cloud shown to Polonius. Politics made strange bedfellows; Cabinets were sometimes the oddest hybrids. One serviceably industrious lawyer, Mr. Henry Sewell, was something or other in nine different Ministries between 1854 and 1872. The premier of one year might be a subordinate minister the next; or some subtle and persistent nature, like that of Sir Frederick Whitaker, might manage chiefs whom he appeared to follow, and be the guiding mind of parties which he did not profess to direct. Lookers-on asked for more stable executives and more definite lines of cleavage. Newly arrived colonists impatiently summed it all up as mere battling of Ins against Outs, and lamented the sweet simplicity of political divisions as they had known them in the mother country.

Chapter XV

GOVERNOR BROWNE'S BAD BARGAIN

"In defence of the colonists of New Zealand, of whom I am one, I say most distinctly and solemnly that I have never known a single act of wilful injustice or oppression committed by any one in authority against a New Zealander."
—*Bishop Selwyn* (1862).

Colonel Gore Browne took the reins from Colonel Wynyard. The one was just such an honourable and personally estimable soldier as the other. But though he did not involve his Parliament in ridicule, Governor Browne did much more serious mischief. In ordinary matters he took the advice of the Stafford Ministry, but in Native affairs the Colonial Office had stipulated that the Governor was to have an over-riding power. He was to take the advice of his ministers, but not necessarily to follow it. To most politicians, as well as the public, the Native Department remained a secret service, though, except as to a sum of £7,000, the Governor, in administering Native affairs, was dependent for supplies on his ministers, and they on Parliament. On Governor Browne, therefore, rests the chief responsibility for a disastrous series of wars which broke out in 1860, and were not finally at an end for ten years. The impatience of certain colonists to buy lands from the Maori faster than the latter cared to sell them was the simple and not too creditable cause of the outbreak. A broad survey of the position shows that there need have been no hurry over land acquisition. Nor was there any great clamour for haste except in Taranaki, where rather less than 3,000 settlers, restricted to 63,000 acres, fretted at the sight of 1,750 Maoris holding and shutting up 2,000,000 acres against them. So high did feeling run there that Bishop Selwyn, as the friend of the Maori, was, in 1855, hooted in the streets of New Plymouth, where the local newspaper wrote nonsense about his "blighting influence." Yet, as he tersely put it in his charge to his angry laity of the district guilty of this unmannerly outburst, the Taranaki Maoris and others of their race had already sold 30,000 acres near New Plymouth for tenpence an acre, a million of acres at Napier for a penny three-farthings an acre, the whole of the territory round Auckland for about fourpence an acre, and the whole South Island below the Kaikouras for a mite an acre. They had also—the bishop might have added—leased large tracts ultimately turned into freeholds. Yet the impatience of the Taranaki settlers, though mischievous, was natural. The Maoris made no use of a hundredth part of their lands. Moreover, members of the Taranaki tribes who were anxious to sell plots to the Whites were threatened, attacked, and even assassinated by their fellow-tribesmen.

Never bullied, and not much interfered with by the Government, the Maori tribes as a whole were prospering. They farmed, and drove a brisk trade with the settlements, especially Auckland, where, in 1858, no less than fifty-three coasting vessels were registered as belonging to Native owners. Still, the growing numbers of the colonists alarmed them. They saw their race becoming the weaker partner. Originating in Taranaki, a league was formed by a number of the tribes against further selling of land. To weld this league together, certain powerful Waikato chiefs determined to have a king. Of them the most celebrated was the son of Hongi's old antagonist, Te Waharoa. This leader, Wiremu Tamihana, usually known as William Thompson, was an educated Christian and a brown-skinned gentleman, far in advance of his race in breadth of view, logical understanding, and persistence. He honestly wanted to be at peace with us, but regarding contact with our race as deadly to his own, desired to organize the Maori as a community dwelling apart from the *Pakeha* on ample and carefully secured territories. Had the Maori race numbered 500,000 instead of 50,000, and been capable of uniting under him for any purpose whatever, he might conceivably have established a counterpart to Basutoland. But the scanty dwindling tribes could not be welded together. New Zealand was, as she is, the land of jealousies, local and personal. It would seem as though every change of wind brought fresh rivalry and division. The Waikato chiefs themselves were at odds. After years of argument and speech-making they came to the point of choosing their king. But they compromised on the old chief, Te Whero Whero. The once famous warrior was now blind, broken, and enfeebled. When, in 1860, he died, they made the still greater mistake of choosing as successor his son Matutaera (Methuselah), better known as Tawhiao, a dull, heavy, sullen-looking fool, who afterwards became a sot. They disclaimed hostility to the Queen, but would sell no land, and would allow no Whites to settle among them except a few mechanics whose skill they wished to use. They even expelled from their villages white men who had married Maori wives, and who now had to leave their families behind. They would not allow the Queen's writ to run beyond their *aukati* or frontier, or let boats and steamers come up their rivers. Amongst themselves the more violent talked of driving the *Pakeha* into the sea. Space will not permit of any sketch of the discussions and negotiations by which attempts were made to deal with the King Movement. Various mistakes were made. Thompson, while still open to conciliation, visited Auckland to see the Governor and ask for a small loan to aid his tribe in erecting a flour-mill. Governor Grey would have granted both the interview and the money with good grace. Governor Browne refused both, and the Waikato chief departed deeply incensed. A much graver error was the virtual repeal of the ordinance forbidding the sale of arms to the natives. Because a certain amount of smuggling went on in spite of it, the insane course was adopted of greatly relaxing its provisions instead of spending money and vigilance in enforcing them. The result was a rapid increase of the guns and powder sold to the disaffected tribes, who are said to have spent £50,000 in buying them between 1857 and 1860. Between July, 1857, and April, 1858, at any rate, 7,849 lbs. of gunpowder, 311 double-barrelled guns, and 441 single-barrelled guns were openly sold to Maoris.

Finally, in 1860, came the Waitara land purchase—the spark which set all ablaze. The name Waitara has been extended from a river both to a little seaport and to the surrounding district in Taranaki, the province where, as already said, feeling on the land difficulty had always been most acute. Enough land had been purchased, chiefly by Grey, to enable the settlement to expand into a strip of about twenty miles along the seashore, with an average depth of about seven miles. During a visit to the district, Governor Browne invited the Ngatiawa natives to sell land. A chief, Teira, and his friends at once offered to part with six hundred acres which they were occupying. The head of their tribe, however, Wiremu Kingi, vetoed the sale. The Native Department and the Governor sent down commissioners, who, after inquiry, decided erroneously that Teira's party had a right to sell, and the head chief none to interfere. A fair price was paid for the block, and surveyors sent to it. The Ngatiawa good-humouredly encountered these with a band of old women well selected for their ugliness, whose appalling endearments effectually obstructed the survey work. Then, as Kingi threatened war, an armed force was sent to occupy the plot. After two days' firing upon a stockade erected there, the soldiers advanced and found it empty. Kingi, thus attacked, astutely made the disputed piece over to the King tribes, and forthwith became their *protege*. Without openly making war, they sent him numbers of volunteer warriors. He became the protagonist of the Maori land league. The Taranaki tribe hard by New Plymouth and the Ngatiruanui further south joined him openly. Hostilities broke out in February, 1860.

It should be mentioned that while all this was going on, the Premier, Mr. Stafford, was absent in England, and that his colleagues supported the Governor's action. Parliament did not assemble until war had broken out, and then a majority of members conceived themselves bound to stand by what had been done. Nevertheless, so great was the doubt about the wisdom and equity of the purchase that most of the North Island members even then condemned it. Most of the South Island members, who had much to lose and nothing to gain by war, thought otherwise. Very heavily has their island had to pay for the Waitara purchase. It was not a crime, unless every purchaser who takes land with a bad title which he believes to be good is a criminal. But, probably wrong technically, certainly needless and disastrous, it will always remain for New Zealand the classic example of a blunder worse than a crime.

Chapter XVI

TUPARA[1] AGAINST ENFIELD

"The hills like giants at a hunting lay,
Chin upon hand, to see the game at bay."

[Footnote 1: *Tupara* (two-barrel), the Maori name for the short double-barrelled guns which were their handiest weapons against us in bush warfare.]

In 1860 the Taranaki settlement was growing to be what it now is—a very pleasant corner of the earth. Curving round the seashore under the lofty, lonely, symmetrical cone of Egmont, it is a green land of soft air and many streams. After long delays and much hope deferred, the colonists—mostly English of the south-west counties—had begun to prosper and to line the coast with their little homesteads standing among peach orchards, grassy fields, and sometimes a garden gay with the flowers of old Devon. Upon this quiet little realm the Maoris swept down, and the labour of twenty years went up in smoke. The open country was abandoned; the settlers took refuge in their town, New Plymouth. Some 600 of their women and children were shipped off to Nelson; about twice as many more who could not be induced to leave stayed huddled up in the little town, and the necessity of keeping a strong force in the place to defend them from a sudden dash by the Maoris hampered the conduct of the campaign. Martial law was proclaimed—destined not to be withdrawn for five years. After a time the town was protected by redoubts and a line of entrenchment. Crowded and ill-drained, it became as unhealthy as uncomfortable. Whereas for sixteen months before the war there had not been a funeral in the district, they were now seen almost daily. On the alarm of some fancied Maori attack, noisy panics would break out, and the shrieks of women and cries of children embarrassed husbands and brothers on whom they called for help, and whose duty as militiamen took them to their posts. The militia of settlers, numbering between four and five hundred, were soon but a minor portion of the defenders of the settlement. When fighting was seen to be inevitable, the Government sent for aid to Australia, and drew thence all the Imperial soldiers that could be spared. The Colony of Victoria, generous in the emergency, lent New Zealand the colonial sloop-of-war *Victoria*, and allowed the vessel not only to transport troops across the Tasman Sea, but to serve for many months off the Taranaki coast, asking payment for nothing except her steaming coal. By the end of the year there were some 3,000 Europeans in arms at the scene of operations, and they probably outnumbered several times over the fluctuating forces of the natives. The fighting was limited to the strip of sea-coast bounded by the Waitara on the north and the Tataramaika plain on the south, with the town of New Plymouth lying about midway between. The coast was open and surf-beaten, the land seamed by ravines or "gulleys," down which the rainfall of Egmont streamed to the shore. Near the sea the soil was—except in the settlers' clearings—covered with tough bracken from two to six feet high, and with other troublesome growths. Inland the great forest, mantling the volcano's flanks, and spreading its harassing network like a far-stretching spider's web, checked European movements. From the first the English officers in command in this awkward country made up their minds that their men could do nothing in the meshes of the bush, and they clung to the more open strip with a caution and a profound respect for Native prowess which epithets can hardly exaggerate, and which tended to intensify the self-esteem of the Maori, never the least self-confident of warriors. A war carried on in such a theatre and in such a temper was likely to drag. There was plenty of fighting, mostly desultory. The Maoris started out of the bush or the bracken to plunder, to cut off stragglers, or to fight, and disappeared again when luck was against them. Thirteen tiresome months saw much marching and counter-marching, frequent displays of courage—more courage than co-operation sometimes,—one or two defeats, and several rather barren successes. For the first eight months the advantage inclined to the insurgents. After that their overweening conceit of their Waikato contingent enabled our superior strength to assert itself. The Maoris, for all their courage and knowledge of the country, were neither clever guerillas nor good marksmen. Their tribal wars had always been affairs of sieges or hand-to-hand encounters. Half the skill displayed by them in intrenching, half the pluck they showed behind stockades, had they been devoted to harassing our soldiers on the march or to loose skirmishing by means of jungle ambuscades, might, if backed by reasonably straight shooting, have trebled our losses and difficulties.

Early in the war we did none too well in an attack upon a hill *pa* at Waireka, a few miles south of New Plymouth. Colonel Murray was sent out from the town with some 300 troops and militia to take it, and at the same time to bring in some families of settlers who had stuck to their farms, and who, if we may believe one of them, did not want to be interfered with. The militia were sent by one route, the troops took another. The Maoris watched the arrangements from the hills, let the militia cross two difficult ravines, and then occupied these, cutting off the Taranaki contingent. The militia officers, however, kept their men together, and passed the day exchanging shots with their enemy and waiting for Colonel Murray to make a diversion by assailing Waireka. This, however, Colonel Murray did not do. He sent

Lieutenant Urquhart and thirty men to clear the ravines aforesaid, and give the militiamen a chance of retreat. But when the latter, still expecting him to attack the *pa*, did not retire, he rather coolly withdrew Urquhart's party and retraced his steps to the town, alleging that his orders had been not to go into the bush, and, in any case, to return by dusk. Great was the excitement amongst the wives, children, and friends of the settlers away in the fight when the soldiers returned without them, and when one terrified woman, who clutched at an officer's arm and asked their whereabouts, got for answer, "My good woman, I don't know"! Loud was the joy when by the light of the moon the militiamen were at length seen marching in. They had been rescued without knowing it by Captain Cracroft and a party of sixty bluejackets from H.M.S. *Niger*. These, meeting Colonel Murray in his retreat, and hearing of the plight of the colonial force, pushed on in gallant indignation, and in the dusk of the evening made that assault upon the *pa* which the Colonel had somehow not made during the day. Climbing the hill, the sailors chanced upon a party of natives, whom they chased before them pell-mell. Reaching the stockade at the heels of the fugitives, the bluejackets gave each other "a back" and scrambled over the palisades, hot to win the £10 promised by the Captain to the first man to pull down the Maori flag. The defenders from their rifle-pits cut at their feet with tomahawks, wounding several nastily; but in a few minutes the scuffle was over, and the *Niger's* people returned victorious to New Plymouth in high spirits. Moreover, their feat caused the main body of the natives to withdraw from the ravines, thus releasing the endangered militia. Among these, Captain Harry Atkinson—in after years the Colony's Premier and best debater—had played the man. Our loss had been small—that of the natives some fifty killed and wounded.

Month followed month, and still the settlers were pent up and the province infested by the marauding Taranaki, Ngatiawa, and Ngatiruanui Maoris, and by sympathisers from Waikato, who, after planting their crops, had taken their guns and come over to New Plymouth to enjoy the sport of shooting *Pakeha*. The farms and homes of the devastated settlement lay a plundered wreck, and the owners complained bitterly of the dawdling and timidity of the Imperial officers, who on their side accused the settlers of unreason in refusing to remove their families, of insolence to Native allies and prisoners, of want of discipline, and of such selfish greed for compensation from Government that they would let their cattle be captured by natives rather than sell them to the commissariat. On the other hand, the natives were far from a happy family. The Waikato had not forgotten that they had been aforetime the conquerors of the Province, now the scene of war, that the Ngatiawa and Taranaki had been their slaves, and that Wiremu Kingi had fled to Cook's Straits to escape their raids. They swaggered among their old foes and servants, and ostentatiously disregarded their advice, much to our advantage.

In June we were defeated at Puké-te-kauere on the Waitara. Three detachments were sent to surround and storm a *pa* standing in the fork of a **Y** made by the junction of two swampy ravines. The plan broke down; the assailants went astray in the rough country and had to retreat; Lieutenant Brooks and thirty men were killed and thirty-four wounded. The Maori loss was little or nothing.

In August General Pratt came on the scene from Australia. He proceeded to destroy the plantations and to attack the *pas* of the insurgents. He certainly took many positions. Yet so long and laborious were his approaches by sapping, so abundant his precautions, that in no case did the natives stay to be caught in their defences. They evacuated them at the last moment, leaving the empty premises to us. Once, however, with an undue contempt for the British soldier, a contingent, newly arrived from the Waikato, occupied a dilapidated *pa* at Mahoe-tahi on the road from New Plymouth to Waitara. Their chief, Tai Porutu, sent a laconic letter challenging the troops to come and fight. "Make haste; don't prolong it! Make haste!" ran the epistle. Promptly he was taken at his word. Two columns marched on Mahoe-tahi from New Plymouth and Waitara respectively. Though the old *pa* was weak, the approaches to it were difficult, and had the Maoris waylaid the assailants on the road, they might have won. But at the favourable moment Tai Porutu was at breakfast and would not stir. He paid for his meal with his life. Caught between the 65th regiment and the militia, the Maoris were between two fires. Driven out of their *pa*, they tried to make a stand behind it in swamp and scrub. Half a dozen well-directed shells sent them scampering thence to be pursued for three miles. They lost over 100, amongst whom were several chiefs. Our killed and wounded were but 22. Here again Captain Atkinson distinguished himself. Not only did he handle his men well, but a prominent warrior fell by his hand.

This was in November, 1860. For five months General Pratt, in the face of much grumbling, went slowly on sapping and building redoubts. He always reached his empty goal; but the spectacle of British forces worming their way underground and sheltering themselves behind earthworks against the fire of a few score or hundred invisible savages who had neither artillery nor long-range rifles was not calculated to impress the public imagination.

On the 23rd January, 1861, our respectful prudence again tempted the Maoris to rashness. They tried a daybreak attack on one of the General's redoubts. But, though they had crept into the ditch without discovery, and, scrambling thence, swarmed over the parapet with such resolution that they even gripped the bayonets of the soldiers with their hands, they were attacked, in the flank and rear, by parties running up to the rescue from neighbouring redoubts, and fled headlong, leaving fifty killed and wounded behind. In March hostilities were stopped after a not too brilliant year, in which our casualties in fighting had been 228, beside certain settlers cut off by marauders. Thompson, the king-maker, coming down from the Waikato, negotiated a truce. There seemed yet a fair hope of peace. Governor Browne had indeed issued a bellicose manifesto proclaiming his intention of stamping out the King Movement. But before this could provoke a general war, Governor Browne was recalled and Sir George Grey sent back from the Cape to save the position. Moreover, the Stafford Ministry, which headed the war party amongst colonists, fell in 1862, and Sir William Fox, the friend of peace, became Premier.

For eighteen months Grey and his Premier laboured for peace. They tried to conciliate the Kingite chiefs, who would not, for a long time, meet the Governor. They withdrew Governor Browne's manifesto. They offered the natives local self-government. At length the Governor even made up his mind to give back the Waitara land. But a curse seemed to cling to those unlucky acres. The proclamation of restitution was somehow delayed, and meanwhile Grey sent troops to resume possession of another Taranaki block, that of Tataramaika, which fairly belonged to the settlers, but on which Maoris were squatting. Under orders from the King natives, the Ngatiruanui retaliated by surprising and killing a party of soldiers, and the position in the province became at once hopeless. The war beginning again there in 1863 smouldered on for more than three long and wearisome years.

But the main interest soon shifted from Taranaki. In the Waikato, relations with the King's tribes were drifting from bad to worse. Grey had been called in too late. His *mana* was no longer the influence it had been ten years before. His diplomatic advances and offers of local government were met with sheer sulkiness. The semi-comic incident of Sir John Gorst's newspaper skirmish at Te Awamutu did no good. Gorst was stationed there as Commissioner by the Government, as an agent of peace and conciliation. In his charge was an industrial school. It was in the heart of the King Country. The King's advisers must needs have an organ—a broad-sheet called the *Hokioi*, a word which may be paraphrased by Phoenix. With unquestionable courage, Gorst, acting on Grey's orders, issued a sheet in opposition, entitled *Te Pihoihoi Mokémoké*, or The Lonely Lark. Fierce was the encounter of the rival birds. The Lark out-argued the Phoenix. But the truculent Kingites had their own way of dealing with *lèse majesté*. They descended on the printing-house, and carried off the press and type of *Te Pihoihoi Mokémoké*. The press they afterwards sent back to Auckland; of the type, it is said, they ultimately made bullets. Gorst, ordered to quit the King

Country, refused to budge without instructions. The Maoris gave him three weeks to get them and depart, and very luckily for him Grey sent them.

The Governor pushed on a military road from Auckland to the Waikato frontier—a doubtful piece of policy, as it irritated the natives, and the Waikato country, as experience afterwards showed, could be best invaded with the help of river steamers. The steamers were, however, not procured at that stage. About the same time as the Gorst incident in the Upper Waikato, the Government tried to build a police-station and barracks on a plot of land belonging to a friendly native lower down the river. The King natives, however, forbade the erection, and, when the work went on, a party of them paddled down, seized the materials and threw them into the stream.

War Map

It was now clear that war was coming. The utmost anxiety prevailed in Auckland, which was only forty miles from the frontier and exposed to attack both from sea and land. Moreover, some hundreds of natives, living quite close to the town, had arms, and were ascertained to be in communication with the Waikatos. The Governor attempted to disarm them, but the plan was not well carried out, and most of them escaped with their weapons to the King Country. The choice of the Government then lay between attacking and being attacked. They learned, beyond a doubt, that the Waikatos were planning a march on Auckland, and in a letter written by Thompson about this time he not only stated this, but said that in the event of an assault the unarmed people would not be spared. By the middle of the year 1863, however, a strong force was concentrated on the border, just where the Waikato River, turning from its long northward course, abruptly bends westward towards the sea. No less than twelve Imperial Regiments were now in New Zealand, and their commander, General Sir Duncan Cameron, a Crimean veteran, gained a success of some note in Taranaki. He was a brave, methodical soldier, destitute of originality, nimbleness or knowledge of the country or of savage warfare. In July, the invasion of the Waikato was ordered. On the very day before our men advanced, the Maoris had begun what they meant to be their march to Auckland, and the two forces at once came into collision. In a sharp fight at Koheroa the natives were driven from their entrenchments with some loss, and any forward movement on their part was effectually stopped. But, thanks to what seemed to the colonists infuriating slowness, the advance up the Waikato was not begun until the latter part of October, and the conquest of the country not completed until February.

To understand the cause of this impatience on the part of the onlookers, it should be mentioned that our forces were now, as usual in the Maori wars, altogether overwhelming. The highest estimate of the fighting men of the King tribes is two thousand. As against this, General Cameron had ultimately rather more than ten thousand Imperial troops in the Colony to draw upon. In addition to that, the colonial militia and volunteers were gradually recruited until they numbered nearly as many. About half of these were, at any rate after a short time, quite as effectual as the regulars for the peculiar guerilla war which was being waged. In armament there was no comparison between the two sides. The *Pakeha* had Enfield rifles and a good supply of artillery. The Maoris were armed with old Tower muskets and shot-guns, and were badly off both for powder and bullets, while, as already said, they were not very good marksmen. Their artillery consisted of two or three old ship's guns, from which salutes might have been fired without extreme danger to their gunners. If the war in the Waikato, and its off-shoot the fighting in the Bay of Plenty, had been in thick forest and a mountainous country, the disparity of numbers and equipment might have been counterbalanced. But the Waikato country was flat or undulating, clothed in fern and with only patches of forest. A first-class high road—the river—ran right through it. The sturdy resistance of the natives was due first to their splendid courage and skilful use of rifle-pits and earthworks, and in the second place to our want of dash and tactical resource. Clever as the Maori engineers were, bravely as the brown warriors defended their entrenchments, their positions ought to have been nothing more than traps for them, seeing how overwhelming was the white force. The explanation of this lies in the Maori habit of taking up their positions without either provisions or water. A greatly superior enemy, therefore, had only to surround them. They then, in the course of two or three days at the outside, had either to surrender at discretion or try the desperate course of breaking through the hostile lines.

REWI, THE WAIKATO LEADER
Photo by J. MARTIN, Auckland

General Cameron preferred the more slap-dash course of taking entrenchments by assault. A stubborn fight took place at Rangiriri, where the Maoris made a stand on a neck of land between the lake and the Waikato River. Assaulted on two sides, they were quickly driven from all their pits and earthworks except one large central redoubt. Three times our men were sent at this, and three times, despite a fine display of courage, they were flung back with loss. The bravest soldier cannot—without wings—surmount a bank which rises eighteen feet sheer from the bottom of a broad ditch. This was seen next day. The attack ceased at nightfall. During the dark hours the redoubt's defenders yelled defiance, but next morning they surrendered, and, marching out, a hundred and eighty-three laid down their arms. Our loss was one hundred and thirty-two killed and wounded; the Maori loss was fifty killed, wounded unknown. By January,

General Cameron had passed beyond Ngaruawahia, the village which had been the Maori King's head-quarters, and which stood at the fine river-junction where the brown, sluggish Waipa loses its name and waters in the light-green volume of the swifter Waikato. Twice the English beat the enemy in the triangle between the rivers. A third encounter was signalised by the most heroic incident in the Colony's history. Some three hundred Maoris were shut up in entrenchments at a place called Orakau. Without food, except a few raw potatoes; without water; pounded at by our artillery, and under a hail of rifle bullets and hand grenades; unsuccessfully assaulted no less than five times—they held out for three days, though completely surrounded. General Cameron humanely sent a flag of truce inviting them to surrender honourably. To this they made the ever-famous reply, "Enough! We fight right on, for ever!" (Heoi ano! Ka whawhai tonu, aké, aké, aké.) Then the General offered to let the women come out, and the answer was, "The women will fight as well as we." At length, on the afternoon of the third day, the garrison assembling in a body charged at quick march right through the English lines, fairly jumping (according to one account) over the heads of the men of the Fortieth Regiment as they lay behind a bank. So unexpected and amazing was their charge, that they would have got away with but slight loss had they not, when outside the lines, been headed and confronted by a force of colonial rangers and cavalry. Half of them fell; the remainder, including the celebrated war-chief Rewi, got clear away. The earthworks and the victory remained with us, but the glory of the engagement lay with those whose message of "Aké, aké, aké," will never be forgotten in New Zealand.

The country round the middle and lower Waikato was now in our hands, and the King natives were driven to the country about its upper waters. They were not followed. It was decided to attack the Tauranga tribe, which had been aiding them. Tauranga lies on the Bay of Plenty, about forty miles to the east of the Waikato. It was in the campaign which now took place there that there occurred the noted repulse at the Gate *Pa*. The Maoris, entrenched on a narrow neck of land between two swamps, were invested by our forces both in the front and rear We were, as usual, immensely the stronger in numbers. Our officers, non-commissioned officers and drummers by themselves almost equalled the garrison. After a heavy though not always very accurate bombardment, General Cameron decided to storm the works. The attacking parties of soldiers and sailors charged well enough and entered the front of the defences, and the Maoris, hopeless and endeavouring to escape, found themselves shut in by the troops in their rear. Turning, however, with the courage of despair, they flung themselves on the assailants of their front. These, seized with an extraordinary panic, ran in confusion, breaking from their officers and sweeping away their supports. The assault was completely repulsed, and was not renewed. In the night the defenders escaped through the swamps, leaving us the empty *pa*. Their loss was slight. Ours was one hundred and eleven, and amongst the killed were ten good officers. As a defeat it was worse than Ohaeawai, for that had been solely due to a commander's error of judgment.

The blow stung the English officers and men deeply, and they speedily avenged it. Hearing that the Tauranga warriors were entrenching themselves at Te Rangi, Colonel Greer promptly marched thither, caught them before they had completed their works, and charging into the rifle-pits with the bayonet, completely routed the Maoris. The temper of the attacking force may be judged from the fact that out of the Maori loss of one hundred and forty-five no less than one hundred and twenty-three were killed or died of wounds. The blow was decisive, and the Tauranga tribe at once submitted.

Chapter XVII

THE FIRE IN THE FERN

"But War, of its majestic mask laid bare,
The face of naked Murder seemed to wear."

From the middle of 1864, to January, 1865, there was so little fighting that it might have been thought that the war was nearing its end. The Waikato had been cleared, and the Tauranga tribes crushed. Thompson, hopeless of further struggling ceased to resist the irresistible, made his peace with us and during the short remainder of his life was treated as became an honourable foe. Nevertheless, nearly two years of harassing guerilla warfare were in store for the Colony. Then there was to be another imperfect period of peace, or rather exhaustion, between the October, 1866, and June, 1868, when hostilities were once more to blaze up and only to die out finally in 1870. This persistency was due to several causes, of which the first was the outbreak, early in 1864, of a curious superstition, the cult of the Hau-Haus. Their doctrine would be hard to describe. It was a wilder, more debased, and more barbaric parody of Christianity than the Mormonism of Joe Smith. It was an angry reaction, a kind of savage expression of a desire to revolt alike from the Christianity and civilization of the *Pakeha* and to found a national religion. For years it drove its votaries into purposeless outbreaks, and acts of pitiless and ferocious cruelty. By the Hau-Haus two white missionaries were murdered—outrages unknown before in New Zealand. Their murderous deeds and the reprisals these brought about gave a darker tinge to the war henceforth. Their frantic faith led to absurdities as well as horrors. They would work themselves up into frenzy by dances and incantations, and in particular by barking like dogs—hence their name. At first, they seem to have believed that the cry *Hau! Hau!* accompanied by raising one hand above the head with palm turned to the front, would turn aside the *Pakeha's* bullets.

It was in April, 1864, that they first appeared in the field. A Captain Lloyd, out with a reconnoitring party in Taranaki, fell, rather carelessly, into an ambuscade, where he and six of his people were killed and a dozen wounded. When Captain Atkinson and his rangers came up at speed to the rescue, they found that the heads of the slain had been cut off and carried away. Lloyd's, it appears, was carried about the island by Hau-Hau preachers, who professed to find in it a kind of diabolical oracle, and used it with much effect in disseminating their teaching. One of these prophets, or preachers, however, had a short career. Three weeks after Lloyd's death, this man, having persuaded himself and his dupes that they were invulnerable, led them against a strong and well-garrisoned redoubt at Sentry Hill, between New Plymouth and Waitara. Early one fine morning, in solid column, they marched deliberately to within 150 yards of the fort, and before straight shooting undeceived them about the value of their charms and passes, thirty-four of the poor fanatics were lying beside their prophet in front of the redoubt. A number more were carried off hurt or dying, and thenceforward the Taranaki natives were reduced to the defensive.

In the summer of the same year another prophet met his death in the most dramatic fight of the war, that by which the friendly natives of the Wanganui district saved it from a Hau-Hau raid by a conflict fought on an island in the Wanganui River, after a fashion which would have warmed the heart of Sir Walter Scott had he been alive to hear of a combat so worthy of the clansmen in "The Fair Maid of Perth." It came about a month after the repulse at the Gate *Pa*. For months the friendlies had been guarding the passage of the river against a strong Hau-Hau force. At last, tired of waiting, they challenged the enemy to a fair fight on the island of Moutua. It was agreed that neither side should attempt to take advantage of the other by surprise or ambuscade. They landed at opposite ends of the islet. First came the friendlies, 100 strong; 50 formed their first line under three brave chiefs; 50 stood in reserve under Haimona (Simon) Hiroti; 150 friends watched them from one of the river banks. Presently the Hau-Haus sprang from their canoes on to the river-girt arena, headed by their warrior-prophet Matené (Martin). After much preliminary chanting of incantations and shouting of defiance, the Hau-Haus charged. As they came on, the friendly natives, more than half believing them to be invulnerable, fired so wildly that every shot missed. Three of the Wanganui leaders fell, and their line wavered and broke. In vain a fourth chief, Tamihana, shot a Hau-Hau with each barrel of his *tupara*, speared a third, and cleft the skull of yet another with his tomahawk. Two bullets brought him down. It was Haimona Hiroti who saved the day. Calling on the reserve, he stopped the flying, and, rallying bravely at his appeal, they came on again. Amid a clash of tomahawks and clubbed rifles, the antagonists fought hand to hand, and fought well. At length our allies won. Fifty Hau-Haus died that day, either on the island or while they endeavoured to escape by swimming. Twenty more were wounded. The Hau-Hau leader, shot as he swam, managed to reach the further shore. "There is your fish!" said Haimona, pointing the prophet out to a henchman, who, *meré* in hand plunged in after him, struck him down as he staggered up the bank, and swam back with his head. His flag and ninety sovereigns were amongst the prizes of the winners in the hard trial of strength. The victors carried the bodies of their fallen chiefs back to Wanganui, where the settlers for whom they had died lined the road, standing bareheaded as the brave dead were borne past.

That three such blows as Sentry Hill, Moutua, and Te Rangi had not a more lasting effect was due, amongst other things, to the confiscation policy.

To punish the insurgent tribes, and to defray in part the cost of the war, the New Zealand Government confiscated 2,800,000 acres of native land. As a punishment it may have been justified; as a financial stroke it was to the end a failure. Coming as it did in the midst of hostilities, it did not simplify matters. Among the tribes affected it bred despair, amongst their neighbours apprehension, in England unpleasant suspicions. At first both the Governor and the Colonial Office endorsed the scheme of confiscation. Then, when Mr. Cardwell had replaced the Duke of Newcastle, the Colonial Office changed front and condemned it, and their pressure naturally induced the Governor to modify his attitude.

An angry collision followed between him and his ministers, and in November, 1864, the Ministry, whose leaders were Sir William Fox and Sir Frederick Whitaker, resigned. They were succeeded by Sir Frederick Weld, upon whose advice Grey let the confiscation go on. Weld became noted for his advocacy of what was known as the Self-reliance Policy—in other words, that the Colony should dispense with the costly and rather cumbrous Imperial forces, and trust in future to the militia and Maori auxiliaries. And, certainly, when campaigning began again in January, 1865, General Cameron seemed to do his best to convert all Colonists to Weld's view. He did indeed appear with a force upon the coast north of Wanganui. But his principal feat was the extraordinary one of consuming fifty-seven days in a march of fifty-four miles along the sea beach, to which he clung with a tenacity which made the natives scornfully name him the Lame Seagull. At the outset he pitched his camp so close to thick cover that the Maoris twice dashed at him, and though of course beaten off, despite astonishing daring, they killed or wounded forty-eight soldiers. After that the General went to the cautious extreme. He declared it was useless for regulars to follow the natives into the forest, and committed himself to the statement that two hundred natives in a stockade could stop Colonel Warre with five hundred men from joining him. He declined to assault the strong Weraroa *pa*—the key to the west coast. He hinted depressingly that 2,000 more troops might be required from England. In vain Sir George Grey urged him to greater activity. The only result was a long and acrid correspondence between them. From this—to one who reads it now—the General seems to emerge in a damaged condition. The best that can be said for him is that he and many of his officers were sick of the war, which they regarded as an iniquitous job, and inglorious to boot. They knew that a very strong party in England, headed by the Aborigines Protection Society, were urging this view, and that the Colonial Office, under Mr. Cardwell, had veered round to the same standpoint. This is probably the true explanation of General Cameron's singular slackness. The impatience and indignation of the colonists waxed high. They had borrowed three millions of money to pay for the war. They were paying £40 a year per man for ten thousand Imperial soldiers. They naturally thought this too much for troops which did not march a mile a day.

Whatever the colonists thought of Grey's warfare with his ministers, they were heartily with him in his endeavours to quicken the slow dragging on of the military operations. He did not confine himself to exhortation. He made up his mind to attack the Weraroa *pa* himself. General Cameron let him have two hundred soldiers to act as a moral support. With these, and somewhat less than five hundred militia and friendly Maoris, the Governor sat down before the fort, which rose on a high, steep kind of plateau, above a small river. But though too strong for front attack, it was itself liable to be commanded from an outwork on a yet higher spur of the hills. Bringing common sense to bear, Grey quietly despatched a party, which captured this, and with it a strong reinforcement about to join the garrison. The latter fled, and the bloodless capture of Weraroa was justly regarded as among the most brilliant feats of the whole war. The credit fairly belonged to Grey, who showed, not only skill, but signal personal daring. The authorities at home must be assumed to have appreciated this really fine feat of his, for they made the officer commanding the two hundred moral supports a C.B. But Grey, it is needless to say, by thus trumping the trick of his opponent the General, did not improve his own relations with the Home authorities. He did, however, furnish another strong reason for a self-reliant policy. Ultimately, though gradually, the Imperial troops were withdrawn, and the colonists carried on the war with their own men, as well as their own money.

MAJOR KEMP
MEIHA KEPA TE RANGI-HIWINUI

In January, 1866, however, after General Cameron had by resignation escaped from a disagreeable position, but while the withdrawal of the troops was still incomplete, his successor, General Chute, showed that under officers of determination and energy British soldiers are by no means feeble folk even in the intricacies of the New Zealand bush. Setting out from the Weraroa aforesaid on January 3rd with three companies of regulars, a force of militia, and 300 Maoris under the chief Kepa, or Kemp, he began to march northward through the forest to New Plymouth. At first following the coast he captured various *pas* by the way, including a strong position at Otapawa, which was fairly stormed in the face of a stout defence, during which both sides suffered more than a little. There, when one of the buttons on Chute's coat was cut off by a bullet, he merely snapped out the remark, "The niggers seem to have found me out." Both the coolness and the words used were characteristic of the hard but capable soldier. Further on the route Kemp in one day of running skirmishes took seven villages. Arriving at the southern side of Mount Egmont, the General decided to march round its inland flank through a country then almost unknown except to a few missionaries. Encumbered with pack-horses, who were checked by every flooded stream, the expedition took seven days to accomplish the sixty miles of the journey. But they did it, and met no worse foes than continual rain, short commons, deep mud, and the gloomy silence of the saturated forest, which then spread without a break over a country now almost entirely taken up by thriving dairy-farmers. Turning south again from New Plymouth by the coast-road, Chute had to fight but once in completing a march right round Mount Egmont, and thenceforward, except on its southern verge, long-distracted Taranaki saw no more campaigning.

Other districts were less fortunate. By the early part of 1865 the Hau-Hau craze was at work on the east as well as the west coast. It was in the country round the Wanganui River to the west, and in the part of the east coast, between Tauranga on the Bay of Plenty and Hawkes Bay, that the new mischief gave the most trouble. The task of coping with it devolved on the New Zealand Militia, and the warriors of certain friendly tribes, headed by the chiefs called by the Europeans Ropata and Kemp. In this loose and desultory but exceedingly arduous warfare, the irregulars and friendlies undoubtedly proved far more efficient than the regular troops had usually been permitted to be. They did not think it useless to follow the enemy into the bush; far from it. They went there to seek him out. They could march many miles in a day, and were not fastidious as to commissariat. More than once they gained food and quarters for the night by taking them from their opponents. In a multitude of skirmishes in 1865 and 1866, they were almost uniformly victorious. Of the laurels gained in New Zealand warfare, a large share belongs to Ropata, to Kemp, and to Militia officers like Tuke, McDonnell and Fraser. Later in the war, when energetic officers tried to get equally good results out of inexperienced volunteers, and when, too—in some cases—militia discipline had slackened, the consequences were by no means so satisfactory. It did not follow that brave men ready to plunge into the bush were good irregulars merely because they were not regulars. Nor were all friendly natives by any means as effective as the Wanganui and Ngatiporou, or all chiefs as serviceable as Ropata and Kemp.

The east coast troubles began in March, 1865, with the murder at Opotiki, on the Bay of Plenty, of Mr. Volckner, a missionary and the most kindly and inoffensive of mankind. At the bidding of Kereopa, a Hau-Hau emissary, the missionary's people suddenly turned on him, hung him, hacked his body to pieces, and smeared themselves with his blood. At another spot in the same Bay a trading schooner was seized just afterwards by order of another Hau-Hau fanatic, and all on board killed save two half-caste boys. A force of militia soon dealt out condign punishment for these misdeeds, but meanwhile Kereopa and his fellow fire-brands had passed down the coast and kindled a flame which gradually crept southward even to Hawkes Bay. In village after village the fire blazed up, and a rising equal to that in the Waikato seemed imminent. It was, indeed, fortunate that much the ablest warrior on that side of the island at once declared against the craze. This was Ropata Te Wahawaha, then and afterwards the most valuable Maori ally the Government had, and one of the very few captains on either side who went through the wars without anything that could be called a defeat. Without fear or pity, he was a warrior of the older Maori type, who with equal enjoyment could plan a campaign, join in a hand-to-hand tussle, doom a captive to death, or shoot a deserter with his own rifle. As he would not join the Hau-Haus, they and their converts made the mistake of attacking him. After beating them off he was joined by Major Biggs and a company of militia. Together they advanced against the stronghold of the insurgents, perched on a cliff among the Waiapu hills. By scaling a precipice with twenty picked men, Ropata and Biggs gained a crest above the *pa*, whence they could fire down into the midst of their astonished adversaries, over 400 of whom surrendered in terror to the daring handful. But the mischief had run down the coast. Spreading from point to point, dying down and then starting up, it was as hard to put out as fire abroad in the fern. The amiable Kereopa visited Poverty Bay, three days' journey south of the Waiapu, and tried hard to persuade the natives to murder Bishop Williams, the translator of the Scriptures into Maori. Though they shrank from this, the Bishop had to fly, and his flock took up arms, stood a siege in one of their *pas*, and lost over a hundred men before they would surrender to the militia. Further south still the next rising flared up on the northern frontier of the Hawkes Bay province. Once more Ropata stamped it under, and the generalship with which he repaired the mistakes made by others, and routed a body of 500 insurgents was not more remarkable than the cold-blooded promptitude with which after the fight he shot four prisoners of note with his own hand. It took ten months for the spluttering fire to flame up again. Then it was yet another stage further south, within a few miles of Napier, amid pastoral plains, where, if anywhere, peace, it would seem, should have an abiding-place. The rising there was but a short one-act play. To Colonel Whitmore belonged the credit of dealing it a first and final blow at Omaranui, where, with a hastily raised force of volunteers, and some rather useless friendlies, he went straight at the insurgents, caught them in the open, and quickly killed, wounded, or captured over ninety per cent. of their number.

After this there was a kind of insecure tranquillity until June, 1868. Then fighting began again near the coast between Wanganui and Mount Egmont, where the occupation of confiscated lands bred bitter feelings. Natives were arrested for horse-stealing. Straggling settlers were shot. A chief, Titokowaru, hitherto insignificant, became the head and front of the resistance. In June a sudden attack was made by his people upon some militia holding a tumble-down redoubt—an attack so desperate that out of twenty-three in the work, only six remained unwounded when help came, after two hours' manful resistance. Colonel McDonnell, then in command on the coast, had proved his dash and bravery in a score of bush-fights. In his various encounters he killed ten Maoris with his own hand. He was an expert bushman, and a capital manager of the friendly natives. But during the eighteen months of quiet the trained militia which had done such excellent work in 1865 and 1866, had been in part dispersed. The force which in July McDonnell led into the bush to attempt Titokowaru's *pa*, at Ngutu-o-te-manu (Beak-of-the-bird) was to a large extent raw material. The Hau-Haus were found fully prepared. Skilfully posted, they poured in a hot cross-fire, both from the *pa* and from an ambush in the neighbouring thickets. Broken into two bodies, McDonnell's men were driven to make a long and painful retreat, during which two died of exhaustion. They lost twenty-four killed and twenty-six wounded. McDonnell resigned in disgust. Whitmore, who replaced him, demanded better men, and got them, but to meet no better success. At Moturoa his assault on another forest stockade failed under a withering fire; the native contingent held back sulkily; and again our men retreated, with a loss this time of forty-seven, of which twenty-one were killed. This was on November 5th. Before Whitmore could try again he was called to the other side of the island by evil tidings from Poverty Bay.

These had their cause in the strangest story of the Maori wars. Amongst the many blunders in these, some of the oddest were the displays of rank carelessness which repeatedly led to the escape of Maori prisoners. Three times did large bodies get away and rejoin their tribes—once from Sir George Grey's island estate at Kawau, where they had been turned loose on parole; once from a hulk in Wellington Harbour, through one of the port-holes of which they slipped into the sea on a stormy night; the third time from the Chatham Islands. This last escape, which was in July, 1868, was fraught with grave mischief.

Fruitlessly the officer in charge of prisoners there had protested against being left with twenty men to control three hundred and thirty captives. The leader of these, Te Kooti, one of the ablest as well as most ferocious partisans the colonists ever had to face, had been deported from Poverty Bay to the Chathams two years before, without trial. Unlike most of his fellow prisoners he had never borne arms against us. The charge against him was that he was in communication with Hau-Hau insurgents in 1865. His real offence seems to have been that he was regarded by some of the Poverty Bay settlers as a disagreeable, thievish, disaffected fellow, and there is an uncomfortable doubt as to whether he deserved his punishment. During his exile he vowed vengeance against those who had denounced him, and against one man in particular. In July, 1868, the schooner *Rifleman* was sent down to the Chathams with supplies. The prisoners took the chance thus offered. They surprised the weak guard, killed a sentry who showed fight, and seized and tied up the others, letting the women and children escape unharmed. Going on board the *Rifleman*, Te Kooti gave the crew the choice between taking his people to New Zealand and instant death. They chose the former, and the schooner set sail for the east coast of

New Zealand with about one hundred and sixty fighting men, and a number of women and children. The outbreak and departure were successfully managed in less than two hours. When head winds checked the runaways, Te Kooti ordered an old man, his uncle, to be bound and thrown overboard as a sacrifice to the god of winds and storms. The unhappy human sacrifice struggled for awhile in the sea and then sank. At once the wind changed, the schooner lay her course, and the *mana* of Te Kooti grew great. After sailing for a week, the fugitives had their reward, and were landed at Wharé-onga-onga (Abode-of-stinging-nettles), fifteen miles from Poverty Bay. They kept their word to the crew, whom they allowed to take their vessel and go scot-free. Then they made for the interior. Major Biggs, the Poverty Bay magistrate, got together a force of friendly natives and went in pursuit. The Hau-Haus showed their teeth to such effect that the pursuers would not come to close quarters. Even less successful was the attempt of a small band of White volunteers. They placed themselves across Te Kooti's path; but after a long day's skirmishing were scattered in retreat, losing their baggage, ammunition, and horses. Colonel Whitmore, picking them up next day, joined them to his force and dragged them off after him in pursuit of the victors. It was winter, and the weather and country both of the roughest. The exhausted volunteers, irritated by Whitmore's manner, left him half-way. For himself the little colonel, all wire and leather, knew not fatigue. But even the best of his men were pretty well worn out when they did at last catch a Tartar in the shape of the enemy's rearguard. The latter made a stand under cover, in an angle of the narrow bed of a mountain-torrent floored with boulders and shut in by cliffs. Our men, asked to charge in single file, hung back, and a party of Native allies sent round to take the Hau Haus in flank made off altogether. Though Te Kooti was shot through the foot, the pursuit had to be given up. The net result of the various skirmishes with him had been that we had lost twenty-six killed and wounded, and that he had got away.

Whitmore went away to take command on the west coast. Thus Te Kooti gained time to send messengers to the tribes, and many joined him. He spoke of himself as God's instrument against the *Pakeha*, preached eloquently, and kept strict discipline amongst his men. In November, after a three months' lull, he made his swoop on his hated enemies the settlers in Poverty Bay, and in a night surprise took bloody vengeance for his sojourn at the Chathams. His followers massacred thirty-three white men, women and children, and thirty-seven natives. Major Biggs was shot at the door of his house. Captain Wilson held out in his till it was in flames. Then he surrendered under promise of life for his family, all of whom, however, were at once bayonetted, except a boy who slipped into the scrub unnoticed. McCulloch, a farmer, was shot as he sat milking. Several fugitives owed their lives to the heroism of a friendly chief, Tutari, who refused to gain his life by telling their pursuers the path they had taken. The Hau Haus killed him and seized his wife, who, however, adroitly saved both the flying settlers and herself by pointing out the wrong track. Lieutenant Gascoigne with a hasty levy of friendly Natives set out after the murderers, only to be easily held in check at Makaretu with a loss of twenty-eight killed and wounded. Te Kooti, moreover, intercepted an ammunition train and captured eight kegs of gunpowder. Fortifying himself on a precipitous forest-clad hill named Ngatapa, he seemed likely to rally round him the disaffected of his race. But his red star was about to wane. Ropata with his Ngatiporou now came on the scene. A second attack on Makaretu sent the insurgents flying. They left thirty-seven dead behind, for Ropata gave no quarter, and had not his men loitered to plunder, Te Kooti, who, still lame, was carried off on a woman's back, must have been among their prizes. Pushing on to Ngatapa, Ropata found it a very formidable stronghold. The *pa* was on the summit of an abrupt hill, steep and scarped on two sides, narrowing to a razor-backed ridge in the rear. In front three lines of earthwork rose one above another, the highest fourteen feet high, aided and connected by the usual rifle-pits and covered way. Most of Ropata's men refused to follow him against such a robbers' nest, and though the fearless chief tried to take it with the faithful minority, he had to fall back, under cover of darkness, and return home in a towering passion. A month later his turn came. Whitmore arrived. Joining their forces, he and Ropata invested Ngatapa closely, attacked it in front and rear, and took the lowest of the three lines of intrenchment. A final assault was to come next morning. The Hau Haus were short of food and water, and in a desperate plight. But one cliff had been left unwatched, and over that they lowered themselves by ropes as the storming party outside sat waiting for the grey dawn. They were not, however, to escape unscathed. Ropata at once sent his men in chase. Hungry and thirsty, the fugitives straggled loosely, and were cut down by scores or brought back. Short shrift was theirs. The Government had decided that Poverty Bay must be revenged, and the prisoners were forthwith shot, and their bodies stripped and tossed over a cliff. From first to last at Ngatapa the loss to the Hau Haus was 136 killed outright, ours but 22, half of whom were wounded only. It was the last important engagement fought in New Zealand, and ended all fear of a general rising. Yet in one respect the success was incomplete: Te Kooti once more escaped. This time he reached the fastnesses of the wild Urewera tribe, and made more than one bloodstained raid thence. In April he pounced on Mohaka, at the northern end of the Hawkes Bay Province, killed seven whites, fooled the occupants of a Native *pa* into opening their gates to him, and then massacred 57 of them. But the collapse of the insurrection on the West Coast enabled attention to be concentrated upon the marauder. He fell back on the plateau round Lake Taupo. There, in

June, 1869, he outwitted a party of militia-men by making his men enter their camp, pretending to be friendlies. When the befooled troopers saw the trick and tried to seize their arms, nine were cut down. McDonnell, however, was at the heels of the Hau Haus, and in three encounters in the Taupo region Te Kooti was soundly beaten with a loss of 50 killed. He became a hunted fugitive. Ropata and Kemp chased him from district to district, backwards and forwards, across and about the island, for a high price had been put on his head. For three years the pursuit was urged or renewed. Every band Te Kooti got together was scattered. His wife was taken; once he himself was shot in the hand; again and again the hunters were within a few yards of their game. Crossing snow-clad ranges, wading up the beds of mountain torrents, hacking paths through the tangled forest, they were ever on his track, only to miss him. It was in the Uriwera wilderness that Te Kooti lost his congenially bloodthirsty crony Kereopa, who was caught there and hung. Left almost without followers, he himself at last took refuge in the King Country, where he stayed quiet and unmolested. In the end he received a pardon, and died in peace after living for some twenty years after his hunters had abandoned their chase.

Colonel Whitmore, crossing to the Wanganui district after the fall of Ngatapa, had set off to deal with Titokowaru. He, however, threw up the game and fled to the interior, where he was wisely left alone, and, except for the fruitless pursuit of Te Kooti, the year 1870 may be marked as the end of warfare in New Zealand.

The interest of the Maori struggle, thus concluded, does not spring from the numbers engaged. To a European eye the combats were in point of size mere battles of the frogs and mice. What gave them interest was their peculiar and picturesque setting, the local difficulties to be met, and the boldness, rising at moments to heroism, with which clusters of badly armed savages met again and again the finest fighting men of Europe. It was the race conflict which gave dignity to what Lieutenant Gudgeon in his chronicle truthfully reduces to "expeditions and skirmishes grandiloquently styled campaigns". Out of a multitude of fights between 1843 and 1870, thirty-seven (exclusive of the raid on Poverty Bay, which was a massacre) may be classed as of greater importance than the rest. Out of these we were unmistakably beaten nine times, and a tenth encounter, that of Okaihau, was indecisive. Of twenty-seven victories, however, those of Rangi-riri and Orakau were dearly bought; in the double fight at Nukumaru we lost more than the enemy, and at Waireka most of our forces retreated, and only heard of the success from a distance. Two disasters and six successes were wholly or almost wholly the work of native auxiliaries. The cleverness and daring of the Maori also scored in the repeated escapes of batches of prisoners.

By 1870 it was possible to try and count the cost of the ten years' conflict. It was not so easy to do so correctly. The killed alone amounted to about 800 on the English side and 1,800 on the part of the beaten natives. Added to the thousands wounded, there had been many scores of "murders" and heavy losses from disease, exposure and hardship. The Maoris were, for the most part, left without hope and without self-confidence. The missionaries never fully regained their old moral hold upon the race, nor has it shown much zeal and enthusiasm in industrial progress. On the other side, the colonists had spent between three and four millions in fighting, and for more than fifteen years after the war they had to keep up an expensive force of armed police. There had been destruction of property in many parts of the North Island, and an even more disastrous loss of security and paralysis of settlement. Since 1865, moreover, the pastoral industry in the south had been depressed by bad prices. It is true that some millions of acres of Maori land had been gained by confiscation, but of this portions were handed over to loyal natives. Much more was ultimately given back to the insurgent tribes, and the settlement of the rest was naturally a tardy and difficult process. Farmers do not rush upon land to be the mark of revengeful raids. The opening of the year 1870 was one of New Zealand's dark hours.

Nevertheless, had the colonists but known it, the great native difficulty was destined to melt fast away. Out of the innumerable perplexities, difficulties, and errors of the previous generation, a really capable Native Minister had been evolved. This was Sir Donald McLean, who, from the beginning of 1869 to the end of 1876, took the almost entire direction of the native policy. A burly, patient, kindly-natured Highlander, his Celtic blood helped him to sympathize with the proud, warlike, clannish nature of the Maori. It was largely owing to his influence that Ropata and others aided us so actively against Te Kooti. It was not, however, as a war minister, but as the man who established complete and lasting peace through New Zealand, that his name should be remembered. By liberal payment for service, by skilful land purchases, by showing respect to the chiefs, and tact and good humour with the people, McLean acquired a permanent influence over the race. The war party in the Colony might sneer at his "Flour and Sugar Policy"; but even the dullest had come to see by this time that peace paid. Into the remnant of the King Country McLean never tried to carry authority. He left that and the Urewera country further east discreetly alone. Elsewhere the Queen's writ ran, and roads, railways, and telegraphs, coming together with a great tide of settlement, made the era of war seem like an evil dream. It is true that the delays in redeeming promises concerning reserves to be made and given back from the confiscated Maori territory were allowed to remain a grievance for more than another decade, and led, as late as 1880, to interference by the natives with road making in some of this lost land of theirs in Taranaki. There, round a prophet named Te Whiti, flocked numbers of natives sore with a sense of injustice. Though Te Whiti was as pacific as eccentric, the Government, swayed by the alarm and irritation thus aroused, took the extreme step of pouring into his village of Parihaka an overwhelming armed force. Then, after reading the Riot Act to a passive and orderly crowd of men, women and children, they proceeded to make wholesale arrests, to evict the villagers and to destroy houses and crops. Public opinion, which had conjured up the phantom of an imminent native rising, supported the proceeding. There was no such danger, for the natives were virtually not supplied with arms, and the writer is one of a minority of New Zealanders who thinks that our neglect to make the reserves put us in the wrong in the affair. However, as the breaking up of Parihaka was at last followed up by an honourable and liberal settlement of the long-delayed Reserves question, it may be classed as the last of the long series of native alarms. There will be no more Maori wars. Unfortunately, it has become a question whether in a hundred years there will be any more Maoris. They were perhaps, seventy thousand when the Treaty of Waitangi was signed; they and the half-castes can scarcely muster forty-three thousand now.

Chapter XVIII

GOLD-DIGGERS AND GUM-DIGGERS

"Fortune, they say, flies from us: she but wheels
Like the fleet sea-bird round the fowler's skiff,
Lost in the mist one moment, and the next
Brushing the white sail with a whiter wing
As if to court the aim. Experience watches,
And has her on the turn."

When the Waitara war broke out the white population did not number
more than seventy-five thousand. When Te Kooti was chased into the King
Country it had grown to nearly four times that sum, in the face of debt,
doubt, and the paralyzing effects of war. A great ally of settlement had
come upon the scene. In 1861 profitable goldfields were discovered in
Otago. The little Free Church colony, which in thirteen years had scarcely
increased to that number of thousands, was thunderstruck at the news. For
years there had been rumours of gold in the river beds and amongst the
mountains of the South Island. From 1857 to 1860 about £150,000 had
been won in Nelson. In 1858, a certain Asiatic, Edward Peters, known to
his familiars as Black Pete, who had somehow wandered from his native
Bombay through Australia to Otago, had struck gold there; and in March,
1861, there was a rush to a short-lived goldfield at the Lindis, another spot
in that province. But it was not until the winter of that year that the
prospector, Gabriel Read, found in a gully at Tuapeka the indubitable signs
of a good alluvial field. Digging with a butcher's knife, he collected in ten
hours nearly five-and-twenty pounds' worth of the yellow metal. Then he
sunk hole after hole for some distance, finding gold in all. Unlike most
discoverers, Read made no attempt to keep his fortune to himself, but
wrote frankly of it to Sir John Richardson, the superintendent of the
province. For this he was ultimately paid the not extravagant reward of
£1,000. The good Presbyterians of Dunedin hardly knew in what spirit to
receive the tidings. But some of them did not hesitate to test the field. Very
soberly, almost in sad solemnity, they set to work there, and the result
solved all doubts. Half Dunedin rushed to Tuapeka. At one of the country
kirks the congregation was reduced to the minister and precentor. The news
went across the seas. Diggers from Australia and elsewhere poured in by
the thousand. Before many months the province's population had doubled,
and the prayerful and painful era of caution, the day of small things, was
whisked away in a whirl of Victorian enterprise. For the next few years the

history of Otago became a series of rushes. Economically, no doubt, "rush" is the proper word to apply to the old stampedes to colonial goldfields. But in New Zealand, at any rate, the physical methods of progression thither were laborious in the extreme. The would-be miner tramped slowly and painfully along, carrying as much in the way of provisions and tools as his back would bear. Lucky was the man who had a horse to ride, or the rudest cart to drive in. When, as time went on, gold was found high up the streams amongst the ice-cold rivers and bleak tussock-covered mountains of the interior, the hardships endured by the gold-seekers were often very great. The country was treeless and wind-swept. Sheep roamed over the tussocks, but of other provisions there were none. Hungry diggers were thankful to pay half a crown for enough flour to fill a tin pannikin. £120 a ton was charged for carting goods from Dunedin. Not only did fuel fetch siege prices, but five pounds would be paid for an old gin-case, for the boards of a dray, or any few pieces of wood out of which a miner's "cradle" could be patched up. The miners did not exactly make light of these obstacles, for, of the thousands who poured into the province after the first discoveries, large numbers fled from the snow and starvation of the winters, when the swollen rivers rose, and covered up the rich drift on the beaches under their banks. But enough remained to carry on the work of prospecting, and the finds were rich enough to lure new-comers. In the year 1863 the export of gold from Otago rose to more than two millions sterling. Extraordinary patches were found in the sands and drift of the mountain torrents. It is recorded of one party that, when crossing a river, their dog was swept away by the current on to a small rocky point. A digger went to rescue it, and never was humanity more promptly rewarded, for from the sands by the rock he unearthed more than £1,000 worth of gold before nightfall. Some of the more fortunate prospectors had their footsteps dogged by watchful bands bent on sharing their good luck. One of them, however, named Fox, managed to elude this espionage for some time, and it was the Government geologist—now Sir James Hector—who, while on a scientific journey, discovered him and some forty companions quietly working in a lonely valley.

The goldfields of Otago had scarcely reached the zenith of their prosperity before equally rich finds were reported from the west coast of the Canterbury province. From the year 1860 it was known that gold existed there, but the difficulties of exploring a strip of broken surf-beaten coast, cut off from settled districts by range upon range of Alps, and itself made up of precipitous hills, and valleys covered with densest jungle and cloven by the gorges of bitterly cold and impassable torrents, were exceptionally great. More than one of the Government officers sent there to explore were either swept away by some torrent or came back half-crippled by hunger and rheumatism. One surveyor who stuck to his work for months in the soaking, cheerless bush, existing on birds, bush-rats, and roots, was thought a hero, and with cause. Even Maoris dreaded parts of this wilderness, and believed it to be the abode of dragons and a lost tribe of their own race. They valued it chiefly as the home of their much-prized jade or greenstone. Searching for this, a party of them, early in 1864, found gold. Later on in the same year a certain Albert Hunt also found paying gold on the Greenstone creek. Hunt was afterwards denounced as an impostor, and had to fly for his life from a mob of enraged and disappointed gold-seekers; but the gold was there nevertheless. In 1865 the stream which had been pouring into Otago was diverted to the new fields in Westland, and in parties or singly, in the face of almost incredible natural difficulties, adventurous men worked their way to every point of the west coast. In a few months 30,000 diggers were searching its beaches and valleys with such results that it seemed astonishing that the gold could have lain unseen so long. Many lost their lives, drowned in the rivers or starved to death in the dripping bush. The price of provisions at times went to fabulous heights, as much as £150 being paid for a ton of flour, and a shilling apiece for candles. What did prices matter to men who were getting from 1 oz. to 1 lb. weight of gold-dust a day, or who could stagger the gold-buyers sent to their camps by the bankers by pouring out washed gold by the pannikin? So rich was the wash-dirt in many of the valleys, and the black sand on many of the sea-beaches, that for years £8 to £10 a week was regarded as only a fair living wage. In 1866 the west coast exported gold to the value of £2,140,000.

On a strip of sand-bank between the dank bush and the bar-bound mouth of the Hokitika river a mushroom city sprang up, starting into a bustling life of cheerful rashness and great expectations. In 1864 a few tents were pitched on the place; in 1865 one of the largest towns in New Zealand was to be seen. Wood and canvas were the building materials—the wood unseasoned pine, smelling fresh and resinous at first, anon shrinking, warping, and entailing cracked walls, creaking doors, and rattling window-sashes. Every second building was a grog-shanty, where liquor, more or less fiery, was retailed at a shilling a glass, and the traveller might hire a blanket and a soft plank on the floor for three shillings a night. Under a rainfall of more than 100 inches a year, tracks became sloughs before they could be turned into streets and roads. All the rivers on the coast were bar-bound. Food and supplies came by sea, and many were the coasting-craft which broke their backs crossing the bars, or which ended their working-life on shoals. Yet when hundreds of adventurers were willing to pay £5 apiece for the twelve hours' passage from Nelson, high rates of insurance did not deter ship-owners. River floods joined the surf in making difficulties. Eligible town sections bought at speculative prices were sometimes washed out to sea, and a river now runs over the first site of the prosperous town of Westport.

It was striking to note how quickly things settled down into a very tolerable kind of rough order. Among the diggers themselves there was little crime or even violence. It is true that a Greymouth storekeeper when asked "How's trade?" concisely pictured a temporary stagnation by gloomily remarking, "There ain't bin a fight for a week!" But an occasional bout of fisticuffs and a good deal of drinking and gambling, were about the worst sins of the gold-seekers. Any one who objected to be saluted as "mate!" or who was crazy enough to dream of wearing a long black coat or a tall black hat, would find life harassing at the diggings. But, at any rate, in New Zealand diggers did not use revolvers with the playful frequency of the Californians of Mr. Bret Harte. Nor did they shoe the horse of their first Member of Parliament with gold, or do a variety of the odd things done in Australian gold-fields. They laughed heartily when the Canterbury Provincial Government sent over the Alps an escort of strapping mounted policemen, armed to the teeth, to carry away gold securely in a bullet-proof cart. They preferred to send their gold away in peaceful coasting steamers. When, in 1867, one or two Irish rows were dignified with the title of Fenian Riots, and a company of militia were sent down from their more serious Maori work in the North Island to restore order in Hokitika, they encountered nothing more dangerous than a hospitality too lavish even for their powers of absorption. One gang of bushrangers, and one only, ever disturbed the coast. The four ruffians who composed it murdered at least six men before they were hunted down. Three were hung; the fourth, who saved his neck by turning Queen's evidence, was not lynched. No one ever has been lynched in New Zealand. For the rest the ordinary police-constable was always able to deal with the sharpers, drunkards, and petty thieves who are among the camp-followers of every army of gold-seekers. So quietly were officials submitted to that sometimes, when a police-magistrate failed to appear in a goldfields' court through some accident of road or river, his clerk would calmly hear cases and impose fines, or a police-sergeant remand the accused without authority and without resistance. In the staid Westland of to-day it is so impossible to find offenders enough to make a show of filling the Hokitika prison that the Premier, who sits for Hokitika, is upbraided in Parliament for sinful extravagance in not closing the establishment.

No sooner had the cream been skimmed off the southern goldfields than yields of almost equal value were reported from the north. The Thames and Coromandel fields in the east of the Auckland province differed from those in the South Island. They were from the outset not alluvial but quartz mines. So rich, however, were some of the Thames mines that the excitement they caused was as great as that roused by the alluvial patches of Otago and Westland. The opening up of the Northern fields was retarded throughout the sixties by Maori wars, and the demands of peaceful but hard-fisted Maori landlords. £1 a miner had to be paid to these latter for the right to prospect their country. They delayed the opening of the now famous Ohinemuri field until 1875. When on March 3rd of that year the Goldfields' Warden declared Ohinemuri open, the declaration was made to an excited crowd of hundreds of prospectors, who pushed jostling and fighting round the Warden's table for their licenses, and then galloped off on horseback across country in a wild race to be first to "peg out" claims. Years before this, however, the shores of the Hauraki Gulf had been systematically worked, and in 1871 the gold export from Auckland had risen to more than £1,100,000.

New Zealand still remains a gold-producing colony, albeit the days of the solitary adventurer working in the wash-dirt of his claim with pick, shovel, and cradle are pretty nearly over. The nomadic digger who called no man master is a steady-going wage-earner now. Coal-mines and quartz-reefs are the mainstays of Westland. Company management, trade unions, conciliation cases, and laws against Sunday labour have succeeded the rough, free-and-easy days of glittering possibilities for everybody. Even the alluvial fields are now systematically worked by hydraulic sluicing companies. They are no longer poor men's diggings. In Otago steam-dredges successfully search the river bottoms. In quartz-mining the capitalist has always been the organizing and controlling power. The application of cyanide and other scientific improvements has revived this branch of mining within the last four years, and, despite the bursting of the usual number of bubbles, there is good reason to suppose that the £54,000,000 which is so far the approximate yield of gold from the Colony will during the next decade be swelled by many millions.

The gold-digger is found in many parts of the earth; the gum-digger belongs to New Zealand alone. With spade, knife, and gum-spear he wanders over certain tracts of the province of Auckland, especially the long, deeply-indented, broken peninsula, which is the northern end of New Zealand. The so-called gum for which he searches is the turpentine, which, oozing out of the trunk of the kauri pines, hardens into lumps of an amber-like resin. Its many shades of colour darken from white through every kind of yellow and brown to jet. A little is clear, most is clouded. Half a century ago, when the English soldiers campaigning against Heké had to spend rainy nights in the bush without tent or fire, they made shift to get light and even warmth by kindling flame with pieces of the kauri gum, which in those days could be seen lying about on the ground's surface. Still, the chips and scraps which remain when kauri-gum has been cleaned and scraped for market are used in the making of fire-kindlers. But for the resin itself a better use was long ago found—the manufacture of varnish. At the moment when, under Governor Fitzroy, the infant Auckland settlement was at its lowest, a demand for kauri-gum from the United States shone as a gleam of hope to the settlers, while the Maoris near the town became too busied in picking up gum to trouble themselves about appeals to join Heké's crusade against the *Pakeha*. Though the trade seemed to die away so completely that in a book written in 1848 I find it briefly dismissed with the words, "The bubble has burst," nevertheless it is to-day well-nigh as brisk as ever, and has many a time and oft stood Auckland in good stead.

KAURI PINE TREE

The greater kauri pines show smooth grey trunks of from eight to twelve feet in diameter. Even Mr. Gladstone would have recoiled from these giants, which are laid low, not with axes, but with heavy double saws worked on scaffolds six feet high erected against the doomed trees. As the British ox, with his short horns and cube-like form, is the result of generations of breeding with a single eye to meat, so that huge candelabrum, the kauri, might be fancied to be the outcome of thousands of years of experiment in producing the perfection of a timber tree. Its solid column may rise a hundred feet without a branch; its small-leaved patchy foliage seems almost ludicrously scanty; it is all timber—good wood. Clean, soft, easily worked, the saws seem to cut it like cheese. It takes perhaps 800 years for the largest pines to come to their best. So plentiful are they that, though fires and every sort of wastefulness have ravaged them, the Kauri

Timber Company can put 40,000,000 feet of timber through their mills in a year, can find employment for two thousand men, and can look forward to doing so for another twenty years. After that——!

The resin may be found in tree-forks high above the ground. Climbing to these by ropes, men have taken thence lumps weighing as much as a hundredweight. But most and the best resin is found in the earth, and for the last generation the soil of the North has been probed and turned over in search of it, until whole tracts look as though they had been rooted up by droves of wild swine. In many of these tracts not a pine is standing now. How and when the forests disappeared, whether by fire or otherwise, and how soil so peculiarly sterile could have nourished the finest of trees, are matters always in dispute. There is little but the resin to show the locality of many of the vanished forests. Where they once were the earth is hungry, white, and barren, though dressed in deceptive green by stunted fern and manuka. In the swamps and ravines, where they may thrust down their steel-pointed flexible spears as much as eight feet, the roaming diggers use that weapon to explore the field. In the hard open country they have to fall back upon the spade. Unlike the gold-seeker, the gum-digger can hope for no great and sudden stroke of fortune. He will be lucky if hard work brings him on the average £1 a week. But without anything to pay for house-room, fuel, or water, he can live on twelve and sixpence while earning his pound, and can at least fancy that he is his own master. Some 7,000 whites and Maoris are engaged in finding the 8,000 tons or thereabouts of resin, which is the quantity which in a fairly good year England and America will buy at an average price of £60 a ton. About 1,500 of the hunters for gum are Istrians and Dalmatians—good diggers, but bad colonists; for years of work do not attach them to the country, and almost always they take their savings home to the fringing islands and warm bays of the Adriatic.

Chapter XIX

THE PROVINCES AND THE PUBLIC WORKS POLICY

"Members the Treasurer pressing to mob;

Provinces urging the annual job;

Districts whose motto is cash or commotion;

Counties with thirsts which would drink up an ocean;

These be the horse-leech's children which cry,

'Wanted, Expenditure!' I must supply."

—*The Premier's Puzzle.*

Sir George Grey had been curtly recalled in the early part of 1868. His friends may fairly claim that at the time of his departure the Colony was at peace, and that he left it bearing with him the general esteem of the colonists. True, his second term of office had been in some ways the antithesis of his first. He had failed to prevent war, and had made mistakes. But from amid a chaos of confusion and recrimination, four things stand out clearly: (1) he came upon the scene too late; (2) he worked earnestly for peace for two years; (3) the part that he personally took in the war was strikingly successful; (4) he was scurvily treated by the Colonial Office.

He was the last Viceroy who took an active and distinct share in the government of the country. Since 1868, the Governors have been strictly constitutional representatives of a constitutional Sovereign. They have been without exception honourable and courteous noblemen or gentlemen. They have almost always left the Colony with the good wishes of all with whom they have come into contact. They have occasionally by tact exercised a good deal of indirect influence over some of their Ministers. They have sometimes differed with these about such points as nominations to the Upper House, or have now and then reserved bills for the consideration of the Home Government. But they have not governed the country, which, since 1868, has enjoyed as complete self-government as the constitution broadly interpreted can permit.

When peace at last gave the Colonists time to look round, the constitution which Grey and Wakefield had helped to draw up was still working. Not without friction, however. Under the provincial system New Zealand was rather a federation of small settlements than a unified colony. This was in accord with natural conditions, and with certain amendments the system might have worked exceedingly well. But no real attempt was ever made to amend it. Its vices were chiefly financial. The inequalities and jealousies caused by the rich landed estate of the southern provinces bred ill-feeling all round. The irregular grants doled out by the Treasurer to the needier localities embarrassed the giver without satisfying the recipients. The provinces without land revenue looked with hungry eyes at those which had it. There was quarrelling, too, within each little provincial circle. The elective superintendents were wont to make large promises and shadow forth policies at the hustings. Then when elected they often found these views by no means in accord with those of their council and their executive. Yet, but for one great blunder, the provinces should and probably would have existed now.

1870 is usually named as the birth-year of the colonial policy of borrowing and public works. This is not strictly true. In that year the central and provincial exchequers already owed about seven millions and a quarter between them. The provincial debts, at any rate, had been largely contracted in carrying out colonizing work, and some of that work had been exceedingly well done, especially in Canterbury and Otago. What the Central Government did do in 1870 was to come forward boldly with a large and continuous policy of public works and immigration based on borrowed money. The scheme was Sir Julius Vogel's. As a politician this gentleman may not unfairly be defined as an imaginative materialist and an Imperialist of the school of which Cecil Rhodes is the best-known colonial exponent. His grasp of finance, sanguine, kindly nature, quick constructive faculty, and peculiarly persuasive manner rapidly brought him to the front in New Zealand, in the face of personal and racial prejudice. As Treasurer in 1870 he proposed to borrow ten millions to be expended on railways, roads, land purchase, immigration, and land settlement. With great wisdom he suggested that the cost of the railways should be recouped from a public estate created out of the crown lands through which they might pass. With striking unwisdom the Provincialists defeated the proposal. This selfish mistake enabled them to keep their land for five years longer, but it spoilt the public works policy and converted Vogel from the friend into the enemy of the Provinces.

His policy, *minus* the essential part relating to land settlement, was accepted and actively carried out. Millions were borrowed, hundreds of miles of railways and roads were made, immigrants were imported by the State or poured in of their own accord. Moreover, the price of wool had risen, and wheat, too, sometimes yielded enormous profits. Farmers were known who bought open land on the downs or plains of the South Island at £2 an acre, and within twelve months thereafter made a net profit of £5 an acre from their first wheat crop. Labour-saving machinery from the United States came in to embolden the growers of cereals; the export of wheat rose to millions of bushels; and the droning hum of the steam threshing-machine and the whir of the reaper-and-binder began to be heard in a thousand fields from northern Canterbury to Southland. In the north McLean steadfastly kept the peace, and the Colony bade fair to become rich by leaps and bounds. The modern community has perhaps yet to be found which can bear sudden prosperity coolly. New Zealand in the seventies certainly did not. Good prices and the rapid opening up of the country raised the value of land. Acute men quickly bought fertile or well-situated blocks and sold them at an attractive profit. So men less acute began to buy pieces less fertile and not so well situated. Pastoral tenants pushed on the process of turning their leaseholds into freeholds. So rapid did the buying become that it grew to be a feverish rush of men all anxious to secure some land before it had all gone. Of course much of this buying was speculative, and much was done with borrowed money. The fever was hottest in Canterbury, where the Wakefield system of free selection without limit as to area or condition as to occupation, and with the fixed price of £2 an acre, interposed less than no check at all to the speculators. Hundreds of thousands of acres were bought each year. The revenue of the Provincial Council rose to half a million; the country road-boards hardly knew how to spend their money. Speculation, extravagance, reaction—such were the fruits the last years of Wakefield's system bore there. Not that the fault was Gibbon Wakefield's. It rests with the men who could not see that his system, like every other devised for a special purpose, wanted to be gradually changed along with the gradual change of surrounding circumstances.

The southern land revenue, thus swollen, was a glittering temptation to politicians at Wellington. As early as 1874 it was clear that more colonial revenue would be wanted to pay the interest on the growing public debt. Vogel decided to appeal to the old Centralist party and overthrow the Provinces. Their hour was come. The pastoral tenants nearly everywhere disliked the democratic note growing louder in some of them. New settlers were overspreading the country, and to the new settlers the Provincial Councils seemed cumbrous and needless. Fresh from Great Britain and with the ordinary British contempt for the institutions of a small community, they thought it ridiculous that a colony with less than half a million of people should want nine Governments in addition to its central authority. The procedure of the Provincial Councils, where Mr. Speaker took the chair daily and a mace was gravely laid on the table by the clerk, seemed a Lilliputian burlesque of the great Mother of Parliaments at Westminster.

Nevertheless, the Provinces did not fall without a struggle. In both Otago and Auckland the older colonists mostly clung to their local autonomy. Moreover, Sir George Grey had taken up his abode in the Colony, and was living quietly in an islet which he owned near Auckland. Coming out of his retirement, he threw himself into the fight, and on the platform spoke with an eloquence that took his audiences by storm, all the more because few had suspected him of possessing it. Keen was the fight; Major Atkinson, *quondam* militia officer of Taranaki, made his mark therein and rose at a bound to take command of the Centralists; the Provincialists were fairly beaten; the land passed to the Central Government. The management of local affairs was minutely subdivided and handed over to some hundreds of boards and councils which vary a good deal in efficiency, though most of them do their special work fairly enough on accepted lines.

Though colonists join in complaining of the number of these no serious attempt has, however, been yet made to amalgamate them, much less to revive any form of Provincialism. Municipal enterprise has made few attempts in New Zealand to follow, however humbly, in the wake of the great urban councils of England and Scotland. Water companies indeed are unknown, but most of the towns depend upon contractors for their supplies of light; municipal fire insurance is only just being talked of; recreation grounds are fairly plentiful, but are not by any means always managed by the municipality of the place. None of the town councils do anything for the education of the people, and but few think of their entertainment. The rural county councils and road boards concern themselves almost solely with road-making and bridge-building. The control of hospitals and charitable aid, though entirely a public function not left in any way to private bounty, is entrusted to distinct boards. Indeed, the minute subdivision of local administration has been carried to extreme lengths in New Zealand, where the hundreds of petty local bodies, each with its functions, officers, and circle of friends and enemies, are so many stumbling-blocks to thorough—going amalgamation and rearrangement. In New Zealand the English conditions are reversed; the municipal lags far behind the central authority on the path of experiment. This is no doubt due, at least in part, to the difference in the respective franchises. The New Zealand ratepayers' franchise is more restricted than that under which the English councils are elected.

A few words will be in place here about the continuance and outcome of the Public Works policy. Sir Julius Vogel quitted the Colony in 1876, but borrowing for public works did not cease. It has not yet ceased, though it has slackened at times. In 1879 a commercial depression overtook the Colony. The good prices of wool and wheat sank lower and lower; the output of gold, too, had greatly gone down. There had been far too much private borrowing to buy land or to set up or extend commercial enterprises. The rates of interest had often been exorbitant. Then there happened on a small scale what happened in Victoria on a larger scale twelve years later. The boom burst amid much suffering and repentance. In some districts three-fourths of the prominent colonists were ruined, for the price of rural produce continued on the whole to fall relentlessly year after year until 1894. The men who had burdened themselves with land, bought wholly or largely with borrowed money, nearly all went down. Some were ruined quickly, others struggled on in financial agony for a decade or more. Then when the individual debtors had been squeezed dry the turn of their mortgagees came. Some of these were left with masses of unsalable property on their hands. At last, in 1894, the directors of the bank which was the greatest of the mortgagees—the Bank of New Zealand—had to come to the Government of the day to be saved from instant bankruptcy. In 1895 an Act was passed which, while guaranteeing the bank, virtually placed it beneath State control, under which it seems likely gradually to get clear of its entanglements. This was the last episode in the long drama of inflation and depression which was played out in New Zealand between 1870 and 1895. No story of the Colony, however brief, can pretend to be complete which does not refer to this. The blame of it is usually laid upon the public works policy. The money borrowed and spent by the Treasury is often spoken of as having been wasted in political jobs, and as having led to nothing except parliamentary corruption and an eternal burden of indebtedness and taxation. This is but true to a very limited extent. It was not the public borrowing of the Colony, but the private debts of the colonists, which, following the extraordinary fall in the prices of their raw products between 1873 and 1895, plunged so many thousands into disaster. Nine-tenths of the money publicly borrowed by the Colony has been very well spent. No doubt the annual distribution of large sums through the Lands and Public Works departments year after year have had disagreeable effects on public life. In every Parliament certain members are to be pointed out—usually from half-settled districts—who hang on to the Ministry's skirts for what they can get for their electorates. The jesting lines at the head of this chapter advert to these. But they must not be taken too seriously. It would be better if the purposes for which votes of borrowed money are designed were scrutinized by a board of experts, or at least a strong committee of members. It would be better still if loans had to be specially authorized by the taxpayers. But when the worst is said that can be said of the public works policy, its good deeds still outweigh its evil. It is true that between 1870 and 1898 the public debt has been multiplied six times; but the white population has nearly tripled, the exports have more than doubled, and the imports increased by 75 per cent. Moreover, of the exports at the time when the public works policy was initiated, about half were represented by gold, which now represents but a tenth of the Colony's exports. Again, the product of the workshops and factories of the Colony are now estimated at above ten millions annually, most of which is consumed in New Zealand, and therefore does not figure in the exports. The income of the bread-winners in the Colony and the wealth of the people per head, are now nearly the highest in the world. In 1870 the colonists were without the conveniences and in many cases comforts of modern civilization. They had scarcely any railways, few telegraphs, insufficient roads, bridges and harbours. Education was not universal, and the want of recreation and human society was so great as to lead notoriously to drunkenness and course debauchery. New Zealand is now a pleasant and highly civilized country. That she has become so in the last thirty years is due chiefly to the much-criticised public works policy.

Before parting with the subject of finance, it should be noted that in 1870 the Treasury was glad to borrow at slightly over five per cent. Now it can borrow at three. The fall in the rate of private loans has been even more remarkable. Mortgagors can now borrow at five per cent. who in 1870 might have had to pay nine. This steady fall in interest, coupled with the generally reproductive nature of the public works expenditure, should not be overlooked by those who are appalled by the magnitude of the colonial debts. For the rest, there is no repudiation party in New Zealand, nor is there likely to be any. The growth of the Colony's debt is not a matter which need give its creditors the slightest uneasiness, though no doubt it is something which the New Zealand taxpayers themselves should and will watch with the greatest care. It is quite possible that some special check will ultimately be adopted by these to ensure peculiar caution and delay in dealing with Parliamentary Loan Bills. It may be that some application of the "referendum" may, in this particular instance, be found advisable, inasmuch as the Upper House of the New Zealand Parliament, active as it is in checking general legislation, may not amend, and in practice does not reject, loan bills.

Chapter XX

IN PARLIAMENT

"Shapes of all sorts and sizes, great and small

That stood upon the floor or by the wall,

And some loquacious Vessels were, and some

Listened, perhaps, but never talked at all."

When we come to look at the men as distinct from the measures of the parliament of New Zealand between 1870 and 1890, perhaps the most interesting and curious feature was the Continuous Ministry. With some approach to accuracy it may be said to have come into office in August, 1869, and to have finally expired in January, 1891. Out of twenty-one years and a half it held office for between sixteen and seventeen years. Sir Edward Stafford turned and kept it out for a month in 1872; Sir George Grey for two years, 1877-79; Sir Robert Stout for three years, 1884-7. None of the ministries which thus for longer or shorter periods supplanted it ever commanded strong majorities, or held any thorough control over the House. The Continuous Ministry was a name given to a shifting combination, or rather series of combinations, amongst public men, by which the cabinet was from time to time modified without being completely changed at any one moment. It might be likened to the pearly nautilus, which passes, by gradual growth and movement, from cell to cell in slow succession; or, more prosaically, to that oft-repaired garment, which at last consisted entirely of patches. Like the nautilus, too, it had respectable sailing and floating powers. The continuous process was rather the outcome of rapidly changing conditions and personal exigencies than of any set plan or purpose. With its men its opinions and actions underwent alterations. Naturally the complete transformation which came over the Colony during the two decades between 1870 and 1890, had its effect on the point of view of colonists and their public men. The Continuous Ministry began by borrowing, and never really ceased to borrow; but its efforts at certain periods of the second of these two decades to restrict borrowing and retrench ordinary expenditure were in striking contrast to the lavishness of the years between 1872 and 1877. At its birth under Sir William Fox its sympathies were provincial and mildly democratic. It quickly quarrelled with and overthrew the Provinces, and became identified with Conservatism as that term is understood in New Zealand. From 1869 to 1872 its leaders were Fox, Vogel, and McLean. Fox left it in 1872; Major Atkinson joined it in 1874; Vogel quitted it in 1876; McLean died in 1877. Put out of office by Sir George Grey, it was for a short time led once more by Sir William Fox. It came back again in 1879 as a Hall-Atkinson-Whitaker combination. Hall retired in 1881, but Atkinson and Whitaker, helped by his advice, continued to direct it to the end.

Now for its opponents. Rallying under Sir George Grey in 1876, the beaten Provincialists formed a party of progress, taking the good old name of Liberal. Though Sir George had failed to save their Provinces, his eloquent exhortations rapidly revived in the House of Representatives the democratic tendencies of some of the Councils. Hitherto any concessions to Radicalism or Collectivism made by the House had been viewed in the most easy-going fashion. Vogel in his earlier years had adopted the ballot, and had set up a State Life Insurance Department, which has been successfully managed, and has now about ten millions assured in it. More interesting and valuable still was his establishment of the office of Public Trustee. So well has the experiment worked, that it may be said as a plain truth that in New Zealand, the best possible Trustee, the one least subject to accidents of fortune, and most exempt from the errors which beset man's honesty and judgment, has been found by experience to be the State. The Public Trust Office of the Colony worked at first in a humble way, chiefly in taking charge of small intestate estates. Experience, however, showed its advantages so clearly, that it has now property approaching two millions' worth in its care. Any owner of property, whether he be resident in the Colony or not, wishing to create a trust, may use the Public Trustee, subject, of course, to that officer's consent. Any one who desires so to do may appoint him the executor of his will. Any one about to leave, or who has left the Colony, may make him his attorney. The Public Trustee may step in and take charge, not only of intestate estates, but of an inheritance where no executor has been named under the will, or where those named will not act. He manages and protects the property of lunatics. Where private trust estates become the cause of disputes and quarrels, between trustees and beneficiaries, the parties thereto may relieve themselves by handing over their burden to the public office. The Public Trustee never dies, never goes out of his mind, never leaves the Colony, never becomes disqualified, and never becomes that extremely disagreeable and unpleasant person—a trustee whom you do not trust. In addition to his other manifold duties he holds and administers very large areas of land reserved for the use of certain Maori tribes. These he leases to working settlers, paying over the rents to the Maori beneficiaries. Naturally, the class which has the most cause to be grateful to the Public Trust Office is that composed of widows and orphans and other unbusinesslike inheritors of small properties, persons whose little inheritances are so often mismanaged by private trustees or wasted in law costs.

Another reform carried out by Vogel had been the adoption of the Torrens system of land transfer. Henceforth under the Land Transfer Law, Government officers did nearly all the conveyancing business of the Colony. Land titles were investigated, registered, and guaranteed, and sales and mortgages then became as simple and almost as cheap as the transfer of a parcel of shares in a company.

Even earlier the legislature had done a creditable thing in being the first in the Empire to abolish the scandal of public executions.

1877 may be accounted the birth year of more militant and systematic reform.

Grey's platform speeches in the summer of 1876-77 brought home the new Radicalism to the feelings of the mass of the electors, and to the number, then considerable, who were not electors. For the first time one of the Colony's leaders appealed to the mass of the colonists with a policy distinctly and deliberately democratic. The result was awakening. Then and subsequently Grey advocated triennial parliaments, one man one vote, a land tax, and a land policy based upon the leasing of land rather than its sale, and particularly upon a restriction of the area which any one man might acquire. The definite views of the Radicals bore fruit at once in the session of 1877. It was necessary to establish a national system of education to replace the useful, but ill-jointed work done peacemeal by the Provinces. A bill—and not a bad bill—was introduced by Mr. Charles Bowen, a gentleman honourably connected with the founding of education in Canterbury. This measure the Radicals took hold of and turned it into the free, secular, compulsory system of primary school-teaching of which the Colony is to-day justly proud, and under which the State educates thirteen-fourteenths of the children of the Colony. Now, in 1898, out of an estimated population of about 780,000 all told, some 150,000 are at school or college. Of children between ten and fifteen years of age the proportion unable to read is but 0·68. The annual average of attendance is much higher in New Zealand than in any of the Australian Colonies. The primary school system is excellent on its literary, not so excellent on its technical side. Nearly three-fourths of the Roman Catholic children do not take advantage of it. Their parents prefer to support the schools of their church, though without State aid of any kind. These, and a proportion of the children of the wealthier, are the only exceptions to the general use made of the public schools. It is not likely that any change, either in the direction of teaching religion in these, or granting money to church schools, will be made. Each political party in turn is only too eager to charge the other with tampering with the National system—a sin, the bare hint of which is like suspicion of witchcraft or heresy in the Middle Ages.

Grey gained office in 1877, but with a majority too small to enable him to carry his measures. Ballance, his treasurer, did indeed carry a tax upon land values. But its chief result at the time was to alarm and exasperate owners of land, and to league them against the Radicals, who after a not very brilliant experience of office without power fell in 1879. Thereafter, so utterly had Grey's angry followers lost faith in his generalship, that they deposed him—a humiliation which it could be wished they had seen their way to forego, or he to forgive. Yet he was, it must be confessed, a very trying leader. His cloudy eloquence would not do for human nature's daily food. His opponents, Atkinson and Hall, had not a tithe of his emotional power, but their facts and figures riddled his fine speeches. Stout and Ballance, lieutenants of talent and character, became estranged from him; others of his friends were enough to have damned any government. The leader of a colonial party must have certain qualities which Sir George Grey did not possess. He may dispense with eloquence, but must be a debater; whether able or not able to rouse public meetings, he must know how to conduct wearisome and complicated business by discussion; he must not only have a grasp of great principles, but readiness to devote himself to the mastery of uninteresting minds and unappetizing details; above all, he must be generous and considerate to lieutenants who have their own views and their own followers, and who expect to have their full share of credit and influence. In one word, he should be what Ballance was and Grey was not. Nevertheless, one of Grey's courage, talent, and prestige was not likely to fail to leave his mark upon the politics of the country; nor did he. Though he failed to pass the reforms just mentioned, he had the satisfaction of seeing them adopted and carried into law, some by his opponents, some by his friends. Only one of his pet proposals seems to have been altogether lost sight of, his oft-repeated demand that the Governor of the Colony should be elected by the people.

The Grey Ministry had committed what in a Colonial Cabinet is the one unpardonable crime—it had encountered a commercial depression, with its concomitant, a shrunken revenue. When Hall and Atkinson succeeded Grey with a mission to abolish the land-tax, they had at once to impose a different but more severe burden. They also reduced—for a time—the cost of the public departments by the rough-and-ready method of knocking ten per cent. off all salaries and wages paid by the treasury, a method which, applied as it was at first equally to low and high, had the unpopularity as well as the simplicity of the poll-tax. That retrenchment and fresh taxation were unpleasant necessities, and that Hall and Atkinson more than once tackled the disagreeable task of applying them, remains true and to their credit.

Between 1880 and 1890 the colonists were for the most part resolutely at work adapting themselves to the new order of things—to lower prices and slower progress. They increased their output of wool and coal—the latter a compensation for the falling-off of the gold. They found in frozen meat an export larger and more profitable than wheat. Later on they began, with marked success, to organize co-operative dairy factories and send cheese and butter to England. Public affairs during the decade resolved themselves chiefly into a series of expedients for filling the treasury and carrying on the work of land settlement. Borrowing went on, but more and more slowly. Times did not soon get better.

In 1885 and 1886 the industrial outlook was perhaps at its worst. In 1887, Atkinson and Whitaker, coming again into power, with Hall as adviser, administered a second dose of taxation-cum-retrenchment. They cut down the salaries of the Governor and the ministers, and the size and pay of the elected chamber. They made efforts, more equitable this time, to reduce the cost of the public departments. They stiffened the property-tax, and for the second time raised the Customs Duties, giving them a distinctly Protectionist complexion. The broad result was the achievement of financial equilibrium. For ten years there have been no deficits in New Zealand. Apart from retrenchment, Atkinson had to rely upon the Opposition in forcing his financial measures through against the Free Traders amongst his own following. This strained his party. Moreover, in forming his cabinet in 1887 he had not picked some of his colleagues well. In particular, the absence of Mr. Rolleston's experience and knowledge from the House and the government weakened him. Mr. Rolleston has his limitations, and his friends did the enemy a service when, after his return to public life in 1891, they tried to make a guerilla chief out of a scrupulous administrator. But he was a capable and not illiberal minister of lands, and his value at that post to his party may be gauged by what they suffered when they had to do without him. The lands administration of the Atkinson cabinet became unpopular, and the discontent therewith found a forcible exponent in an Otago farmer, Mr. John McKenzie, a gigantic Gael, in grim earnest in the cause of close settlement, and whose plain-spoken exposures of monopoly and "dummyism" not only woke up the Radicals, but went home to the smaller settlers far and wide. It may be that these things hastened the breaking-down of Sir Harry Atkinson's health in 1890. At any rate fail it did, unhappily. His colleague, Sir Frederick Whitaker, was ageing palpably. Nor did Sir John Hall's health allow him to take office.

THE HON. JOHN MACKENZIE

With their *tres Magi* thus disabled, the Conservative party began to lose ground. More than one cause, no doubt, explains how it was that up to 1891 the Liberals hardly ever had a command of Parliament equal to their hold upon the country. But the abilities of the three men just named had, I believe, a great share in holding them in check. Sir John Hall's devotion to work, grasp of detail, and shrewd judgment were proverbial. He was the most businesslike critic of a bill in committee the House of Representatives ever had, and was all the more effective in politics for his studiously conciliatory manner. Astute and wary, Sir Frederick Whitaker was oftener felt than seen. But with more directness than Whitaker, and more fighting force than Hall, it was Atkinson who, from 1875 to his physical collapse in 1890, was the mainstay of his party. He carried through the abolition of the Provinces; he twice reorganized the finances; he was the protagonist of his side in their battles with Grey, Ballance, and Stout, and they could not easily have had a better. This chief of Grey's opponents was as unlike him in demeanour and disposition as one man can well be to another. The two seemed to have nothing in common, except inexhaustible courage. Grey had been trained in the theory of war, and any part he took therein was as leader. Atkinson had picked up a practical knowledge of bush-fighting by exchanging hard knocks with the Maoris as a captain of militia. Grey was all courtesy; the other almost oddly tart and abrupt. Grey's oratory consisted of high-pitched appeals to great principles, which were sometimes eloquent, sometimes empty. His antagonist regarded Parliament as a place for the transaction of public business. When he had anything to say, he said it plainly; when he had a statement to make, he made it, and straightway went on to the next matter. His scorn of the graces of speech did not prevent him from being a punishing debater. Theories he had—of a quasi-socialistic kind. But his life was passed in confronting hard facts. Outside the House he was a working colonist; inside it a practical politician. The only glory he sought was "the glory of going on," and of helping the Colony to go on. When, with tragic suddenness, he died in harness, in the Legislative Council in 1892, there was not alone sincere sorrow among the circle of friends and allies who knew his sterling character, but, inasmuch as however hard he had hit in debate it had never been below the belt, his opponents joined in regretting that so brave and faithful a public servant had not been spared to enjoy the rest he had well earned.

SIR HARRY ATKINSON

What kind of an assembly, it may be asked, is the New Zealand Parliament which Atkinson's force of character enabled him to lead so long, and which has borne undivided rule over the Colony since 1876? The best answer can be found in the story of the Colony, for the General Assembly, at all events, has never been a *fainéant* ruler. It has done wrong as well as right, but it has always done something. After the various false starts before referred to, it has, since getting fairly to work in 1856, completed forty-three years of talk, toil, legislation and obstruction. It may fairly be claimed that its life has been interesting, laborious and not dishonourable. It has exactly doubled in size since Governor Wynyard's day. Old settlers say that it has not doubled in ability. But old settlers, with all their virtues, are incorrigible *laudatores temporis acti.* The industry of the members, the difficulties they had to cope with in the last generation, and the number and variety and novelty of the questions they have essayed to solve in this, are undoubted. Their work must, of course, be tested by time. Much of it has already borne good fruit, and any that does manifest harm is not likely to cumber the earth long. If laws in colonies are more quickly passed, they are also more easy to amend than in older countries.

The Lower House of a Colonial Parliament resembles, in most ways, the London County Council more than the House of Commons. But in New Zealand members have always been paid—their salary is now £240 a year. Farmers and professional men make up the largest element. The Labour members have never numbered more than half a dozen. At present there are five in each House. In the more important debates speeches are now limited to an hour, otherwise to half an hour. The length of speeches in committee must not exceed ten minutes. About twenty per cent. of the speaking is good; most of it is made with little or no preparation, and suffers—together with its hearers—accordingly. Bores are never shouted or coughed down—the House is too small, and nearly all the members are on friendly terms with each other. Until the adoption of the time limit business was in daily danger of being arrested by speeches of phenomenal length and dreariness. Anthony Trollope, who listened to a debate at Wellington in 1872, thought the New Zealand parliamentary bores the worst he had known. The discussions in Committee are often admirably businesslike, except when there is obstruction, as there frequently is. As elsewhere, special committees do much work and get little thanks therefor. As compared with the House of Commons, the debates would seem to lack dignity; as compared with the proceedings of the Sydney Parliament, they would have appeared models of decorum, at any rate until quite recently. No New Zealand debater would be held great in England, but seven or eight would be called distinctly good. The House supports a strong Speaker, but is disposed to bully weakness in the chair.

For the last thirty years the Maori race has returned four members to the House. They usually speak through an interpreter. In spite of that, when discussing native questions they often show themselves fluent and even eloquent. Outside local and private bills, nearly all important legislation is conducted by Government. Private members often profess to put this down to the jealousy and tyranny of Ministers, but the truth is that Parliament, as a whole, has always been intolerant of private members' bills. There is no direct personal corruption. If the House were as free from small-minded jealousy and disloyalty as it is from bribery and idleness, it would be a very noble assembly. In character, the politicians have been at least equal to the average of their fellow-colonists. But party ties are much looser than in England. Members will sometimes support Governments for what they can get for their districts, or leave them because they have not been given a portfolio. Attempts to form a third party are incessant but unsuccessful. Ministries, if not strangled at the birth—as was the "Clean Shirt" Cabinet—usually last for three years. Since August, 1884, there have virtually been but two changes of the party in power. Reconstructions owing to death or retirement of a Premier have now and then added to the number of apparently new Cabinets. Of the seven or eight Ministers who make up a Cabinet, four or five are usually able and overworked men. The stress of New Zealand public life has told on many of her statesmen. Beside Governor Hobson, McLean, Featherston, Crosbie Ward, Atkinson and Ballance died in harness, and Hall had to save his life by resigning. Most of the Colony's leaders have lived and died poor men. Parliaments are triennial, and about one-third of the constituencies are pretty certain to return new members at a general election. All the elections take place on one day, and if a member—even the leader of a party—loses his seat, he may be cut out for years. This is a misfortune, as experience is a quality of which the House is apt to run short. Block votes frequently prevent elections from being fought on the practical questions of the hour. The contests are inexpensive, and there is very little of the cynical blackmailing of candidates and open subsidising by members which jar so unpleasantly on the observer of English constituencies. Indeed, cynicism is by no means a fault of New Zealand political life. The most marked failings are, perhaps, the savagely personal character of some of its conflicts, and a general over-strained earnestness and lack of sense of proportion or humour. Newspapers and speeches teem with denunciations which might have been in place if hurled at the corruption of Walpole, the bureaucracy of Prussia, the finance of the *Ancien Régime*, or the treatment of native races by the Spanish conquerors of the New World. Nor is bitterness confined to wild language in or out of parliament. The terrible saying of Gibbon Wakefield, fifty years ago, that in Colonial politics "every one strikes at his opponent's heart," has still unhappily some truth in it. The man who would serve New Zealand in any more brilliant fashion than by silent voting or anonymous writing must tread a path set with the thorns of malice, and be satisfied to find a few friends loyal and a few foes chivalrous.

Chapter XXI

SOME BONES OF CONTENTION

"Now who shall arbitrate?

Ten men love what I hate,

Shun what I follow, slight what I receive;

Ten who in ears and eyes

Match me; we all surmise,

They this thing, and I that; whom shall my soul
believe?"

During the ten years beginning in 1879 New Zealand finance was little
more than a series of attempts to avert deficits. In their endeavours to raise
the revenue required for interest payments on the still swelling public debt,
and the inevitably growing departmental expenditure, various treasurers
turned to the Customs. In raising money by duties they received support
both from those who wished to protect local industries and from those who
wished to postpone the putting of heavy taxation upon land. Sir Harry
Atkinson, the treasurer who carried the chief protectionist duties, used to
disclaim being either a protectionist or a free-trader. The net result of
various conflicts has been a tariff which is protectionist, but not highly
protectionist. The duties levied on New Zealand imports represent twenty-
four per cent. of the declared value of the goods. But the highest duties,
those on spirits, wine, beer, sugar, tea, and tobacco, are not intentionally
protectionist; they are simply revenue duties, though that on beer has
undoubtedly helped large and profitable colonial breweries to be
established. English free-traders accept as an axiom that Customs duties
cannot produce increased revenue and at the same time stimulate local
manufactures. Nevertheless, under the kind of compromise by which duties
of fifteen, twenty, and twenty-five per cent. are levied on so many articles, it
does come about that the colonial treasurer gets his revenue while, sheltered
by the fiscal hedge, certain colonial manufactures steadily grow up. The
factories of the Colony now employ some 40,000 hands, and their annual
output is estimated at ten millions sterling. Much of this would, of course,
have come had the Colony's ports been free; but the factories engaged in
the woollen, printing, clothing, iron and steel, tanning, boot, furniture,
brewing, jam-making, and brick and tile-making industries owe their

existence in the main to the duties. Nor would it be fair to regard the Colony's protection as simply a gigantic job managed by the more or less debasing influence of powerful companies and firms. It was adopted before such influences and interests were. It could not have come about, still less could it last, were there not an honest and widespread belief that without duties the variety of industries needful to make a civilized and prosperous nation could not be attained in young countries where nascent enterprises are almost certain to be undercut and undersold by the giant capitalists and cheaper labour of the old world. Such a belief may conceivably be an economic mistake, but those who hold it need not be thought mere directors or tools of selfish and corrupt rings. The Colony will not adopt Free Trade unless a change comes over the public mind, of which there is yet no sign; but it is not likely to go further on the road towards McKinleyism. Its protection, such as it is, was the outcome of compromises, stands frankly as a compromise, and is likely for the present to remain as that.

So long as the Provinces lasted the General Assembly had little or nothing to do with land laws. When, after abolition, the management of the public estate came into the hands of the central authority, the regulations affecting it were a bewildering host. Some fifty-four statutes and ordinances had to be repealed. Nor could uniformity be substituted at once, inasmuch as land was occupied under a dozen different systems in as many different provincial districts. Only very gradually could these be assimilated, and it was not until the year 1892 that one land act could be said to contain the law on the subject, and to be equally applicable to all New Zealand. In the meantime the statute-books of 1877, 1878, 1883, 1885 and 1887 bore elaborate evidence of the complexity of the agrarian question, and the importance attached to it. On it more than on any other difference party divisions were based. Over it feelings were stirred up which were not merely personal, local, or sectional. It became, and over an average of years remained, the matter of chief moment in the Colony's politics. Finance, liquor reform, labour acts, franchise extension may take first place in this or that session, but the land question, in one or other of its branches, is always second. The discussions on it roused an enduring interest in Parliament given to no other subject. The Minister of Lands ranks with the Premier and the Treasurer as one of the leaders in every Cabinet. Well may he do so. Many millions of acres and many thousands of tenants are comprised in the Crown leases alone. Outside these come the constant land sales, the purchases from the Maori tribes, and in recent years the buying back of estates from private owners, and the settlement thereof. These form most, though not all, of the business of the Minister of Lands, his officers, and the administrative district boards attached to his department. If there were no land question in New Zealand, there might be no Liberal Party. It was the transfer of the land from the Provinces to the central Parliament in 1876 which chiefly helped Grey and his lieutenants to get together a democratic following.

A NEW ZEALAND SETTLER'S HOME
Photo by WINCKLEMAN

Slowly but surely the undying agrarian controversy passed with the Colony's progress into new stages. In the early days we have seen the battle between the "sufficient price" of Gibbon Wakefield and the cheap land of Grey, the good and evil wrought by the former, the wide and lasting mischief brought about by the latter. By 1876 price had ceased to be the main point at issue. It was agreed on all hands that town and suburban lands parted with by the Crown should be sold by auction at fairly high upset prices; and that rural agricultural land should be divided into classes—first, second, and third— and should not be sold by auction, but applied for by would-be occupants prepared to pay from £2 to 10s. an acre, according to quality. More and more the land laws of the Colony were altered so as to favour occupation by small farmers, who were not compelled to purchase their land for cash, but permitted to remain State tenants at low rentals, or allowed to buy the freehold by gradual instalments, termed deferred payments. Even the great pastoral leaseholds were to some extent sub-divided as the leases fell in. The efforts of the land reformers were for many years devoted to limiting the acreage which any one person could buy or lease, and to ensuring that any person acquiring land should himself live thereon, and should use and improve it, and not leave it lying idle until the spread of population enabled him to sell it at a profit to some monopolist or, more often, some genuine farmer. As early as 1856 Otago had set the example of insisting on an outlay of 30s. an acre in improvement by each purchaser of public land. Gradually the limiting laws were made more and more stringent, and were partly applied even to pastoral leases. Now, in 1898, no person can select more than 640 acres of first-class or 2,000 acres of second-class land, including any land he is already holding. In other words, no considerable landowner can legally acquire public land. Pastoral "runs"—*i.e.*, grazing leases—must not be larger than such as will carry 20,000 sheep or 4,000 cattle, and no one can hold more than one run. The attempts often ingeniously made to evade these restrictions by getting land in the names of relatives, servants, or agents are called "dummyism," and may be punished by imprisonment— never inflicted—by fines, and by forfeiture of the land "dummied."[1]

[Footnote 1: Many a good story is founded on the adventures of land-buyers in their endeavours to evade the spirit and obey the letter of land regulations. In 1891 a rhymester wrote in doggerel somewhat as follows of the experiences of a selector who "took up" a piece of Crown land—

"On a certain sort of tenure, which his fancy
much preferred,
That convenient kind of payment which is
known as the 'deferred.'

"Now the laws in wise New Zealand with
regard to buying land,
Which at divers times and places have been
variously planned,
Form a code that's something fearful,
something wonderful and grand.

"You may get a thousand acres, and you
haven't got to pay
Aught but just a small deposit in a friendly sort
of way.

"But you mustn't own a freehold, and you
mustn't have a run,
And you mustn't be a kinsman of a squatter
owning one;

"But must build a habitation and contentedly
reside,
And must satisfy the Land Board that you pass
the night inside.

"For if any rash selector on his section isn't
found
He is straightway doomed to forfeit all his title
to the ground."]

The political battles over the land laws of New Zealand during the sixteen years since 1882 have not, however, centred round the limitation of the right of purchase, or insistence on improvements, so much as round the respective advantages of freehold and perpetual leasehold, and round the compulsory repurchase of private land for settlement. Roughly speaking, the political party which has taken the name of Liberal has urged on the adoption of the perpetual lease as the main or sole tenure under which State lands should in the future be acquired. As a rule the party which the Liberals call Conservative has advocated that would-be settlers should be allowed to choose their tenure for themselves, and to be leaseholders or freeholders as they please. Then there have arisen, too, important questions affecting the perpetual lease itself. Should the perpetual leaseholders retain the right of converting at any time their leasehold into a freehold by paying down the cash value of their farm, or should the State always retain the fee simple? Next, if the State should retain this, ought there to be periodical revisions of the rent, so as to reserve the unearned increment for the public? Fierce have been the debates and curious the compromises arrived at concerning these debatable points. The broad result has been that the sale of the freehold of Crown lands, though not entirely prohibited, has been much discouraged, and that the usual tenure given now is a lease for 999 years at a rent of four per cent. on the prairie value of the land at the time of leasing. As this tenure virtually hands over the unearned increment to the lessee, it is regarded by the advanced land reformers with mixed feelings. From their point of view, however, it has the advantage of enabling men with small capital to take up land without expending their money in a cash purchase. Inasmuch, too, as transfers of a lease can only be made with the assent of the State Land Board for the district—which assent will only be given in case the transfer is to a *bona fide* occupier not already a landowner—land monopoly is checked and occupancy for use assured. Meanwhile there is plenty of genuine settlement; every year sees many hundred fresh homes made and tracts reclaimed from the wilderness.

PICTON—QUEEN CHARLOTTE'S SOUND
Photo by HENRY WRIGHT

Quite as keen has been the fighting over the principle of State repurchase of private lands with or without the owner's consent. It was a favourite project of Sir George Grey's; but it did not become law until he had left public life, when it was carried by the most successful and determined of the Liberal Ministers of Lands, John McKenzie, who has administered it in a way which bids fair to leave an enduring mark on the face of the Colony. Under this law £700,000 has been spent in buying-forty-nine estates, or portions of estates, for close settlement. The area bought is 187,000 acres. A few of these have, at the time of writing, not yet been thrown open for settlement; on the rest 2,252 human beings are already living. They pay a rent equal to 5.2 per cent. on the cost of the land to the Government. Even taking into account interest on the purchase money of land not yet taken up, a margin remains in favour of the Treasury. Nearly 700 new houses and £100,000 worth of improvements testify to the genuine nature of the occupation. As a rule there is no difficulty in buying by friendly arrangement between Government and proprietor. The latter is commonly as ready to sell as the former to buy. The price is usually settled by bargaining of longer or shorter duration. Twice negotiations have failed, and the matter has been laid before the Supreme Court, which has statutory power to fix the price when the parties fail to agree. It must be remembered that as a rule large holdings of land mean something quite different in New Zealand from anything they signify to the English mind. In England a great estate is peopled by a more or less numerous tenantry. In New Zealand it is, as a rule, not peopled at all. Sheep roam over its grassy leagues, cared for by a manager and a few shepherds. Natural and proper as this may be on the wilder hills and poorer soils, it is easy to see how unnatural and intolerable it appears in fertile and accessible districts. In 1891 there were nearly twelve and a half million acres held in freehold. Of these rather more than seven millions were in the hands of 584 owners, none of whom held less than five thousand acres. In spite of land-laws, land-tax, and time, out of thirty-four million acres of land occupied under various tenures, twenty-one millions are held in areas of more than five thousand acres.

Much the largest of the estates purchased by the Government came into their hands in an odd way, and not under the Act just described. The Cheviot property was an excellent example of what the old cheap-land regulations led to. It was a fine tract of 84,000 acres of land, on which up to 1893 some forty human beings and about 60,000 sheep were to be found. Hilly but not mountainous, grassy, fertile, and lying against the sea-shore, it was exactly suited for fairly close settlement. Under the provisions of the land-tax presently to be described, a landowner who thinks the assessors have over-valued his property may call upon the Government to buy it at his own lower valuation. A difference of £50,000 between the estimate of the trustees who held the Cheviot estate and that of the official valuers caused the former to give the Government of the day the choice between reducing the assessment or buying the estate. Mr. McKenzie, however, was just the man to pick up the gauntlet thus thrown down. He had the Cheviot bought, cut up, and opened by roads. A portion was sold, but most leased; and within a year of purchase a thriving yeomanry, numbering nearly nine hundred souls and owning 74,000 sheep, 1,500 cattle, and 500 horses, were at work in the erstwhile empty tract. Four prosperous years have since added to their numbers, and the rent they pay more than recoups the Treasury for the interest on its outlay in the purchase and settlement.

In 1886, John Ballance, then Minister of Lands, made a courageous endeavour to place a number of workmen out of employment on the soil in what were known as village settlements. In various parts of the Colony blocks of Crown land were taken and divided into allotments of from twenty to fifty acres. These were let to the village settlers on perpetual lease at a rental equal to five per cent. on the prairie value of the land. Once in a generation there was to be a revision of the rental. The settlers, many of whom were quite destitute, were helped at first not only by two years' postponement of their rent, but by small advances to each to enable them to buy seed, tools, food, and building material. Ballance was fiercely attacked in 1887 for his experiment, and his opponents triumphantly pointed to the collapse of certain of his settlements. Others, however, turned out to be successes, and by last accounts the village settlers and their families now number nearly five thousand human beings, occupying 35,000 acres in allotments of an average size of twenty-four acres. Most of them divide their time between tilling their land and working for wages as shearers, harvesters, or occasionally mechanics. Some £27,000 has been lent them, of which they still owe about £24,000. As against this the Government has been paid £27,000 in rent and interest, and the improvements made by the settlers on their allotments are valued at about £110,000, and form very good security for their debts to the Treasury. Of late years Mr. McKenzie has been aiding the poorer class of would-be farmers by employing them at wages to clear the land of which they afterwards become tenants. The money paid them is, of course, added to the capital value of the land.

For the last five years Liquor has disputed with Land the chief place in the public interest. It has introduced an element of picturesque enthusiasm and, here and there, a passion of hatred rarely seen before in New Zealand politics. It brought division into the Liberal Party in 1893, at the moment when the Progressive movement seemed to have reached its high-water mark, and the feeling it roused was found typified in the curious five years' duel between Mr. Seddon and Sir Robert Stout, which began in 1893 and ended only with Sir Robert's retirement at the beginning of the present year. It has strangely complicated New Zealand politics, is still doing so, and is the key to much political manoeuvring with which it might seem to have nothing whatever to do.

For many years total abstainers in New Zealand have grown in numbers. Though for the last thirty years drinking and drunkenness have been on the decline among all classes of colonists, and though New Zealanders have for a long time consumed much less alcohol per head than Britons do, that has not checked the growth of an agitation for total prohibition, which has absorbed within itself probably the larger, certainly the more active, section of temperance reformers.[1] In 1882 a mild form of local option went on to the statute-book, while the granting of licenses was handed over to boards elected by ratepayers. For the next ten years no marked result roused attention. Then, almost suddenly, the Prohibition movement was seen to be advancing by leaps and bounds. Two clergymen, the Rev. Leonard Isitt and the Rev. Edward Walker, were respectively the voice and the hand of the Prohibitionists. As a speaker Mr. Isitt would perhaps be the better for a less liberal use of the bludgeon, but his remarkable energy and force on the platform, and his bold and thorough sincerity, made him a power in the land. Mr. Walker had much to do with securing tangible results for the force which Mr. Isitt's harangues aroused, and in which the Liberal Party was to a large extent enrolled. In 1893 the temperance leaders thought themselves strong enough to make sweeping demands of Parliament. Ballance, the Liberal Premier, had just died; his party was by many believed to be disorganized. In Sir Robert Stout, the Brougham of New Zealand public life, the Prohibitionists had a spokesman of boundless energy and uncommon hitting power in debate. He tabled a Bill briefly embodying their complete demands, and it was read a second time. Old parliamentary hands knew full well that the introduction of so controversial and absorbing a measure in the last session before a General Election meant the sacrifice for that year, at least, of most of the policy bills on labour, land, and other matters. But, whether it would or would not have been better to postpone Licensing Reform to a Parliament elected to deal with it, as matters came to stand, there was no choice. The Ministry tried to deal with the question on progressive, yet not unreasonable, lines. A Local Option Bill was passed, therefore, and nearly every other important policy measure, except the Female Franchise Bill, went by the board—blocked or killed in one Chamber or the other. The hurried Government licensing measure of 1893 had of course to be expanded and amended in 1895 and 1896. Now, though it has failed to satisfy the more thorough-going Prohibitionists, it embraces a complete and elaborate system of local option. Except under certain extraordinary conditions, the existing number of licenses cannot be increased. The licensing districts are coterminous with the Parliamentary electorates. The triennial licensing poll takes place on the same day as the General Election, thus ensuring a full vote. Every adult male and female resident may vote: (1) to retain all existing licenses; or (2) to reduce the number of licenses, and (3) to abolish all licenses within the district. To carry No. 3 a majority of three to two is requisite. No compensation is granted to any licensed house thus closed. Two local option polls have been held under this law. The first resulted in the closing of some seventy houses and the carrying of a total prohibition of retail liquor sales in the district of Clutha. Limited Prohibition has been the law in Clutha for some four years. The accounts of the results thereof conflict very sharply. In the writer's opinion—given with no great confidence—the consumption of beer and wine there has been greatly reduced, that of spirits not very greatly. There is much less open drunkenness. In certain spots there is sly grog-selling with its concomitants of expense, stealthy drinking, and perjury. The second general Licensing Poll was held in December, 1896. Then for the first time it was taken on the same day as the Parliamentary elections. In consequence the Prohibitionist vote nearly doubled. But the Moderate vote more than trebled, and the attacking abstainers were repulsed all along the line, though they, on their side, defeated an attempt to recapture Clutha.

[Footnote 1: In 1884 the consumption of liquor among New Zealanders per head was—beer, 8.769 gallons; wine, 0.272 gallons; spirits, 0.999 gallons. The proportions had fallen in 1895 to 7.421 gallons of beer, 0.135 of wine, and 0.629 of spirits.]

The Prohibitionists are now disposed, it is believed, to make the fullest use in future of their right to vote for the reduction of the number of licensed houses. They still, however, object to the presence of the Reduction clause in the Act, and unite with the publicans in the wish to restrict the alternatives at the Local Option polls to two—total Prohibition and the maintenance of all existing licensed houses. They have also decided to oppose having the Licensing Poll on General Election day. Strongest of all is their objection to the three to two majority required to carry total and immediate Prohibition. These form the line of cleavage between them and a great many who share their detestation of the abuses of the liquor traffic.

Chapter XXII

EIGHT YEARS OF EXPERIMENT

"For I remember stopping by the way

To watch a potter thumping his wet clay."

In 1890 a new force came into the political field—organized labour. The growth of the cities and of factories in them, the decline of the alluvial and more easily worked gold-fields, and the occupation of the more fertile and accessible lands, all gradually tended to reproduce in the new country old-world industrial conditions. Even the sweating system could be found at work in holes and corners. There need be no surprise, therefore, that the labour problem, when engaging so much of the attention of the civilized world, demanded notice even in New Zealand. There was nothing novel there in the notion of extending the functions of the State in the hope of benefiting the community of the less fortunate classes of it. Already in 1890, the State was the largest landowner and receiver of rents, and the largest employer of labour. It owned nearly all the railways and all the telegraphs just as it now owns and manages the cheap, popular, and useful system of telephones. It entirely controlled and supported the hospitals and lunatic asylums, which it managed humanely and well. It also, by means of local boards and institutions, controlled the whole charitable aid of the country—a system of outdoor relief in some respects open to criticism. It was the largest trustee, managed the largest life insurance business, did nearly all the conveyancing, and educated more than nine-tenths of the children.

THE HON. JOHN BALLANCE

It will thus be seen that the large number of interesting experiments sanctioned by the New Zealand Parliament since 1890 involved few new departures or startling changes of principle. The constitution was democratic: it has simply been made more democratic. The functions of the State were wide; they have been made yet wider. The uncommon feature of the last eight years has been not so much the nature as the number and degree of the changes effected and the trials made by the Liberal-Labour fusion which gained power under Mr. Ballance at the close of 1890 and still retains office. The precise cause of their victory was the wave of socialistic, agrarian, and labour feeling which swept over the English-speaking world at the time, and which reached New Zealand.

The oft-repeated assertion that the Australasian maritime strike of August, 1890, was not only coincident with the forming of Labour Parties in various colonies, but was itself the chief cause thereof, is not true Colonial Labour Parties have, no doubt, been influenced by two noted strikes, themselves divided by the width of the world. I mean the English dockers' strike and our own maritime strike. But the great Thames strike may be said rather to have given a fillip to Colonial Trades Unionism, apart from politics altogether, than to have created any Party. As for the other conflict, though the utter rout of the colonial maritime strikers in 1890 undoubtedly sent Trades Unionists to the ballot-box sore and with a keen desire to redress the balance by gaining political successes, it was not the sole or the chief cause of their taking to politics. Before it took place New Zealand politicians knew the Labour organizations were coming into their field. The question was what they would do. The Opposition of 1889-90, though not without Conservative elements—the remnants of a former coalition—was mainly Radical. It had always supported Sir George Grey in his efforts to widen the franchise, efforts which in 1889 were finally crowned by the gain of one-man-one-vote. And in 1889 it choose as its head, John Ballance, perhaps the only man who could head with success a Liberal-Labour fusion. A journalist, but the son of a North Irish farmer, he knew country life on its working side. His views on the land question were not therefore mere theories, but part of his life and belief. Though not a single-taxer, he advocated State tenancy, as opposed to freehold, and his extension of village settlements had made him amongst New Zealand workmen a popular Lands Minister. Experience had made him a prudent financier, a humane temper made him a friend of the Maori. His views on constitutional reform were advanced, on liquor and education reactionary. In Labour questions apart from land settlement he took no special part. He was an excellent debater and a kindly, courteous, considerate chief. In Ballance and his followers in 1890 New Zealand Labour Organizations found a ready-made political Party from which they had much to hope. With it, therefore, they threw in their lot. The result showed the power the agrarian feeling of Unionism and of one-man-one-vote. In New Zealand, all the elections for the House of Representatives take place on one day. In 1890 the day was the 5th December. On the 6th it was clear enough that Ballance would be the Colony's next Premier. His defeated opponents made a short delay, in order to commit the huge tactical mistake of getting the Governor to make seven additions to the Upper House. Then they yielded, and on 24th January, 1891, he took office.

Within his cabinet, he had the staunchest of lieutenants in Mr. John McKenzie aforesaid, whose burly strength combined with that of Mr. Seddon, now Premier, to supply the physical fighting force lacking in their chief. Mr. Cadman, another colleague, was an administrator of exceptional assiduity. But none of these had held office before, and outside his cabinet Ballance had to consolidate a party made up largely of raw material. Amongst it was a novel and hardly calculable element, the Labour Members. At the elections, however, no attempt had been made to reserve the Labour vote for candidates belonging exclusively to Trades Unions, or who were workmen. Of some score of Members who owed their return chiefly to the Labour vote, and who had accepted the chief points of the Labour policy, six only were working mechanics. Moreover, though the six were new to Parliament, several of their closest allies had been there before, and were old members of the Ballance Party. Not only, therefore, was a distinct Labour Party not formed, but there was no attempt to form one. For the rest, any feeling of nervous curiosity with which the artisan parliamentarians were at first regarded soon wore off. They were without exception men of character, intelligence, and common-sense. They behaved as though their only ambition was to be sensible Members of Parliament. As such, they were soon classed, and lookers-on were only occasionally reminded that they held a special brief.

Anything like a detailed history of the struggles which followed would be out of place here. Nor is it possible yet to sum up the results of changes, none of which are eight years old. A mere enumeration of them would take some space: a succinct description would require a fairly thick pamphlet. Some were carried after hot debate; some after very little. Some were resolutely contested in the popular chamber, and were assented to rather easily in the Upper House; others went through the Lower House without much difficulty, but failed again and again to run the gauntlet of the nominated chamber. The voting of some was on strict party lines: in other instances leading Opposition Members like Captain Russell frankly accepted the principle of measures. Some were closely canvassed in the newspapers and country; others were hardly examined outside Parliament. But, roughly speaking, the chief experiments of the last eight years not already dealt with many be divided into three sections. These relate to (1) Finance; (2) Constitutional Reform; (3) Labour. One of the first and—to a New Zealander's eyes—boldest strokes delivered was against the Property Tax. This, the chief direct tax of the Colony, was an annual impost of 1d. in the £ on the capital value of every citizen's possessions, less his debts and an exemption of £500. Its friends claimed for this tax that it was no respecter of persons, but was simple, even-handed, and efficient. The last it certainly was, bringing as it did into the Treasury annually about as many thousands as there are days in the year. But inasmuch as different kinds of property are by no means equally profitable, and therefore the ability of owners to pay is by no means equal, the simplicity of the Property Tax was not by many thought equity. The shopkeeper, taxed on unsaleable stock, the manufacturer paying on plant and buildings as much in good years as in bad, bethought them that under an Income Tax they would at any rate escape in bad seasons when their income might be less or nothing. The comfortable professional man or well-paid business manager paid nothing on their substantial and regular incomes. The working-farmer settling in the desert felt that for every pound's worth of improvements made by muscle and money he would have to account to the tax-collector at the next assessment. Nevertheless the Conservative politicians rallied round the doomed tax. It was a good machine for raising indispensable revenue.

Moreover, it did not select any class of property-owners or any description of property for special burdens. This suited the landowners, who dreaded a Land Tax, for might not a Land Tax contain the germ of that nightmare of the larger colonial landowner—the Single Tax? It suited also the wealthy, who feared graduated taxation, and the lawyers, doctors, agents, and managing directors, whose incomes it did not touch. So when in the autumn the rumour went round that the Ballance Ministry meant to abolish the Property Tax and bring forward Bills embodying a Progressive Land Tax, and Progressive Income Tax, the proposal was thought to represent the audacity of impudence or desperation. When the rumour proved true, it was predicted that the farmers throughout the length and breath of the country would rise in wrath and terror, scared by the very name of Land Tax. Nevertheless Parliament passed the Bills, with the addition of a light Absentee Tax. The smaller farmers, at any rate, took the appeals of the Property Taxers with apathy, suspecting that under a tax on bare land values they would pay less than under a Property Tax which fell on land, improvements, and live stock as well. Since 1891, therefore, progression or graduation has been in New Zealand a cardinal principle of direct taxation.

Land pays no Income Tax, and landowners who have less than £500 worth of bare land value pay no Land Tax. This complete exemption of the very small land owners forms an almost insuperable barrier to the progress of singletaxers. On all land over £500 value 1d. in the £ is paid. The mortgaged farmer deducts the amount of his mortgage from the value of his farm and pays only on the remainder. The money-lender pays 1d. in the £ on the mortgage, which for this purpose is treated as land. An additional graduated tax begins on holdings worth, £5,000. At that stage it is an eighth of a penny. By progressive steps it rises until, on estates assessed at £210,000, it is 2d. Thus under the graduated and simple Land Tax together, the holders of the largest areas pay 3d. in the £, whilst the peasant farmers whose acres are worth less than £500 pay nothing. The owner who pays graduated tax pays upon the whole land value of his estate with no deduction for mortgage. The Graduated Tax brings in about £80,000 a year; the 1d. Land Tax about £200,000; the Income Tax about £70,000. The assessment and collection cause no difficulty. South Australia had a Land Tax before New Zealand; New South Wales has imposed one since. Both differ from New Zealand's.

Income earners pay on nothing up to £300 a year. Between £300 and £1,300 the tax is 6d. all round; over £1,300 it rises to a shilling. Joint-stock companies pay a shilling on all income.

Another law authorizes local governing bodies to levy their rates on bare land values. Three times the Bill passed the Lower House, only to be rejected in the Upper. It became law in 1896. The adoption of the principle permitted by it is hedged about by various restrictions but some fourteen local bodies have voted in favour thereof.

The unexampled and, till 1895, continuous fall of prices in the European markets made it hard for colonial producers to make both ends meet. The cultivator found his land depreciated because, though he grew more than before, he got less for it. As the volume of produce swelled, so the return for it sank as by some fatal compensation. To pay the old rates of interest is for the mortgaged farmer, therefore, an impossibility. Various schemes for using the credit of the State to reduce current rates of interest have been before the public in more than one colony. The scheme of the New Zealand Government is contained in the Advances to Settlers Act, 1894. Under it a State Board may lend Government money on leasehold and freehold security, but not on urban or suburban land, unless occupied for farming or market-gardening. The loan may amount to three-fifths of the value of the security when freehold, and one-half when leasehold. The rate of interest charged is 5 per cent., but the borrower pays at the rate of 6 per cent. in half-yearly instalments, the extra 1 per cent. being by way of gradual repayment of the principal. Mortgagees must in this way repay the principal in 73 half-yearly instalments, provided they care to remain indebted so long. If able to wipe off their debts sooner, they can do so. The Act came into force in October, 1894. Machinery for carrying it out was quickly set up; applications for loans came in freely, and about a million has been lent, though the State Board, in its anxiety to avoid bad security, has shown a proper spirit of caution.

With one exception, the constitutional changes of the eight years may be dismissed in a very few words. The Upper Chamber, or Legislative Council of New Zealand, is nominative and not elective, nor is there any fixed limit to its numbers. Liable, thus, to be diluted by Liberal nominees, it is not so strong an obstacle to the popular will as are the Elective Councils of certain Australian Colonies. Prior to 1891, however, the nominations in New Zealand were for life. This was objected to for two reasons. A Councillor, who at the age of sixty might be a valuable adviser, might twelve years later be but the shadow of his former self. Moreover, experience showed that Conservatism was apt to strengthen in the nominated legislator's mind with advancing years. So a seven years' tenure has been substituted for life tenure. Then, again, in 1891 the Liberal majority in the Colony was scarcely represented in the Council at all. In important divisions, Government measures passed by decisive majorities in the popular Chamber could only muster two, three, four, or five supporters in the Council. This not only meant that a hostile majority could reject and amend as it pleased, but that measures were not even fairly debated in the Upper House. Only one side was heard. In 1892 the Ballance Ministry, therefore, asked the Governor to call twelve fresh Councillors. His Excellency demurred to the number. As there was about to be a change of Governors the matter stood over. The new Governor proved as unwilling as his predecessor. Ballance held that in this matter, as in others, the constitutional course was for the Governor to take the advice of his Ministers. His Excellency thought otherwise. By mutual consent the matter was referred to the Colonial Office, where Lord Ripon decided in favour of the Premier. Twelve new Councillors were nominated. Though this submission to the arbitration of the Colonial Office was attacked not only by colonial Conservatives but by Sir George Grey, it was highly approved of both by the Lower House and the mass of the electors, and was regarded as one of Ballance's most important successes.

Another he did not live to see achieved. His Electoral Bill, wrecked twice in the Council, was only passed some months after his death. Under it the one-man-one-vote was carried to its complete issue by the clause providing for one man one registration; that is to say, that no voter could register on more than one roll. Consequently property-owners were not only cut down to one vote in one district at a general election, but were prevented from voting in another district at a by-election. The right to vote by letter was extended from seamen to shearers. But much the greatest extension of the franchise was the giving it to women. This was a curious example of a remarkable constitutional change carried by a Parliament at the election of which the question had scarcely been discussed. Labour, Land, and Progressive Taxation had been so entirely the ascendant questions at the General Election of 1890, that it came as a surprise to most to learn next year that the House of Representatives was in favour of women's suffrage. Even then it was not generally supposed that the question would be settled. Sir John Hall, however, its consistent friend, brought it up in the House, and Ballance, an equally earnest supporter, at once accepted it. After that, the only doubts as to its becoming law sprang from the attitude of the Legislative Council, and from the scruples of certain persons who thought that so great a change should be definitely submitted to the constituencies. Feeling was both strengthened and exacerbated by the enthusiasm of the Prohibition lodges, some of whose members at the same time demanded that the Government should pass the measure, and emphatically assured every one that its passing would forthwith bring about the Government's downfall and damnation. There is no doubt that many of the Ministry's opponents believed this, and that to their mistake was due the escape of the Bill in the Council. It was passed on the eve of the General Elections by the narrowest possible majority. The rush of the women on to the rolls; the interest taken by them in the elections; the peaceable and orderly character of the contests; and the Liberal majority returned at two successive General Elections are all matters of New Zealand history.

Most of the women voters show as yet no disposition to follow the clergy in assailing the national system of free, secular, and compulsory education. They clearly favour temperance reform, but are by no means unanimous for total prohibition. On the whole, the most marked feature of their use of the franchise is their tendency to agree with their menkind. Families, as a rule, vote together, and the women of any class or section are swayed by its interests, prejudices, or ideals to just about the same extent as the males thereof. Thus, the friends and relatives of merchants and professional men, large landowners, or employers of labour, usually vote on one side; factory girls, domestic servants, wives of labourers, miners, artisans, or small farmers, on the other. Schoolmistresses are as decidedly for secular education as are schoolmasters. It is too soon to pronounce yet with anything like confidence on the results of this great experiment. We have yet to see whether female interest in politics will intensify or fade. At present, perhaps, the right of every adult woman to vote is more remarkable for what it has not brought about than for what it has. It has not broken up existing parties, unsexed women, or made them quarrel with their husbands, or neglect their households. It has not interfered with marriage, or society, or the fashion of dress. The ladies are not clamouring to be admitted to Parliament. They do less platform-speaking than Englishwomen do, though many of them study public affairs—about which, to say truth, they have much to learn. Observers outside the Colony need not suppose that New Zealand women are in the least degree either "wild," or "new," or belong to any shrieking sisterhood. Though one or two have entered learned professions, most of them are engaged in domestic duties. Those who go out into the world do so to work unassumingly as school teachers, factory hands, or household servants. As school teachers they are usually efficient, as domestic servants civil and hard-working, as factory hands neat, industrious, and moral. It is true that they are, without exception, educated to the extent of having had at least good primary school teaching. But though they read—clean, healthy English books—this, so far from making them inclined to favour frantic or immoral social experiments, should have, one may hope, just the opposite effect. Far from being a spectacled, angular, hysterical, uncomfortable race, perpetually demanding extravagant changes in shrill tones, they are, at least, as distinguished for womanly modesty, grace, and affection, as Englishwomen in any other part of the Empire.

There are some who connect the appearance of women in the political arena with the recent passing of an Infants' Life Protection Act, the raising of the age of consent to fifteen, the admission of women to the Bar, the appointment of female inspectors to lunatic asylums, factories, and other institutions, improvements in the laws dealing with Adoption of Children and Industrial Schools, a severe law against the keepers of houses of ill-fame, and with the new liquor laws and the Prohibitionist movement which is so prominent a feature of New Zealand public life.

A handy volume issued by the Government printer contains most of the Labour Laws of New Zealand. They are now twenty-six in number, comprising Acts, amending Acts, and portions of Acts. Their aim is not the abolition of the wages system, but, as far as may be to make that system fair and tolerable, and in protecting the labourer to protect the fair employer. Some twenty of these laws have been passed during the last seven years. Of these an Employers' Liability Act resembles Mr. Asquith's ill-fated Bill. Worked in conjunction with a law for the inspection of machinery and a thorough-going system of factory inspection, it has lessened accidents without leading to litigation. It neither permits contracting-out nor allows employers to escape liability by means of letting out contracts.

A Truck Act declares the right of every wage-earner to be paid promptly, in full, in the current coin of the realm, and to be allowed to spend wages as they choose. Two more enactments deal with the earnings of the workmen of contractors and sub-contractors, make them a first charge on all contract money, give workers employed on works of construction a lien thereon, and compel a contractor's employer to hold back at least one-fourth of the contract money for a month after the completion of a contract, unless he shall be satisfied that all workmen concerned have been paid in full. A Wages Attachment Act limits without entirely abolishing a creditor's right to obtain orders of court attaching forthcoming earnings.

The Factories Act of 1894, slightly extended by an amending Act in 1896, consolidates and improves upon no less than four previous measures, two of which had been passed by the Ballance Government. As compared with similar European and American laws, it may fairly claim to be advanced and minute. Under its pivot clause all workshops, where two or more persons are occupied, are declared to be factories, must register, pay an annual fee, and submit to inspection at any hour of the night or day. A master and servant working together count as two hands. Inspectors have absolute power to demand such cubic space, ventilation, and sanitary arrangements generally as they may consider needful to preserve life and health. The factory age is fourteen; there are no half-timers; and, after a struggle, the Upper House was induced to pass a clause enforcing an education test before any child under fifteen should be allowed to go to factory work. This is but logical in a country wherein primary education is not only free, but compulsory. Children under sixteen must be certified by an inspector to be physically fit for factory life. Women and children under eighteen may not work before 7.45 a.m. or after 6 p.m., nor more than forty-eight hours per week. Whether time-workers or piece-workers, they are equally entitled to the half-holiday after 1 p.m. on Saturday. In the case of time-workers, this half-holiday is to be granted without deduction of wages. The rates of pay and hours of work in factories have to be publicly notified and returned to the inspectors. Overtime may be permitted by inspectors on twenty-eight days a year, but overtime pay must be not less than 6d. an hour extra. The factory-owners who send work out have to make complete returns thereof. All clothing made outside factories for sale is to be ticketed "tenement made," and any person removing the ticket before sale may be fined. No home work may be sublet. A peculiar feature in the Act relates to the board and lodging provided on sheep stations for the nomadic bands of shearers who traverse colonies, going from wool-shed to wool-shed during the shearing season. The huts in which these men live are placed under the factory inspectors, who have power to call upon station-owners to make them decent and comfortable. The Act has clauses insisting on the provision of a separate dining-room for women workers, of fire-escapes, and protection against dangerous machinery. Girls under fifteen may not work as type-setters; young persons of both sexes are shut out of certain dangerous trades; women may not work in factories within a month after their confinement. Such are the leading features of the Factories Act. It is strictly enforced, and has not in any way checked the growth of manufactures in the colony.

The laws which regulate retail shops do not aim at securing what is known as early closing. A weekly half-holiday for all, employer and employed alike; a fifty-four hours' working week for women and young persons; seats for shop girls, and liberty to use them; sanitary inspection of shops. These were the objects of those who framed the acts, and these have been attained. Under a special section merchants' offices must close at 5 o'clock p.m. during two-thirds of each month. On the weekly half-holiday shops in towns must be closed at 1 o'clock, but each town chooses its own day for closing. Nearly all choose Wednesday or Thursday, so as not to interfere with the Saturday market-day of the farmers. Much feeling was stirred up by the passing of this Act, but it has since entirely died away.

Until 1894 the legal position of Trade Unionists in New Zealand was much less enviable than that of their brethren in England. The English Act of 1875 repealing the old Labour Conspiracy law and modifying the common law doctrine relating thereto, had never been enacted in New Zealand. The Intimidation law (6 George IV.) was still in force throughout Australasia; the common law doctrine relating thereto had not been in any way softened. Within the last few years Australian Trade Unionists had found the old English law unexpectedly hunted up for the purpose of putting them into gaol. Three short clauses and a schedule, passed in 1894, swept from the Statute-Book and the common law of New Zealand all laws and doctrines specially relating to conspiracy among members of Trades Unions who in future will only be amenable to such conspiracy laws as affect all citizens.

In New Zealand most domestic servants and many farm hands and gardeners are engaged through Servants' Registry Offices. A law, passed in 1895, provides for the inspection of these, and regulates the fees charged therein. Office-keepers have to be of good character; have to register and take out a license; have to keep books and records which are officially inspected. They are not allowed to keep lodging-houses or to have any interest in such houses.

To certain students the most interesting and novel of the New Zealand labour laws is that which endeavours to settle labour disputes between employers and Trade Unions by means of public arbitration instead of the old-world methods of the strike and the lock-out. Under this statute, which was passed in 1894, the Trade Unions of the Colony have been given the right to become corporate bodies able to sue and be sued. In each industrial locality a Board of Conciliation is set up, composed equally of representatives of employers and workmen, with an impartial chairman. Disputes between Trade Unions and employers—the Act deals with no others—are referred first of all to these Boards. The exclusion of disputes between individuals, or between unorganized workmen and their masters, is grounded on the belief that such disputes are apt to be neither stubborn nor mischievous enough to call for State interference; moreover, how could an award be enforced against a handful of roving workmen, a mere nebulous cluster of units? At the request of any party to an industrial dispute the District Board can call all other parties before it, and can hear, examine, and recommend. It is armed with complete powers for taking evidence and compelling attendance. Its award, however, is not enforceable at law, but is merely in the nature of friendly advice. Should all or any of the parties refuse to accept it, an appeal lies to the Central Court of Arbitration, composed of a judge of the Supreme Court sitting with two assessors representing capital and labour respectively. The trio are appointed for three years, and in default of crime or insanity can only be removed by statute. Their court may not be appealed from, and their procedure is not fettered by precedent. No disputant may employ counsel unless all agree to do so. The decisions of this Court are binding in law, and may be enforced by pains and penalties. The arbitration law has been in active operation for about three years, during which time some thirty-five Labour disputes have been successfully settled. As a rule, the decisions of the Local Conciliation Boards are not accepted. Either some of the parties refuse to concur, or some of the recommendations are objected to by all those on one side or the other. In nearly all cases the awards of the Arbitration Court have been quietly submitted to. In three minor cases proceedings have been taken for penalties. Twice these have been dismissed on technical grounds. In the third instance a small penalty was imposed. All the important Labour disputes of the last three years have been brought before the tribunals set up under the Act. The only strike which has occurred and has attracted any attention during this period was by certain unorganized bricklayers working for the government. As the Act applied to neither side an attempt was made to settle the dispute by voluntary arbitration. Some of the men, however, refused to accept the arbitrators' award, and lost their work. But of strikes by Trades Unions there have been none, and there should be none so long as the Act can be made to work.

As to the kind of questions arbitrated upon, they comprise most of the hard nuts familiar to students of the Labour problem. Among them are hours of labour, holidays, the amount of day wages, the price to be paid for piece-work, the proportion of apprentices to skilled artizans, the facilities to be allowed to Trade Union officials for interviews with members, the refusal of Unionists to work with non-Union men, and the pressure exerted by employees to induce workmen to join private benefit societies. A New Zealand employer, it may be mentioned, cannot take himself outside the Act of discharging his Union hands, or even by gradually ceasing to engage Union men, and then pleading that he has none left in his employ. A Union, whose members are at variance with certain employers in a trade, may bring all the local employees engaged in that trade into court, so that the same award may be binding on the whole trade in the district.

Most of the references have been anything but trivial affairs, either as to the numbers of workmen concerned, or the value of the industries, or importance of the points in dispute. It is wrong to suppose that the operation of the Act is confined to industries protected by high customs duties, or to workers in factories. It may be applied wherever workers are members of legally constituted bodies, set up either under the Trade Union Act, or under the Arbitration Statute itself. Unions who want to make use of it, register under it; and some eighty have already done so. Trade Unions who do not specially register may nevertheless be brought before the Arbitration Court by the employers of their members. So far the Act has met with a remarkable measure of success. The Trade Unions are enthusiastic believers in it,—rather too enthusiastic, indeed, for they have shown a tendency to make too frequent a use of it. Some of their officials, too, would do well to be more brief and businesslike in the conduct of cases. On the other hand, employers in most of the localities have made a serious mistake in refusing to elect representatives for the local Conciliation Boards, and thus forcing the Government to nominate members. This has weakened the Boards, has hindered them from having the conciliatory character they ought to have, and has led in part to the frequent appeals to the Central Court of which the employers themselves complain. The lawyers claim to have discovered that the penalty clauses of the Act are badly drafted, and some of them assert that unless these are amended, they will be able to drive a coach and six through the statute. No doubt technical amendments will be required from time to time. What is still more requisite is an understanding between the more reasonable leaders on both sides of industry, by which arrangements may be made for the more effectual and informal use of the Conciliation Boards. Meanwhile it savours of the absurd to talk and write—as certain fault-finders have done—as though every arbitration under the Act were a disturbance of industry as ruinous as a prolonged strike. Other critics have not stickled to assert that it has mischievously affected the volume of the Colony's industries, a statement which is simply untrue. It is the reviving prosperity of the Colony during the last three years which has led the Trade Unions to make so much use of the Act. In place of striking on a rising market, as they do in other countries, they have gone to arbitration. Public opinion in New Zealand has never been one-sided on the question. It has all along been prepared to give this important experiment a fair trial, and is quite ready to have incidental difficulties cured by reasonable amendment.

The Shipping and Seamen's Act, 1894, and the amending Acts of the two following years, mitigate the old-fashioned severity of punishments for refusal of duty, assaults on the high seas, and other nautical offences. The forecastle and the accommodation thereof become subject to the *fiat* of the Government inspector, as are factories on shore. Regular payment of wages is stipulated for, overcrowding amongst passengers is forbidden. Complete powers are given to the marine authorities to enforce not only a full equipment of life-boats and life-saving appliances, but boat-drill. Deck loading is restricted, and the Plimsoll mark insisted on. But the portion of the Act which gave rise to the intensest opposition was the proviso by which all sailing vessels are obliged to carry a certain complement of able seamen and ordinary seamen, according to their tonnage, while steamers must carry a given number of able seamen, ordinary seamen, firemen, trimmers, and greasers, according to their horse-power. Foreign vessels, while engaging in the New Zealand coasting-trade, have to pay their crews the rate of wages current on the coast. Parliament was warned that the passing of this Act would paralyze the trade of the Colony, but passed it was—with certain not unreasonable amendments—and trade goes on precisely as before.

In 1891, moreover, the colonial laws relating to mining generally, and to coal-mining especially, were consolidated and amended. An interesting feature in the New Zealand Coal Mines' Act is the provision by which mine-owners have to contribute to a fund for the relief of miners or the families of miners in cases where men are injured or killed at work. Every quarter the owners have to pay a halfpenny per ton on the output, if it be bituminous coal; and a farthing a ton, if it be lignite. Payment is made into the nearest Post Office Savings Bank and goes to the credit of an account called "The Coal Miners' Relief Fund." From 1891 mineral rights are reserved in lands thereafter alienated by the Crown.

Most of the Labour laws are watched and administered by the Department of Labour, a branch of the public service created in 1891. It costs but £7,000 or £8,000 a year, much of which is recouped by factory fees and other receipts. It also keeps labour statistics, acts as a servants' registry office, and by publishing information, and by shifting them from congested districts, endeavours to keep down the numbers of the unemployed. In this, though it is but a palliative, it has done useful and humane work, aided—so far as the circulation of labour goes—by the State-owned railways.

(rear) TE WAHAROA ------ HENARE KAIHAU, M.H.R. ------ HON.
JAMES CARROLL, M.H.R
(front) RIGHT HON. R.J. SEDDON (*Premier*) ------ MAHUTA (*The Maori*
"King")
Photo by BEATTIE & SANDERSON, Auckland.

From what has gone before, readers will readily understand that the New Zealand Government has usually in its employ several thousand labourers engaged in road-making, bridge-building, draining, and in erecting and repairing public buildings. To avoid the faults of both the ordinary contract and the day-wage system, a plan, clumsily called The Co-operative Contract System, has been adopted by the present Premier, Mr. Seddon. The work is cut up into small sections, the workmen group themselves in little parties of from four to eight men, and each party is offered a section at a fair price estimated by the Government's engineers. Material, when wanted, is furnished by the Government, and the tax-payer thus escapes the frauds and adulteration of old contract days. The result of the system in practice is that where workmen are of, at any rate, average industry and capacity, they make good, sometimes excellent, wages. In effect they are groups of piece-workers, whose relation with each other is that of partners. Each band elects a trustee, with whom the Government officials deal. They are to a large extent their own masters, and work without being driven by the contractor's foreman. They are not encouraged to work more than eight hours a day; but as what they get depends on what they do, they do not dawdle during those hours, and if one man in a group should prove a loafer, his comrades, who have to suffer for his laziness, soon get rid of him. The tendency is for first-class men to join together, and for second-class men to similarly arrange themselves. Sometimes, of course, the officers, in making estimates of the price to be paid for work, make mistakes, and men will earn extravagantly high wages, or get very poor returns. But as the sections are small, this does not last for long, and the balance is redressed. After some years' experience, it seems fairly proved that the average of earnings is not extravagant, and that the taxpayer loses nothing by the arrangement as compared with the old contract system, while the change is highly popular with workmen throughout the Colony.

Those who know anything of politics anywhere, will not need to be told that the changes and experiments here sketched have been viewed with suspicion, alarm, contempt, or anger, by a large class of wealthy and influential New Zealanders. It is but fair that, in a sketch like this, some emphasis should be laid upon their dissent and protests. Into the personal attacks of which very much of their criticism has consisted this is not the place to enter. A summary of the Conservative view of the progressive work ought, however, to have a place. Disqualified as I might be thought to be from attempting it, I prefer to make use of an account written and published in 1896 by an English barrister, who, in the years 1894-95, spent many months in the Colony studying with attention its politics and public temper. As his social acquaintanceships lay chiefly among the Conservatives, he had no difficulty in getting frank expressions of their views. In the following sentences he sums up the more moderate and impersonal of these, as he heard and analysed them:—

"... It must not be supposed that the Conservatives of New Zealand, any more than those of the mother country, are apologists for 'sweating.' Indeed, as Mr. Reeves himself has acknowledged, the labour legislation with which he is associated was inaugurated by the Government's predecessors, and in carrying his Bills he had the cordial support of Captain Russell, the leader of the Opposition. At the same time it is urged that this protective legislation has been carried to an unreasonable extent, and people allege, no doubt with a certain amount of exaggeration, that they feel themselves regulated in all the relations of life. The measure which has created the most irritation seems to be the Shop Assistants Act. Employers say that Mr. Reeves has made every man 'a walking lawsuit,' and that they are chary of having one about their premises. Moreover, this constant succession of labour laws, and the language of some of their supporters, have created, so they say, in the minds of the working classes the impression that the squatters, manufacturers, and the classes with which they associate, are tyrants and oppressors, and their lives are embittered by the feeling that they are regarded as enemies of the people. Further, they say that the administrative action of the Government tends to keep up the price of labour, that the price of labour is unreasonably high, and that this fact, coupled with the necessity of keeping all the provisions of the labour laws in mind, and the spirit which they have generated, makes them disinclined to employ labour in the improvement of their lands. As to the Government's land policy, while it is admitted that small settlers are desirable, it is not admitted that large properties are necessarily a curse. What is resented more fiercely than anything else is the fact that they are liable to have their own properties appropriated at the arbitrary will of the Minister of lands, and though the Government promises to work the law reasonably, neither this nor any other of their declarations is regarded with confidence. It is asserted that the Government is flooding the country with incompetent settlers, who imagine that anyone can get a living out of the land; that the resumed properties have been purchased and cut up in such a way that a cry for a reduction of rents will soon become inevitable, and that the Cheap Money Scheme has created a class of debtors, who, in conceivable circumstances, might be able to apply effectual political pressure for the reduction of their interest. In point of fact they do not share the Progressist idea, that much can be done by legislation to ameliorate the condition of the masses of the population, nor do they see that in a country like New Zealand, where labour is dear, food cheap, and the climate mild and equable, their condition need necessarily be so deplorable. They still cherish the old theories of individualism. The humanitarian ideals of Mr. Reeves, not being idealists, they regard with little interest. What they see is the Government of their Colony, which they had been accustomed to control, in the hands of men whose characters they despise or detest, and the House of Representatives, which was once the most dignified and distinguished assembly in the Colonies, now become (in their circle at any rate) a byword of reproach—full of men who vote themselves for a three months' session salaries which many of them would be unable to earn in any other walk of life."

Despite the Socialistic tendency of the Acts thus denounced, it must not be thought that there is any strong party of deliberate State Socialists in the Colony at all corresponding to the following of Bebel and Liebknecht in Germany, or even the Independent Labour Party in England. There is not. The reforms and experiments which show themselves so many in the later chapters of the story of New Zealand have in all cases been examined and taken on their merits, and not otherwise. They are the outcome of a belief which, though much more boldly trusted and acted upon by the Progressives than by the Conservatives, is not now the monopoly of one political party. The leaders of the rival parties, the robust Mr. Seddon and the kindly Captain Russell, both admit one main principle. It is that a young democratic country, still almost free from extremes of wealth and poverty, from class hatreds and fears and the barriers these create, supplies an unequalled field for safe and rational experiment in the hope of preventing and shutting out some of the worst social evils and miseries which afflict great nations alike in the old world and the new.

To sum up the experiments themselves, it may be said that the Colony has now reached the stage when the State, without being in any way a monopolist, is a large and active competitor in many fields of industry. Where it does not compete it often regulates. This very competition must of course expose it to the most severe tests and trials. Further progress will chiefly depend on the measure of success with which it stands these, and on the consequent willingness or unwillingness of public opinion to make trial of further novelties.

Chapter XXIII

THE NEW ZEALANDERS

"No hungry generations tread thee down."

Some 785,000 whites, browns, and yellows are now living in New Zealand. Of these the browns are made up of about 37,000 Maoris and 5,800 half-castes. The Maoris seem slowly decreasing, the half-castes increasing rather rapidly. 315,000 sheep, 30,000 cattle, many horses, and much land, a little of which they cultivate, some of which they let, support them comfortably enough. The yellows, some 3,500 Chinese, are a true alien element. They do not marry—78 European and 14 Chinese wives are all they have, at any rate in the Colony. They are not met in social intercourse or industrial partnership by any class of colonists, but work apart as gold-diggers, market-gardeners, and small shop-keepers, and are the same inscrutable, industrious, insanitary race of gamblers and opium-smokers in New Zealand as elsewhere. At one time they were twice as numerous. Then a poll-tax of £10 was levied on all new-comers. Still, a few score came in every year, paying the tax, or having it paid for them; and about as many went home to China, usually with £200 or more about them. In 1895 the tax was raised to £50, and this seems likely to bring the end quickly. Despised, disliked, dwindling, the Chinese are bound soon to disappear from the colony.

Of the 740,000 whites, more than half have been born in the country, and many are the children, and a few even the grandchildren, of New Zealand-born parents. An insular race is therefore in process of forming. What are its characteristics? As the Scotch would say—what like is it? Does it give any signs of qualities, physical or mental, tending to distinguish it from Britons, Australians, or North Americans? The answer is not easy. Nothing is more tempting, and at the same time more risky, than to thus generalize and speculate too soon. As was said at the outset, New Zealand has taken an almost perverse delight in upsetting expectations. Nevertheless, certain points are worth noting which may, at any rate, help readers to draw conclusions of their own.

The New Zealanders are a British race in a sense in which the inhabitants of the British Islands scarcely are. That is to say, they consist of English, Scotch, and Irish, living together, meeting daily, intermarrying, and having children whose blood with each generation becomes more completely blended and mingled. The Celtic element is larger than in England or in the

Scottish lowlands. As against this there is a certain, though small, infusion of Scandinavian and German blood; very little indeed of any other foreign race. The Scotch muster strongest in the south and the Irish in the mining districts. In proportion to their numbers the Scotch are more prominent than other races in politics, commerce, finance, sheep farming, and the work of education. Among the seventy European members of the New Zealand House of Representatives there is seldom more than one Smith, Brown, or Jones, and hardly ever a single Robinson; but the usual number of McKenzies is three. The Irish do not crowd into the towns, or attempt to capture the municipal machinery, as in America, nor are they a source of political unrest or corruption. Their Church's antagonism to the National Education system has excluded many able Catholics from public life. The Scandinavians and Germans very seldom figure there. Some 1,700 Jews live in the towns, and seem more numerous and prominent in the north than in the south. They belong to the middle class; many are wealthy. These are often charitable and public-spirited, and active in municipal rather than in parliamentary life.

MAORIS CONVEYING GUESTS IN A CANOE
Photo by Beattie & Sanderson, Auckland.

Among the Churches the Church of England claims 40 per cent. of the people; the Presbyterians 23 per cent.; other Protestants, chiefly Methodists, 17 per cent.; and Catholics 14. Methodists seem increasing rather faster than any other denomination. Though the National School system is secular, it is not anti-Christian. 11,000 persons teach 105,000 children in Sunday-schools. In the census returns about two per cent. of the population object or neglect to specify their religion; only about one per cent. style themselves as definitely outside the Christian camp.

The average density of population throughout the Colony's 104,000 square miles is somewhat less than eight to the mile. Two-thirds of the New Zealanders live in the country, in villages, or in towns of less than 5,000 inhabitants. Even the larger towns cover, taken together, about seventy square miles of ground—not very cramping limits for a quarter of a million of people. Nor is there overcrowding in houses; less than five persons to a house is the proportion. There are very few spots in the towns where trees, flower gardens, and grass are not close at hand, and even orchards and fields not far away. The dwelling-houses, almost all of wood, seldom more than two storeys high, commonly show by their shady verandahs and veiling creepers that the New Zealand sun is warmer than the English. Bright, windy, and full of the salt of the ocean, the air is perhaps the wholesomest on earth, and the Island race naturally shows its influence. Bronzed faces display on every side the power of sun and wind. Pallor is rare; so also is the more delicate pink and white of certain English skins. The rainier, softer skies of the western coasts have their result in smoother skins and better complexions on that side of the Islands than in the drier east. On the warm shores of Auckland there are signs of a more slightly-built breed, but not in the interior, which almost everywhere rises quickly into hill or plateau. Athletic records show that the North Islanders hold their own well enough against Southern rivals. More heavily built as a rule than the Australians, the New Zealanders have darker hair and thicker eyebrows than is common with the Anglo-Saxon of Northern England and Scotland. Tall and robust, the men do not carry themselves as straight as the nations which have been through the hands of the drill-sergeant. The women—who are still somewhat less numerous than the males—are as tall, but not usually as slight, as those of the English upper classes. To sum up, the New Zealand race shows no sign of beating the best British, or of producing an average equal to that best; but its average is undoubtedly better than the general British average. The puny myriads of the manufacturing towns have no counterpart in the Colony, and, if humanitarian laws can prevent it, never should. The birth-rate and death-rate are both strikingly low: the latter, 9.14 per 1,000, is the lowest in the world. The birth-rate has fallen from 37.95 in 1881 to 25.96 in 1897. The yearly number of births has in effect remained the same for sixteen years, though the population has grown thirty per cent. larger in the period. The gain by immigration is still appreciable, though not large.

Their speech is that of communities who are seldom utterly illiterate, and as seldom scholarly. I have listened in vain for any national twang, drawl, or peculiar intonation. The young people, perhaps, speak rather faster than English of the same age, that is all. On the other hand, anything like picturesque, expressive language within the limits of grammar is rarely found. Many good words in daily use in rural England have been dropped in the Colony. Brook, village, moor, heath, forest, dale, copse, meadow, glade are among them. Young New Zealanders know what these mean because they find them in books, but would no more think of employing them in speaking than of using "inn," "tavern," or "ale," when they can say "hotel," "public-house," or "beer." Their place is taken by slang. Yet if a nation is known by its slang, the New Zealanders must be held disposed to borrow rather than to originate, for theirs is almost wholly a mixture of English, American, and Australian. Most of the mining terms come from California; most of the pastoral from Australia, though "flat" and "creek" are, of course, American. "Ranche" and "gulch" have not crossed the Pacific; their place is taken by "run" and "gulley." On the other hand, "lagoon" has replaced the English "pond," except in the case of artificial water. Pasture is "feed," herd and flock alike become "mob." "Country" is used as a synonym for grazing; "good country" means simply good grazing land. A man tramping in search of work is a "swagman" or "swagger," from the "swag" or roll of blankets he carries on his back. Very few words have been adopted from the vigorous and expressive Maori. The convenient "mana," which covers prestige, authority, and personal magnetism; "wharé," a rough hut; "taihoa," equivalent to the Mexican *manana*; and "ka pai," "'tis good," are exceptions. The South Island colonists mispronounce their beautiful Maori place-names murderously. Even in the North Island the average bushman will speak of the pukatea tree as "bucketeer," and not to call the poro-poro shrub "bull-a-bull" would be considered affectation. There is or was in the archives of the Taranaki Farmers' Club a patriotic song which rises to the notable lines—

"And as for food, the land is full

Of that delicious bull-a-bull!"

In Canterbury you would be stared at if you called Timaru anything but "Timmeroo." In Otago Lake Wakatipu becomes anything, from "Wokkertip" to "Wackatipoo"; and I have heard a cultured man speak of Puke-tapu as "Buck-a-tap."

The intellectual average is good. Thanks in great part to Gibbon Wakefield's much-abused Company, New Zealand was fortunate in the mental calibre of her pioneer settlers, and in their determined efforts to save their children from degenerating into loutish, half-educated provincials. Looking around in the Colony at the sons of these pioneers, one finds them on all sides doing useful and honourable work. They make upright civil servants, conscientious clergymen, schoolmasters, lawyers, and journalists, pushing agents, resourceful engineers, steady-going and often prosperous farmers, and strong, quick, intelligent labourers. Of the "self-reverence, self-knowledge, self-control" needful to make a sound race they have an encouraging share. Of artistic, poetic, or scientific talent, of wit, originality, or inventiveness, there is yet but little sign. In writing they show facility often, distinction never; in speech fluency and force of argument, and even, sometimes, lucidity, but not a flash of the loftier eloquence. Nor has the time yet arrived for Young New Zealand to secure the chief prizes of its own community—such posts and distinctions as go commonly to men fairly advanced in years. No native of the country has yet been its Prime Minister or sat amongst its supreme court judges or bishops. A few colonial-born have held subordinate Cabinet positions, but the dozen leading Members of Parliament are just now all British-born. So are the leading doctors, engineers, university professors, and preachers; the leading barrister is a Shetlander. Two or three, and two or three only, of the first-class positions in the civil service are filled by natives. On the whole, Young New Zealand is, as yet, better known by collective usefulness than by individual distinction.

The grazing of sheep and cattle, dairying, agriculture, and mining for coal and gold, are the chief occupations. 47,000 holdings are under cultivation. The manufactures grow steadily, and already employ 40,000 hands. A few figures will give some notion of the industrial and commercial position. The number of the sheep is a little under 20,000,000; of cattle, 1,150,000; of horses, 250,000. The output of the factories and workshops is between £10,000,000 and £11,000,000 sterling a year; the output of gold, about £1,000,000; that of coal, about 900,000 tons. The export of wool is valued at £4,250,000. Among the exports for 1897 were: 2,700,000 frozen sheep and lambs; 66,000 cwt. cheese, and 71,000 cwt butter; £433,000 worth of kauri gum; £427,000 worth of grain. The exports and imports of the Colony for the year 1897 were a little over £10,000,000 and £8,000,000 sterling respectively. It would appear that, taking a series of years, about three-quarters of the Colony's trade has been with the mother-country, and nearly all the remainder with other parts of the Empire. The public debt is about £44,000,000; the revenue, £5,000,000. The State owns 2,061 miles of railway.

Socially the colonists are what might be expected from their environment. Without an aristocracy, without anything that can be called a plutocracy, without a solitary millionaire, New Zealand is also virtually without that hopeless thing, the hereditary pauper and begetter of paupers. It may be doubted whether she has a dozen citizens with more than £10,000 a year apiece. On the other hand, the average of wealth and income is among the highest in the world.

A RURAL STATE SCHOOL
Photo by BEATTIE & SANDERSON, Auckland.

Education is universal. The lectures of the professors of the State University—which is an examining body, with five affiliated colleges in five different towns—are well attended by students of both sexes. The examiners are English; the degrees may be taken by either sex indifferently. Not two per cent. of the Colony's children go to the secondary schools, though they are good and cheap. It is her primary education that is the strength and pride of New Zealand. It is that which makes the list of crimes light. Criminals and paupers are less often produced than let in from the outside. The regulations relating to the exclusion of the physically or mentally tainted are far too lax, and will bring their own punishment. The colonists, honestly anxious that their country shall in days to come show a fine and happy race, are strangely blind to the laws of heredity. They carelessly admit those whose children to the third and fourth generation must be a degrading influence. On the other hand, the Colony gains greatly by the regular and deliberate importation of English experts. Every year a small but important number of these are engaged and brought out. They vary from bishops and professors to skilled artizans and drill-instructors; but whatever they are, their quality is good, and they usually make New Zealand the home of their families.

With wealth diffused, and caste barriers unknown, a New Zealander, when meeting a stranger, does not feel called upon to act as though in dread of finding in the latter a sponge, toady, or swindler. Nor has the colonist to consider how the making of chance acquaintances may affect his own social standing. In his own small world his social standing is a settled thing, and cannot be injured otherwise than by his own folly or misconduct. Moreover, most of the Islanders are, or have been, brought face to face with the solitude of nature, and many of all classes have travelled. These things make them more sociable, self-confident, and unsuspicious than the middle classes of older countries. Such hospitality as they can show is to them a duty, a custom, and a pleasure.

The Islanders are almost as fond of horses and athletics as their Australian cousins. They are not nearly such good cricketers, but play football better, are often good yachtsmen, and hold their own in rowing, running, jumping, and throwing weights. Fox-hunting is a forbidden luxury, as the fox may not be imported. But they have some packs of harriers, and ride to them in a way which would not be despised in the grass counties at Home. There are fair polo teams too. They are just as fond of angling and shooting as the race elsewhere. Capital trout-fishing, some good deer-shooting, and a fine supply of rabbits, hares, and wild ducks help to console the sportsman for the scarcity of dangerous game. As might be expected in an educated people passionately fond of out-door exercises, well fed and clothed, and with sun and sea air for tonics, drink is not their national vice. Gambling, especially over horse races, has more claim to that bad eminence. Perhaps that is one of the reasons why the land rings with denunciations of drink, while comparatively little has until quite lately been said against gambling.

Of colonial art there is not much to be said. Sculpture is represented by an occasional statue brought from England. Architecture in its higher form is an unknown quantity. Painting is beginning to struggle towards the light, chiefly in the form of water-colour drawings. Political satire finds expression in cartoons, for the most part of that crude sort which depicts public men as horrific ogres and malformed monsters of appalling disproportions. Music, reading, and flower gardening are the three chief refining pastimes. The number and size of the musical societies is worthy of note. So are the booksellers' shops and free libraries. The books are the same as you see in London shops. There is no colonial literature. As for flowers, New Zealanders promise to be as fond of them as the Japanese. There is a newspaper of some description in the Islands to about every 1,500 adults. Every locality may thus count upon every item of its local news appearing in print. The Colonists who support this system may be assumed to get what they want, though, of course, under it quality is to some extent sacrificed to number. As a class the newspapers are honest, decent, and energetic as purveyors of news. Every now and then public opinion declares itself on one side, though the better known newspapers are on the other. But on the average their influence is not slight. There is no one leading journal. Of the four or five larger morning newspapers, the *Otago Daily Times* shows perhaps the most practical knowledge of politics and grasp of public business. It is partisan, but not ferociously so, except in dealing with some pet aversion, like the present Minister of Lands. You may read in it, too, now and then, what is a rarity indeed in colonial journalism—a paragraph written in a spirit of pure, good-natured fun.

The working classes are better, the others more carelessly, dressed than in England. The workpeople are at the same time more nomadic and thriftier. Amongst the middle classes, industrious as they are, unusual thrift is rare. Their hospitality and kindliness do not prevent them from being hard bargainers in business.

Compared with the races from which they have sprung, the Islanders seem at once less conventional, less on their guard, and more neighbourly and sympathetic in minor matters. In politics they are fonder of change and experiment, more venturesome, more empirical, law-abiding, but readier to make and alter laws. Hypercritical and eaten up by local and personal jealousies in public life, they are less loyal to parties and leaders, and less capable of permanent organization for a variety of objects. They can band themselves together to work for one reform, but for the higher and more complex organization which seeks to obtain a general advance along the line of progress by honourable co-operation and wise compromise, they show no great aptitude. In politics their pride is that they are practical, and, indeed, they are perhaps less ready than Europeans to deify theories and catchwords. They are just as suspicious of wit and humour in public men, and just as prone to mistake dulness for solidity. To their credit may be set down a useful impatience of grime, gloom, injustice, and public discomfort and bungling.

In social life they are more sober and more moral, yet more indifferent to the opinion of any society or set. Not that they run after mere eccentrics; they have a wholesome reserve of contempt for such. British in their dislike to take advice, their humbler position among the nations makes them more ready to study and learn from foreign example. Though there is no division into two races as in London, it would be absurd to pretend that social distinctions are unknown. Each town with its rural district has its own "society." The best that can be said for this institution is that it is not, as a rule, dictated to by mere money. It is made up of people with incomes mostly ranging from £500 to £2,000, with a sprinkling of bachelors of even more modest means. Ladies and gentlemen too poor to entertain others will nevertheless be asked everywhere if they have either brightness or intellect, or have won creditable positions. You see little social arrogance, no attempt at display. Picnics, garden parties, and outings in boats and yachts are amongst the pleasanter functions. A yacht in New Zealand means a cutter able to sail well, but quite without any luxury in her fittings. The indoor gatherings are smaller, more kindly, less formal, less glittering copies of similar affairs in the mother country.

Brilliant talkers there are none. But any London visitor who might imagine that he was about to find himself in a company of clownish provincials would be much mistaken. A very large proportion of colonists have travelled and even lived in more lands than one. They have encountered vicissitudes and seen much that is odd and varied in nature and human nature. In consequence they are often pleasant and interesting talkers, refreshingly free from mannerism or self-consciousness.

They both gain and lose by being without a leisured class; it narrows their horizon, but saves them from a vast deal of hysterical nonsense, social mischief and blatant self-advertising. Though great readers of English newspapers and magazines, and much influenced thereby in their social, ethical, and literary views, their interest in English and European politics is not very keen. A cherished article of their faith is that Russia is England's irreconcileable foe, and that war between the two is certain. Both their geographical isolation and their constitution debar them from having any foreign policy. In this they contentedly acquiesce. Loyal to the mother country, resolved not to be absorbed in Australia, they are torpid concerning Imperial Federation. Their own local and general politics absorb any interest and leisure not claimed by business and pastimes. Their isolation is, no doubt, partly the cause of this. It takes their steamers from four to six days to reach Australia, and nearly as long to travel from one end of their own land to the other. Most of them can hardly hope to see Europe, or even Asia or America, or any civilized race but their own. This is perhaps the greatest of their disadvantages. Speedier passage across the oceans which divide them from the rest of the human race must always be in the forefront of their aims as a nation.

Industrious, moral, strong, it is far too soon to complain of this race because it has not in half a century produced a genius from amongst its scanty numbers. Its mission has not been to do that, but to lay the foundations of a true civilization in two wild and lonely, though beautiful, islands. This has been a work calling for solid rather than brilliant qualities—for a people morally and physically sound and wholesome, and gifted with "grit" and concentration. There is such a thing as collective ability. The men who will carve statues, paint pictures, and write books will come, no doubt, in good time. The business of the pioneer generations has been to turn a bloodstained or silent wilderness into a busy and interesting, a happy, if not yet a splendid, state.

BIBLIOGRAPHY

Books about New Zealand are numerous enough. A critic need not be fastidious to regret that most of them are not better written, useful and interesting as they are in the mass. Every sort of information about the country is to be got from them, but not always with pleasure or ease. To get it you must do a good deal of the curst hard reading which comes from easy writing. And even then, for the most part, it is left to your own imaginative power to see—

"The beauty, and the wonder, and the power,

The shapes of things, their colours, lights, and shades,

Changes, surprises."

The undoubted and agreeable exceptions, too, require in you some knowledge of the Islands, if they are to be enjoyed. How is that knowledge to be obtained? A hard-headed student with a hearty appetite for facts might, of course, start with F.J. Moss's careful and accurate school history and the latest Government Year Book in his hand, and would soon be well on his way. Those who like easier paths to knowledge may try Edward Wakefield's "New Zealand After Fifty Years," or Gisborne's "Colony of New Zealand." When one comes to periods, districts, or special subjects, the choice is much wider.

To begin at the beginning; "Tasman's Log" is little but dry bones; of Cook and Crozet I have written elsewhere. Of the writers who tell of Alsatian days, none is worth naming in the same breath with Maning. Personally I like Polack and Savage the best of them, despite the lumbering pretentiousness and doubtful veracity of the former. Earle and Major Cruise are more truthful than readable—conditions which are exactly reversed in the case of Rutherford. If, as is said, Lord Brougham helped to write Rutherford's narative, he did his work very well; but after the exposure of its "facts" by Archdeacon W.L. Williams, it can only be read as the yarn of a runaway sailor, who had reasons for not telling the whole truth, and a capacity and knowledge of local colour which would have made him a capital romance-writer, had he been an educated man. As a picture of the times, Rutherford's story in the "Library of Entertaining Knowledge" will always, however, be worth reading.

The missionaries have not been as fortunate in their chroniclers as they deserve. The tumid cant of Nicholas is grotesque enough to be more amusing than the tract-and-water style of Yate and Barret Marshall, or the childishness of Richard Taylor. Much better in every way are Buller's

(Wesleyan) "Forty Years In New Zealand," and Tucker's "Life and Episcopate of George Augustus Selwyn."

Among the descriptions of the country as it was when the colonists found it, Edward Shortland's account of the whalers and Maoris of the South Island, Jerningham Wakefield's of the founding of the New Zealand Company's settlements, Dieffenbach's travels, and Bidwill's unpretending little pamphlet telling of his tramp to the volcanoes and hot lakes in 1842, seem to me at once to tell most and be easiest to read.

On the Maoris, their myths, legends, origin, manners, and customs, William Colenso is admittedly the chief living authority. For his views it is necessary to go to pamphlets, and to search the Transactions of the New Zealand Institute, where much other good material will also reward the seeker. To John White's ill-jointed but invaluable compilation "The Ancient History of the Maori," every student henceforth will have to turn. The selections therein from the papers of Stack on the South Island Maoris, from Travers' "Life of Te Rauparaha," and Wilson's "Story of Te Waharoa," are less stony than the more genealogical portions. Sir George Grey's collection of the historical and legendary traditions of the race has not been superseded. Messrs. Percy Smith and Edward Tregear edit the valuable journal of the Polynesian Association; the former has made a special study of the origin and wanderings of the Maori race, the latter has produced the Comparative Maori-Polynesian Dictionary. General Robley has written the book on Maori tattooing; Mr. Hamilton is bringing out in parts what promises to be a very complete and worthily illustrated account of Maori art.

As narratives of the first twenty years of the Colony two books stand out from among many: Thomson's "Story of New Zealand," and Attorney— General Swainson's "New Zealand and its Colonization." It would not be easy to find a completer contrast than the gossipy style of the chatty army medico and the dry, official manner of the precise lawyer, formerly and for upwards of fifteen years Her Majesty's Attorney-General for New Zealand, as he is at pains to tell you on his title-page. But Swainson's is the fairest and most careful account of the time from the official, philo-Maori and anti-Company side, and may be taken as a safe antidote to Jerningham Wakefield, Sir W.T. Power, Hursthouse, and others. A comparison with Rusden, when the two are on the same ground, shows Swainson to be the better writer all round. Of Rusden's "History of New Zealand" no one doubts the honest intent. The author, believing the Maori to be a noble, valiant, and persecuted race, befriended by the missionaries and those who took missionary advice, and robbed and cheated by almost all others, says so in three long, vehement, sincere, but not fascinating volumes, largely composed of extracts from public papers and speeches. Sweeping condemnation of the Public Works policy, of Radical reforms, and recent

Socialistic experiments, complete his tale. The volumes have their use, but are not a history of New Zealand.

Of early days in the pastoral provinces we get contemporary sketches by Samuel Butler, L.J. Kennaway, Lady Barker, and Archdeacon Paul. Butler's is the best done picture of the country, Kennaway's the exactest of the settlers' every-day rough-and-tumble haps and mishaps, and Lady Barker's the brightest. One of the volumes of General Mundy's "Our Antipodes" gives a nice, light sketch of things as they were in the North Island in the first years of Governor Grey. Dr. Hocken's recent book has at once become the recognised authority on the first years of Otago, and also has interesting chapters on the South Island before settlement. Fitzgerald's selections from Godley's writings and speeches is made more valuable by the excellent biographical sketch with which it opens. Dr. Richard Garnett's admirable "Life of Gibbon Wakefield" is the event of this year's literature from the point of view of New Zealanders.

Of the books on the Eleven Years' War from 1860 to 1871, Sir William Fox's easily carries away the palm for vigour of purpose and performance. Sir William was in hot indignation when he wrote it, and some of his warmth glows in its pages. It is a pity that he only dealt with the years 1863-65. Generals Carey and Alexander supply the narrative of the doings of the regulars; Lieutenant Gudgeon that of the militia's achievements. General Carey handles the pen well enough; not so his gallant brother-soldier. Of Gudgeon's two books I much prefer the Reminiscences, which on the whole tell more about the war than any other volume one can name. Sir John Gorst describes the King Movement and his own experiences in the King's country. Swainson takes up his parable against the Waitara purchase.

Gisborne's "Rulers and Statesmen of New Zealand," though not a connected history, is written with such undoubted fairness and personal knowledge, and in so workmanlike, albeit good—natured, a way, as to have a permanent interest. Most of the many portraits which are reproduced in its pages are correct likenesses, but it is the pen pictures which give the book its value.

Of volumes by travellers who devote more or less space to New Zealand, the most noteworthy are Dilke's brilliant "Greater Britain," the volumes of Anthony Trollope, and Michael Davitt, and Froude's thoughtful, interesting, but curiously inaccurate "Oceana." Mennell's serviceable "Dictionary of Australasian Biography" gives useful details concerning the pioneer colonists.

Scientific students may be referred to the Works of Hooker and Dieffenbach, to Von Haast's "Geology of Canterbury and Westland," Kirk's "New Zealand Forest Flora," Sir Walter Buller's "Birds of New Zealand,"

Hudson's "New Zealand Entomology," and to the papers of Hector, Hutton and Thompson.

Dr. Murray Moore has written, and written well, for those who may wish to use the country as a health resort.

Mountaineers and lovers of scenery should read Green's "High Alps of New Zealand," and T. Mackenzie's papers on West Coast Exploration. Mannering Fitzgerald and Harper are writers on the same topic. Murray's guide book will, of course, be the tourist's main stay. Delisle Hay's Brighter Britain deals in lively fashion with a settler's life in the bush north of Auckland and in the Thames goldfields. Reid and Preshaw have written of the Westland gold-seekers; Pyke of the Otago diggings. Domett's "Ranolf and Amohia" is not only the solitary New Zealand poem which has achieved any sort of distinction, but is also an interesting picture of Maori life and character.

The Official Year-Book is a mass of well-arranged information, and the economic enquirer may be further referred to Cumin's "Index of the Laws of New Zealand," and to the numerous separate annual reports of the Government offices and departments. Historical students must, of course, dive pretty deeply into the parliamentary debates and appendices to the journals of the House of Representatives, into the bulky reports and correspondence relating to New Zealand published in London by the Imperial authorities, and into the files of the larger newspapers The weekly newspapers of the Colony are especially well worth consulting. For the rest, Collier's New Zealand Bibliography (Wellington), and the library catalogues of the N.Z. Parliament and of the Royal Colonial Institute, London, are the best lists of the books and pamphlets on New Zealand.

Booksophile
Your Local Online Bookstore

Buy Books Online from
www.Booksophile.com

Explore our collection of books written in various languages and uncommon topics from different parts of the world, including history, art and culture, poems, autobiography and bibliographies, cooking, action & adventure, world war, fiction, science, and law.

Add to your bookshelf or gift to another lover of books - first editions of some of the most celebrated books ever published. From classic literature to bestsellers, you will find many first editions that were presumed to be out-of-print.

Free shipping globally for orders worth US$ 100.00.

Use code "Shop_10" to avail additional 10% on first order.

Visit today
www.booksophile.com